마이갓 5 Step 모의고사 공부법

1 ● **Vocabulary** 필수 단어 암기 & Test
① 단원별 필수 단어 암기 ② 영어 → 한글 Test ③ 한글 → 영어 Test

2 ● **Text** 지문과 해설
① 전체 지문 해석 ② 페이지별 필기 공간 확보 ③ N회독을 통한 지문 습득

3 ● **Practice 1** 빈칸 시험 (w/ 문법 힌트)
① 해석 없는 반복 빈칸 시험 ② 문법 힌트를 통한 어법 숙지
③ 주요 문법과 암기 내용 최종 확인

4 ● **Practice 2** 빈칸 시험 (w/ 해석)
① 주요 내용/어법/어휘 빈칸 ② 한글을 통한 내용 숙지
③ 반복 시험을 통한 빈칸 암기

5 ● **Quiz** 객관식 예상문제를 콕콕!
① 수능형 객관식 변형문제 ② 100% 자체 제작 변형문제 ③ 빈출 내신 문제 유형 연습

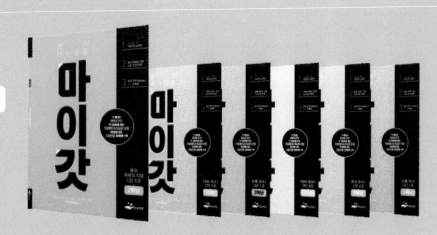

영어 내신의 끝
마이갓 모의고사 고1, 2

1 등급을 위한 5단계 노하우
2 모의고사 연도 및 시행월 별 완전정복
3 내신변형 완전정복

영어 내신의 끝
마이갓 교과서 고1, 2

1 등급을 위한 10단계 노하우
2 교과서 레슨별 완전정복
3 영어 영역 마스터를 위한 지름길

마이갓 교재
보듬책방 온라인 스토어 (https://smartstore.naver.com/bdbooks)

마이갓 10 Step 영어 내신 공부법

Vocabulary

필수 단어 암기 & Test
① 단원별 필수 단어 암기
② 영어 → 한글 Test
③ 한글 → 영어 Test

Grammar

단원별 중요 문법과 연습 문제
① 기초 문법 설명
② 교과서 적용 예시 소개
③ 기초/ Advanced Test

Text

지문과 해설
① 전체 지문 해석
② 페이지별 필기 공간 확보
③ N회독을 통한 지문 습득

Practice 3

빈칸 시험 (w/ 해석)
① 주요 내용/어법/어휘 빈칸
② 한글을 통한 내용 숙지
③ 반복 시험을 통한 빈칸 암기

Practice 2

빈칸 시험 (w/ 해석)
① 주요 내용/어법/어휘 빈칸
② 한글을 통한 내용 숙지
③ 반복 시험을 통한 빈칸 암기

Practice 1

어휘 & 어법 선택 시험
① 시험에 나오는 어법 어휘 공략
② 중요 어법/어휘 선택형 시험
③ 반복 시험을 통안 포인트 숙지

Quiz

객관식 예상문제를 콕콕!
① 수능형 객관식 변형문제
② 100% 자체 제작 변형문제
③ 빈출 내신 문제 유형 연습

Final Test

주관식 서술형 예상문제
① 어순/영작/어법 등
　 주관식 서술형 문제 대비!
② 100% 자체 제작 변형문제

전체 영작 연습

직접 영작 해보기
① 주어진 단어를 활용한
　 전체 서술형 영작 훈련
② 쓰기를 통한 내용 암기

학교 기출 문제

지문과 해설
① 단원별 실제 학교 기출
　 문제 모음
② 객관식부터 서술형까지
　 완벽 커버!

23년 고1
9월 모의고사

마이갓

연습과 실전 모두 잡는 내신대비 완벽

| workbook |

보듬영어

2023 고1

9월

WORK BOOK

———

2023년 고1 9월 모의고사 내신대비용 WorkBook & 변형문제

CONTENTS

2023 고1 9월 WORK BOOK

—

보듬영어

Voca

❶ voca	❷ text	❸ [/]	❹ ____	❺ quiz 1	❻ quiz 2	❼ quiz 3	❽ quiz 4	❾ quiz 5

18	chemistry	화학, 교감(交感)		share	지분, 몫, 주식; 공유하다, 나누다
	local	지역의, 지방의; 지역민, 현지인		priority	우선(권), 우선 사항
	encourage	장려[격려]하다, 촉구하다		principle	원리, 원칙, 신념, 신조
	be interested in	~에 관심[흥미]이 있다		make up	차지하다, 만들어내다, 화해하다
	experiment	실험, 시험, 시도; 실험하다, 시도하다		act on	~에 작용하다, ~을 따라 행동하다
	look for	~을 모집하다, ~을 찾다		respect	존중하다; 존중, 관련, 주의, (측)면, (-s) 안부
	recommend	추천하다; 권고하다		compassion	연민
	department	부서, 매장		concern	~에 관련되다, 걱정하다; 관심사, 걱정
	be sure	확신하다, 반드시 ~하도록 하다		suffering	고통, 괴로움, 고난; 괴로워하는, 고통을 겪는
	participant	참여자, 참가자		courage	용기, 담력
	look forward to -ing	~하기를 고대하다		decision	결정, 결심, 판결
19	climb	올라가다, 기어오르다	21	doubt	의심, 불확실성; 의심하다
	take a risk	위험을 무릅쓰다, 모험하다		correct	교정하다; 정확한, 올바른
	definitely	확실히, 틀림없이		pressure	압력, 압박, 스트레스; 압력을 가하다
	persuade	설득하다, 확신시키나		indeed	실제로, 사실
	deceptively	믿을 수 없게도		similarly	유사하게, 마찬가지로
	barren	불모의, 메마른		process	과정, 절차; 처리하다, 가공하다
	cliff	절벽, 낭떠러지		useless	쓸모없는, 소용없는, 헛된
	end up with	결국 ~하게 되다		perceive	인지하다, 감지하다
	get to	~에 도착하다		publish	게재하다, 출간하다, 발표하다
	tremble	떨다, 흔들리다; 떨림, 진동		receive	받다, 받아들이다
	exhaustion	탈진, 고갈, 소진		intend	~할 작정이다, 의도하다
	freeze	얼다, 얼어붙다		complete	완성[완료]하다; 완전한
	fright	놀람, 공포, 두려움		publication	출판(물), 발행
20	overhear	우연히 듣다, 엿듣다	22	negotiate	협상하다, 헤쳐 나가다

Voca

| ❶ voca | ❷ text | ❸ [/] | ❹ _____ | ❺ quiz 1 | ❻ quiz 2 | ❼ quiz 3 | ❽ quiz 4 | ❾ quiz 5 |

	traditional	전통적인, 고풍의		increase	(수량이) 늘다, 증가하다; 증가
	approach	접근하다; 접근(법)		productivity	생산성
	be likely to V	~하기 쉽다, ~할 가능성이 있다		spillover	파급
	win-win	모두에게 유리한		advantage	이익, 이점; 이롭게 하다
	agreement	합의, 동의		up to	~까지, ~의 책임인
	negotiation	협상, 교섭, 절충, 극복		degree	정도, 도, 학위
	probably	아마		variety	변화, 다양(성), 품종
	deal with	~을 처리[해결]하다, 다루다		excessive	과도한, 지나친, 터무니없는
	transaction	거래, 매매, 처리		lower	낮은, 하부의; 낮추다, 내리다, 떨어뜨리다
	increasingly	점점, 더욱 더		diversity	다양(성)
	repeatedly	반복적으로, 되풀이하여		impact	영향, 효과, 충격; 영향[충격]을 주다
	spouse	배우자, 남편, 아내		affect	~에 영향을 미치다, ~인 척하다; 정서
	colleague	동료, 동업자		multicultural	다문화의
	client	고객, 의뢰인		region	지역, 지방
	essential	근본적인, 본질적인, 필수적인		range	범위, 영역, 다양성; 정렬시키다
	achieve	달성하다, 이루다, 성취하다		goods	상품
	maintain	유지하다, 주장하다		on the other hand	한편, 반면에
	healthy	건강한, 건전한		feature	특징, 특집, 용모; 특집으로 하다, 특징으로 삼다
	at the same time	반면에, 동시에		identity	정체(성), 신원, 고유성, 독자성
	interdependent	상호 의존적인		ethnic	민족의, 인종의
	outcome	결과(물)		conflict	분쟁, 충돌, 갈등; 충돌하다, 다투다
	acceptable	받아들일 만한, 용인되는		foreign	외국의, 대외적인
23	interaction	상호 작용		nationality	국적
	host	주인, 진행자; 주최하다, 진행하다, 접대하다	24	development	발달, 발전, 성장
	population	인구, 개체 수		construction	건축, 구성, 공사

Voca

| ❶ voca | ❷ text | ❸ [/] | ❹ ___ | ❺ quiz 1 | ❻ quiz 2 | ❼ quiz 3 | ❽ quiz 4 | ❾ quiz 5 |

	carve	조각하다, 새기다		include	포함하다, 포괄하다
	ancestor	조상, 선조		tool	도구, 연장
	multiple	다양한, 다수의, 많은; 배수		material	재료, 물질; 물질의, 육체의, 중요한
	so ~ that ...	아주 ~해서 ...하다		be limited to	~에 제한되다, ~에 국한되다
	innovator	혁신가		at least	적어도, 최소한
	force	강요하다; 힘, 세력		refund	반환, 환불; 환불하다
	settle	해결[결정]하다, 정착하다, 진정시키다	28	awareness	자각, 의식, 인식
	construct	건설하다, 구성[조립]하다		marine	바다의, 해양의
25	state	상태, 국가, 주; 진술하다		conservation	보존, 보호
	except for	~을 제외하고, ~이 없으면		wildlife	야생 동물; 야생 동물의
	decrease	감소; 감소하다		pollution	오염, 공해
26	classical	고전의, 고전적인		guideline	가이드라인, 지침, 지표
	go on to V	(한 가지 일을 하고 나서) 이어서 ~하다		submission	제출, 진술, 복종, 항복, 굴복
	serve	제공[기여]하다, 복무하다, 적합하다		deadline	(마감) 기한, 최종 기한
	military	군(대)의, 군사(상)의; 군대		entry	참가, 출품(작), 입구, 참가자
	composition	구성, 구조, 작곡, 작품		announce	발표하다, 알리다
	composer	작곡가	29	exist	존재하다, 실존하다
	admire	감탄하다, 존경하다, 열망하다		comment	비평[논평]하다, 설명하다
	hire	고용하다, 빌리다, 임차하다		discuss	토론하다, 논의하다
	perform	수행하다, 행동하다, 공연[연주]하다		manage	경영[관리]하다, 운영하다, 간신히 ~하다
	expressive	표현이 풍부한, 표현력이 있는		successfully	성공적으로
	inspire	영감을 주다, 고무시키다, 격려하다		go for	~을 위해 가다, ~에 해당되다, 선택하다
	generation	세대, 대, 발생		professional	프로, 전문가; 전문적인, 직업의
27	offering	공물, 제물, 헌납, 제공		specialized	전문적인, 특수화된
	registration	등록 (서류), 기재		stranger	낯선 사람, 이방인

Voca

| ❶ voca | ❷ text | ❸ [/] | ❹ _____ | ❺ quiz 1 | ❻ quiz 2 | ❼ quiz 3 | ❽ quiz 4 | ❾ quiz 5 |

	expertise	전문 지식[기술]		distance	거리, 간격, 차이
	executive	집행의, 경영의; 임원, 경영진		destination	목적지, 행선지
	management	관리, 경영(진)		solely	오직, 단독으로
	criticism	비평, 비판, 비난		logic	논리, 이론
	surgery	외과, (외과) 수술		odds	확률
	prepare	준비하다, 대비하다, (약을) 조제하다		dye	염료; 염색하다
	organization	조직, 단체, 구조		crash	고장 내다, 추락[충돌]하다; 추락, 충돌, 굉음
30	particularly	특히, 상세히		possibly	아마, 혹시, (부정문에서) 아무리 해도, 도저히
	sense	느끼다, 감지하다; 감각, 느낌, 분별		involve	포함[수반]하다, 필요로 하다, 관련시키다
	security	안전, 안심, 보안, 보증		favor	찬성하다, 호의를 베풀다; 호의, 은혜
	routine	일상적인; 일과, 습관적인 동작		pay attention to	~에 주목하다
	disrupt	방해하다, 교란[붕괴]시키다; 혼란된, 분열된		risk	위험; 위험을 무릅쓰다
	familiar	익숙한, 친숙한, 친밀한		make sure	반드시 (~하도록) 하다, 확인하다, 확신하다
	take away	빼앗다, 가져가다	32	similarity	유사성, 닮음
	literal	원문 어구에 충실한, 문자 그대로의		spot	발견하다, 찾아내다; 장소, 반점
	beforehand	사전에, 미리		imaginary	가공의, 가상의, 상상의
	establish	설립하다, 수립하다, 제정하다		ladder	사다리, (출세의) 수단; 출세하다
	focus on	~에 집중하다, 초점을 맞추다		point out	지적하다, 언급하다
	adjust to	~에 맞추다, 적응하다		employ	고용하다, 사용[이용]하다
	contribute to	~에 기여[공헌]하다, ~의 원인이 되다		interpret	해석하다, 통역하다, 설명하다
31	terrified	놀란, 겁먹은		evidence	증거, 징후
	stem from	~에서 생기다, 유래하다		somehow	여하튼, 어쩌면
	lack	부족, 결핍; ~가 부족하다		define	정의하다, 한계 짓다, 한정하다
	passenger	승객, 여객, 통행인		humanity	인류, 인간성, 인간애
	potential	가능성이 있는, 잠재적인; 가능성, 잠재력		beat	치다, 때리다, 패배시키다; 고동, 맥박, 박자

Voca

| ❶ voca | ❷ text | ❸ [/] | ❹ _____ | ❺ quiz 1 | ❻ quiz 2 | ❼ quiz 3 | ❽ quiz 4 | ❾ quiz 5 |

	cognitive	인지의, 인식의		strategy	전략, 전술, 계획, 방법
	task	일, 과업; ~에 과중한 부담을 주다		opposite	반대(되는 사람[것]); 반대의
	species	종, 종류		to one's surprise	~에게 놀랍게도
	precise	정확한, 정밀한		enthusiastic	열정적인, 열광적인, 열렬한
	thousands of	수천의, 많은		on the contrary	그와는 반대로, 오히려
	instinct	본능		seek	추구하다, 찾다, 노력하다
	intelligence	지성, 지능, 정보		subject	주제, 과목, 대상; 지배하다, 복종시키다
	trick	요령, 비결		passionate	열정적인, 열렬한
	term	기간, 용어, (-s) 조건, 관점; 말하다		religion	종교
	linguistic	언어의, 언어학의		biography	전기, 전기 문학
	castration	거세		matter	문제, 사안, 물질; 문제가 되다, 중요하다
	tongue	혀, 언어		find out	~을 찾아내다, ~을 발견하다
	disempower	~로부터 힘을 빼앗다	34	refer to	~을 언급[참조]하다, 가리키다
	invent	발명하다, 꾸며내다		intellectual	지적인, 지능의; 지식인
33	engagement	참여, 약속, 약혼, 고용		competence	능력, 역량, 재능
	achievement	업적, 성취		reflect	반영하다, 나타내다, 숙고하다
	provide A with B	A에게 B를 제공하다		brief	간결한, 잠시의; 요약하다; 짧은 보고, 개요
	influence	영향을 미치다; 영향(력)		elegant	고상한, 우아한
	including	~을 포함하여		exceptionally	특별히, 유난히, 예외적으로
	physicist	물리학자		witty	재치 있는, 위트 있는
	significant	상당한, 중요한, 의미심장한		in terms of	~ 면에서, ~에 관하여
	throughout	도처에, ~동안 내내, 처음부터 끝까지		particular	특정한, 개개의; 사항, 상세
	school year	학년, 학년도		attractive	매력적인, 마음을 끄는
	avoid	피하다, 막다		entertain	즐겁게 하다, 환대하다, 품다
	discover	발견하다, 알다, 깨닫다		trend	유행, 경향, 추세, 흐름

Voca

❶ voca　　❷ text　　❸ [/]　　❹ _____　　❺ quiz 1　　❻ quiz 2　　❼ quiz 3　　❽ quiz 4　　❾ quiz 5

	gadget	도구, 장치	36	at a time	한 번에, 한꺼번에
	occur	일어나다, 발생하다, 존재하다		atom	원자
	performance	수행, 성과, 성적, 공연		block	막다, 차단하다; 장애물, 방해물
	measure	측정하다, 평가하다; 척도, 기준, 조치		be made up of	~로 구성되다
	take into account	~을 고려[참작]하다		a variety of	다양한
	outstanding	뛰어난, 두드러진, 미해결된		common	공통의, 흔한, 평범한
	average	평균; 평균의; 평균이 ~가 되다		form	형태, 모양, 양식; 형성하다, 만들다
35	sensory	감각의, 지각의		liquid	액체; 액체의
	nerves	신경질, 우울		source	원천, 근원, (-s) 출처, 정보원
	pick up	태워주다, 알아채다, 찾아오다		twist	꼬다, 비틀다, 왜곡하다; 비틀림, 왜곡
	sensation	감각, 느낌, 기분, 센세이션, 돌풍		display	전시, 과시; 전시하다, 내보이다
	object	~에 반대하다; 목표, 대상, 물체		steady	한결같은, 확고한, 안정된, 착실한
	nerve	신경, 긴장, 담력, 정신력		environment	환경, 주위(의 상황)
	unpleasant	불쾌한, 불편한		individual	개인; 개인의, 개별적인, 독특한
	protective	보호하는, 방어적인		plenty of	많은
	mechanism	기계 장치, 기구, 메커니즘		fit	~에 맞다; 건강한; 어울림
	so that	~하기 위하여		be known as	~로 알려져 있다
	polite	예의 바른, 공손한		crystal lattice	결정격자(결정을 구성하는 원자와 이온의 규칙적인 배열)
	muscle	근육, 힘, 체력		structure	구조, 조직, 체계; 구성하다, 조직화하다
	contract	계약(서); 계약하다, 수축하다	37	pluck	(악기의 현을) 뜯다, 퉁기다
	painful	아픈, 괴로운		string	끈, 줄; 묶다, 꿰다, 연결하다
	function	기능하다, 작용하다; 기능, 작용		naturally	자연스럽게, 본래
	movement	운동, 움직임, 행동		blur	모호하게 하다, 흐리게 하다
	gut	직감적인; 창자, 장, 배짱, 용기		outline	윤곽, 개요; ~의 윤곽을 그리다
	sweat	땀을 흘리다; 땀		in this way	이런 방식으로, 이렇게 해서

Voca

| ❶ voca | ❷ text | ❸ [/] | ❹ _____ | ❺ quiz 1 | ❻ quiz 2 | ❼ quiz 3 | ❽ quiz 4 | ❾ quiz 5 |

	on one's own	혼자, 혼자 힘으로		popularity	인기, 평판, 대중성
	attach	붙이다, 첨부하다, 애착을 갖게 하다		produce	생산[제조]하다, 초래하다; 농산물
	vibration	진동, 흔들림		ensure	확실하게 하다, 보장하다
	pass on	속이다, 이용하다, 물려주다		demand	요구하다, 필요로 하다; 요구, 수요
	wooden	나무로 된, 목재의		status	상태, 지위, 신분
	panel	패널, 토론자단		assume	추정하다, (태도 등을) 취하다, 맡다
	original	초기의, 본래의, 독창적인; 원형, 원작		completely	완전히, 충분히
38	boundary	경계(선), 한계, 범위		require	필요로 하다, 요구하다
	portable	휴대용의, 휴대가 쉬운; 휴대용 기기		purchase	구매, 구입; 구매[구입]하다
	responsibility	책임; 해야 할 일		switch	바꾸다, 전환하다; 스위치, 개폐기
	separate	갈라진, 별개의; 분리하다, 갈라지다	40	judge	판단하다, 심사하다; 판사, 심판
	minimize	최소화하다, 축소하다		based on	~에 근거하여
	account for	(~의 비율을) 차지하다, 설명하다		in general	보통, 대개, 전반적으로
	conduct	~을 하다, 지휘하다, (전기 등을) 전도하다; 행동		investigate	조사하다, 연구하다
	take care of	~을 돌보다, 보살피다		judgment	판단, 판결, 견해
	notice	알아채다, 주목하다; 공지, 안내문, 주목		match	경기, 시합, 호적수; 경쟁시키다, 어울리다
	flexible	융통성이 있는, 유연한, 탄력적인		expectation	기대, 요구, 예상, 가망
	enable	할 수 있게 하다, ~을 가능하게 하다		scrubs	(외과 의사의) 수술복
	distinction	구별, 차이, 특징, 뛰어남, 우수(성)		exception	예외(사항), 제외
	at work	작동 중인, 작용하여		a series of	일련의
	constantly	지속적으로, 끊임없이		article	(신문 등의) 기사, 글, 조항, 물품
	return	수익, 귀환, 반환; 돌아오다		explore	탐구하다, 탐험하다
39	complementary	서로 보완하는, 보충하는		reaction	반응, 반작용, 반발
	product	생산물, 상품, 산물		established	확립된, 입증된, 정착한, 상비의
	consume	소비하다, 섭취하다, 먹다		slightly	약간, 조금

Voca

	affair	일, 사건, 문제		fossil fuel	화석 연료
	bow	고개를 숙이다, 절하다, 굴종하다		pastureland	목초지
	uniqueness	특별함, 고유성		surface	표면, 외관; 표면의; 겉으로 드러나다
	rating	평점, 등급, 평가		load	(짐을) 싣다, (사람을) 태우다; 하중, 짐, 부담
	give a lecture	강연하다		halfway	중간[중도]의, 불완전한
	suggest	제안하다, 암시하다, 시사하다		deliver	배달하다, 전하다, 출산하다
	deviation	일탈	43~45	temple	사원, 신전
41~42	claim	주장[요구]하다, 차지하다; 요구, 주장		worship	숭배하다, 예배하다; 숭배, 예배
	production	생산, 산출물, 연출, 제작, 상연		arrangement	배열, 배치
	greenhouse	온실, 건조실		accommodation	숙박 (시설), 적응, 편의
	emission	배출(물), 배출량, 발산		look after	돌보다
	reduce	줄이다, 낮추다, 감소하다		applicant	신청자, 지원자
	burning	불타는, 화급한, 중대한		go through	겪다, 경험[통과]하다, 자세히 조사[검토]하다
	transportation	교통, 운송, 교통수단		offer	제공하다, 제안하다; 제공, 제안
	fuel	연료; 연료를 가하다, 부채질하다		care for	~을 돌보다, 좋아하다
	transport	운송, 수송; 운반[수송]하다		educate	가르치다, 교육시키다
	wasteful	낭비적인, 비경제적인, 소모성의		confused	혼란을 느끼는
	from a distance	멀리서		bury	묻다, 매장하다
	depending on	~에 따라		path	(작은) 길, 진로, 보도, 경로
	carbon	탄소		trip over	~에 걸려 넘어지다
	generate	발생시키다, 만들어내다, (감정을) 일으키다		remove	제거하다, 없애다, 옮기다
	pound	빻다, 두드리다; (단위) 파운드, 동물 수용소		duty	의무, 임무, 근무, 관세, 세금
	compared to	~에 비해, ~와 비교하여			
	raise	높이다, 올리다, 기르다, 제기하다; 인상			
	feed	먹이를 주다, 먹이다; 먹이			

Voca Test

영 〉한

① voca　　❷ text　　❸ [/]　　❹ ____　　❺ quiz 1　　❻ quiz 2　　❼ quiz 3　　❽ quiz 4　　❾ quiz 5

18	chemistry		share		
	local		priority		
	encourage		principle		
	be interested in		make up		
	experiment		act on		
	look for		respect		
	recommend		compassion		
	department		concern		
	be sure		suffering		
	participant		courage		
	look forward to -ing		decision		
19	climb		21	doubt		
	take a risk		correct		
	definitely		pressure		
	persuade		indeed		
	deceptively		similarly		
	barren		process		
	cliff		useless		
	end up with		perceive		
	get to		publish		
	tremble		receive		
	exhaustion		intend		
	freeze		complete		
	fright		publication		
20	overhear		22	negotiate		

(.hwp) (.pdf) ➔ www.englishmygod.com

Voca Test

영 〉 한

| ❶ voca | ❷ text | ❸ [/] | ❹ _____ | ❺ quiz 1 | ❻ quiz 2 | ❼ quiz 3 | ❽ quiz 4 | ❾ quiz 5 |

	traditional			increase	
	approach			productivity	
	be likely to V			spillover	
	win-win			advantage	
	agreement			up to	
	negotiation			degree	
	probably			variety	
	deal with			excessive	
	transaction			lower	
	increasingly			diversity	
	repeatedly			impact	
	spouse			affect	
	colleague			multicultural	
	client			region	
	essential			range	
	achieve			goods	
	maintain			on the other hand	
	healthy			feature	
	at the same time			identity	
	interdependent			ethnic	
	outcome			conflict	
	acceptable			foreign	
23	interaction			nationality	
	host		24	development	
	population			construction	

Voca Test

	carve				include			
	ancestor				tool			
	multiple				material			
	so ~ that ...				be limited to			
	innovator				at least			
	force				refund			
	settle			28	awareness			
	construct				marine			
25	state				conservation			
	except for				wildlife			
	decrease				pollution			
26	classical				guideline			
	go on to V				submission			
	serve				deadline			
	military				entry			
	composition				announce			
	composer			29	exist			
	admire				comment			
	hire				discuss			
	perform				manage			
	expressive				successfully			
	inspire				go for			
	generation				professional			
27	offering				specialized			
	registration				stranger			

Voca Test

	❶ voca	❷ text	❸ [/]	❹ ____	❺ quiz 1	❻ quiz 2	❼ quiz 3	❽ quiz 4	❾ quiz 5
	expertise				distance				
	executive				destination				
	management				solely				
	criticism				logic				
	surgery				odds				
	prepare				dye				
	organization				crash				
30	particularly				possibly				
	sense				involve				
	security				favor				
	routine				pay attention to				
	disrupt				risk				
	familiar				make sure				
	take away			32	similarity				
	literal				spot				
	beforehand				imaginary				
	establish				ladder				
	focus on				point out				
	adjust to				employ				
	contribute to				interpret				
31	terrified				evidence				
	stem from				somehow				
	lack				define				
	passenger				humanity				
	potential				beat				

Voca Tes

영 > 한

| ❶ voca | ❷ text | ❸ [/] | ❹ ___ | ❺ quiz 1 | ❻ quiz 2 | ❼ quiz 3 | ❽ quiz 4 | ❾ quiz 5 |

	cognitive			strategy	
	task			opposite	
	species			to one's surprise	
	precise			enthusiastic	
	thousands of			on the contrary	
	instinct			seek	
	intelligence			subject	
	trick			passionate	
	term			religion	
	linguistic			biography	
	castration			matter	
	tongue			find out	
	disempower		34	refer to	
	invent			intellectual	
33	engagement			competence	
	achievement			reflect	
	provide A with B			brief	
	influence			elegant	
	including			exceptionally	
	physicist			witty	
	significant			in terms of	
	throughout			particular	
	school year			attractive	
	avoid			entertain	
	discover			trend	

Voca Test

영 ◐ 한

❶ voca	❷ text	❸ [/]	❹ ____	❺ quiz 1	❻ quiz 2	❼ quiz 3	❽ quiz 4	❾ quiz 5

	gadget		36	at a time	
	occur			atom	
	performance			block	
	measure			be made up of	
	take into account			a variety of	
	outstanding			common	
	average			form	
35	sensory			liquid	
	nerves			source	
	pick up			twist	
	sensation			display	
	object			steady	
	nerve			environment	
	unpleasant			individual	
	protective			plenty of	
	mechanism			fit	
	so that			be known as	
	polite			crystal lattice	
	muscle			structure	
	contract		37	pluck	
	painful			string	
	function			naturally	
	movement			blur	
	gut			outline	
	sweat			in this way	

Voca Test

영 〉한

	❶ voca	❷ text	❸ [/]	❹ ____	❺ quiz 1	❻ quiz 2	❼ quiz 3	❽ quiz 4	❾ quiz 5

	on one's own			popularity	
	attach			produce	
	vibration			ensure	
	pass on			demand	
	wooden			status	
	panel			assume	
	original			completely	
38	boundary			require	
	portable			purchase	
	responsibility			switch	
	separate		40	judge	
	minimize			based on	
	account for			in general	
	conduct			investigate	
	take care of			judgment	
	notice			match	
	flexible			expectation	
	enable			scrubs	
	distinction			exception	
	at work			a series of	
	constantly			article	
	return			explore	
39	complementary			reaction	
	product			established	
	consume			slightly	

(.hwp) (.pdf) → www.englishmygod.com

Voca Test

영 ◗ 한

❶ voca ❷ text ❸ [/] ❹ ____ ❺ quiz 1 ❻ quiz 2 ❼ quiz 3 ❽ quiz 4 ❾ quiz 5

	affair			fossil fuel	
	bow			pastureland	
	uniqueness			surface	
	rating			load	
	give a lecture			halfway	
	suggest			deliver	
	deviation		43~45	temple	
41~42	claim			worship	
	production			arrangement	
	greenhouse			accommodation	
	emission			look after	
	reduce			applicant	
	burning			go through	
	transportation			offer	
	fuel			care for	
	transport			educate	
	wasteful			confused	
	from a distance			bury	
	depending on			path	
	carbon			trip over	
	generate			remove	
	pound			duty	
	compared to				
	raise				
	feed				

Voca Test 영 ▶ 한

❶ voca	❷ text	❸ [/]	❹ _____	❺ quiz 1	❻ quiz 2	❼ quiz 3	❽ quiz 4	❾ quiz 5
18		화학, 교감(交感)						
		지역의, 지방의; 지역민, 현지인						
		장려[격려]하다, 촉구하다						
		~에 관심[흥미]이 있다						
		실험, 시험, 시도; 실험하다, 시도하다						
		~을 모집하다, ~을 찾다						
		추천하다; 권고하다						
		부서, 매장						
		확신하다, 반드시 ~하도록 하다						
		참여자, 참가자						
		~하기를 고대하다						
19		올라가다, 기어오르다						
		위험을 무릅쓰다, 모험하다						
		확실히, 틀림없이						
		설득하다, 확신시키다						
		믿을 수 없게도						
		불모의, 메마른						
		절벽, 낭떠러지						
		결국 ~하게 되다						
		~에 도착하다						
		떨다, 흔들리다; 떨림, 진동						
		탈진, 고갈, 소진						
		얼다, 얼어붙다						
		놀람, 공포, 두려움						
20		우연히 듣다, 엿듣다						

❶ voca	❷ text	❸ [/]	❹ _____	❺ quiz 1	❻ quiz 2	❼ quiz 3	❽ quiz 4	❾ quiz 5
		지분, 몫, 주식; 공유하다, 나누다						
		우선(권), 우선 사항						
		원리, 원칙, 신념, 신조						
		차지하다, 만들어내다, 화해하다						
		~에 작용하다, ~을 따라 행동하다						
		존중하다; 존중, 관련, 주의, (측)면, (-s) 안부						
		연민						
		~에 관련되다, 걱정하다; 관심사, 걱정						
		고통, 괴로움, 고난; 괴로워하는, 고통을 겪는						
		용기, 담력						
		결정, 결심, 판결						
21		의심, 불확실성; 의심하다						
		교정하다; 정확한, 올바른						
		압력, 압박, 스트레스; 압력을 가하다						
		실제로, 사실						
		유사하게, 마찬가지로						
		과정, 절차; 처리하다, 가공하다						
		쓸모없는, 소용없는, 헛된						
		인지하다, 감지하다						
		게재하다, 출간하다, 발표하다						
		받다, 받아들이다						
		~할 작정이다, 의도하다						
		완성[완료]하다; 완전한						
		출판(물), 발행						
22		협상하다, 헤쳐 나가다						

Voca Test

❶ voca		❷ text	❸ [/]	❹ ____	❺ quiz 1	❻ quiz 2	❼ quiz 3	❽ quiz 4	❾ quiz 5
		전통적인, 고풍의			(수량이) 늘다, 증가하다; 증가
		접근하다; 접근(법)			생산성
		~하기 쉽다, ~할 가능성이 있다			파급
		모두에게 유리한			이익, 이점; 이롭게 하다
		합의, 동의			~까지, ~의 책임인
		협상, 교섭, 절충, 극복			정도, 도, 학위
		아마			변화, 다양(성), 품종
		~을 처리[해결]하다, 다루다			과도한, 지나친, 터무니없는
		거래, 매매, 처리			낮은, 하부의; 낮추다, 내리다, 떨어뜨리다
		점점, 더욱 더			다양(성)
		반복적으로, 되풀이하여			영향, 효과, 충격; 영향[충격]을 주다
		배우자, 남편, 아내			~에 영향을 미치다, ~인 척하다; 정서
		동료, 동업자			다문화의
		고객, 의뢰인			지역, 지방
		근본적인, 본질적인, 필수적인			범위, 영역, 다양성; 정렬시키다
		달성하다, 이루다, 성취하다			상품
		유지하다, 주장하다			한편, 반면에
		건강한, 건전한			특징, 특집, 용모; 특집으로 하다, 특집으로 삼다
		반면에, 동시에			정체(성), 신원, 고유성, 독자성
		상호 의존적인			민족의, 인종의
		결과(물)			분쟁, 충돌, 갈등; 충돌하다, 다투다
		받아들일 만한, 용인되는			외국의, 대외적인
23		상호 작용			국적
		주인, 진행자; 주최하다, 진행하다, 접대하다	24		발달, 발전, 성장
		인구, 개체 수			건축, 구성, 공사

Voca Test

❶ voca	❷ text	❸ [/]	❹ ____	❺ quiz 1	❻ quiz 2	❼ quiz 3	❽ quiz 4	❾ quiz 5

No.	뜻	No.	뜻
	조각하다, 새기다		포함하다, 포괄하다
	조상, 선조		도구, 연장
	다양한, 다수의, 많은; 배수		재료, 물질; 물질의, 육체의, 중요한
	아주 ~해서 ...하다		~에 제한되다, ~에 국한되다
	혁신가		적어도, 최소한
	강요하다; 힘, 세력		반환, 환불; 환불하다
	해결[결정]하다, 정착하다, 진정시키다	28	자각, 의식, 인식
	건설하다, 구성[조립]하다		바다의, 해양의
25	상태, 국가, 주; 진술하다		보존, 보호
	~을 제외하고, ~이 없으면		야생 동물; 야생 동물의
	감소; 감소하다		오염, 공해
26	고전의, 고전적인		가이드라인, 지침, 지표
	(한 가지 일을 하고 나서) 이어서 ~하다		제출, 진술, 복종, 항복, 굴복
	제공[기여]하다, 복무하다, 적합하다		(마감) 기한, 최종 기한
	군(대)의, 군사(상)의; 군대		참가, 출품(작), 입구, 참가자
	구성, 구조, 작곡, 작품		발표하다, 알리다
	작곡가	29	존재하다, 실존하다
	감탄하다, 존경하다, 열망하다		비평[논평]하다, 설명하다
	고용하다, 빌리다, 임차하다		토론하다, 논의하다
	수행하다, 행동하다, 공연[연주]하다		경영[관리]하다, 운영하다, 간신히 ~하다
	표현이 풍부한, 표현력이 있는		성공적으로
	영감을 주다, 고무시키다, 격려하다		~을 위해 가다, ~에 해당되다, 선택하다
	세대, 대, 발생		프로, 전문가; 전문적인, 직업의
27	공물, 제물, 헌납, 제공		전문적인, 특수화된
	등록 (서류), 기재		낯선 사람, 이방인

(.hwp) (.pdf) → www.englishmygod.com

Voca Test

❶ voca	❷ text	❸ [/]	❹ _____	❺ quiz 1	❻ quiz 2	❼ quiz 3	❽ quiz 4	❾ quiz 5
		전문 지식[기술]			거리, 간격, 차이			
		집행의, 경영의; 임원, 경영진			목적지, 행선지			
		관리, 경영(진)			오직, 단독으로			
		비평, 비판, 비난			논리, 이론			
		외과, (외과) 수술			**확률**			
		준비하다, 대비하다, (약을) 조제하다			염료; 염색하다			
		조직, 단체, 구조			고장 내다, 추락[충돌]하다; 추락, 충돌, 굉음			
30		특히, 상세히			아마, 혹시, (부정문에서) 아무리 해도, 도저히			
		느끼다, 감지하다; 감각, 느낌, 분별			포함[수반]하다, 필요로 하다, 관련시키다			
		안전, 안심, 보안, 보증			찬성하다, 호의를 베풀다; 호의, 은혜			
		일상적인; 일과, 습관적인 동작			~에 주목하다			
		방해하다, 교란[붕괴]시키다; 혼란된, 분열된			위험; 위험을 무릅쓰다			
		익숙한, 친숙한, 친밀한			반드시 (~하도록) 하다, 확인하다, 확신하다			
		빼앗다, 가져가다	32		유사성, 닮음			
		원문 어구에 충실한, 문자 그대로의			발견하다, 찾아내다; 장소, 반점			
		사전에, 미리			가공의, 가상의, 상상의			
		설립하다, 수립하다, 제정하다			사다리, (출세의) 수단; 출세하다			
		~에 집중하다, 초점을 맞추다			지적하다, 언급하다			
		~에 맞추다, 적응하다			고용하다, 사용[이용]하다			
		~에 기여[공헌]하다, ~의 원인이 되다			해석하다, 통역하다, 설명하다			
31		놀란, 겁먹은			증거, 징후			
		~에서 생기다, 유래하다			여하튼, 어쩌면			
		부족, 결핍; ~가 부족하다			정의하다, 한계 짓다, 한정하다			
		승객, 여객, 통행인			인류, 인간성, 인간애			
		가능성이 있는, 잠재적인; 가능성, 잠재력			치다, 때리다, 패배시키다; 고동, 맥박, 박자			

Voca Test

❶ voca	❷ text	❸ [/]	❹ _____	❺ quiz 1	❻ quiz 2	❼ quiz 3	❽ quiz 4	❾ quiz 5
		인지의, 인식의			전략, 전술, 계획, 방법			
		일, 과업; ~에 과중한 부담을 주다			반대(되는 사람[것]); 반대의			
		종, 종류			~에게 놀랍게도			
		정확한, 정밀한			열정적인, 열광적인, 열렬한			
		수천의, 많은			그와는 반대로, 오히려			
		본능			추구하다, 찾다, 노력하다			
		지성, 지능, 정보			주제, 과목, 대상; 지배하다, 복종시키다			
		요령, 비결			열정적인, 열렬한			
		기간, 용어, (-s) 조건, 관점; 말하다			종교			
		언어의, 언어학의			전기, 전기 문학			
		거세			문제, 사안, 물질; 문제가 되다, 중요하다			
		혀, 언어			~을 찾아내다, ~을 발견하다			
		~로부터 힘을 빼앗다	34		~을 언급[참조]하다, 가리키다			
		발명하다, 꾸며내다			지적인, 지능의; 지식인			
33		참여, 약속, 약혼, 고용			능력, 역량, 재능			
		업적, 성취			반영하다, 나타내다, 숙고하다			
		A에게 B를 제공하다			간결한, 잠시의; 요약하다; 짧은 보고, 개요			
		영향을 미치다; 영향(력)			고상한, 우아한			
		~을 포함하여			특별히, 유난히, 예외적으로			
		물리학자			재치 있는, 위트 있는			
		상당한, 중요한, 의미심장한			~ 면에서, ~에 관하여			
		도처에, ~동안 내내, 처음부터 끝까지			특정한, 개개의; 사항, 상세			
		학년, 학년도			매력적인, 마음을 끄는			
		피하다, 막다			즐겁게 하다, 환대하다, 품다			
		발견하다, 알다, 깨닫다			유행, 경향, 추세, 흐름			

(.hwp) (.pdf) ➔ www.englishmygod.com

Voca Test

❶ voca	❷ text	❸ [/]	❹ ____	❺ quiz 1	❻ quiz 2	❼ quiz 3	❽ quiz 4	❾ quiz 5
		도구, 장치	36		한 번에, 한꺼번에			
		일어나다, 발생하다, 존재하다			원자			
		수행, 성과, 성적, 공연			막다, 차단하다; 장애물, 방해물			
		측정하다, 평가하다; 척도, 기준, 조치			~로 구성되다			
		~을 고려[참작]하다			다양한			
		뛰어난, 두드러진, 미해결된			공통의, 흔한, 평범한			
		평균; 평균의; 평균이 ~가 되다			형태, 모양, 양식; 형성하다, 만들다			
35		감각의, 지각의			액체; 액체의			
		신경질, 우울			원천, 근원, (-s) 출처, 정보원			
		태워주다, 알아채다, 찾아오다			꼬다, 비틀다, 왜곡하다; 비틀림, 왜곡			
		감각, 느낌, 기분, 센세이션, 돌풍			전시, 과시; 전시하다, 내보이다			
		~에 반대하다; 목표, 대상, 물체			한결같은, 확고한, 안정된, 착실한			
		신경, 긴장, 담력, 정신력			환경, 주위(의 상황)			
		불쾌한, 불편한			개인; 개인의, 개별적인, 독특한			
		보호하는, 방어적인			많은			
		기계 장치, 기구, 메커니즘			~에 맞다; 건강한; 어울림			
		~하기 위하여			~로 알려져 있다			
		예의 바른, 공손한			결정격자(결정을 구성하는 원자와 이온의 규칙적인 배열)			
		근육, 힘, 체력			구조, 조직, 체계; 구성하다, 조직화하다			
		계약(서); 계약하다, 수축하다	37		(악기의 현을) 뜯다, 퉁기다			
		아픈, 괴로운			끈, 줄; 묶다, 꿰다, 연결하다			
		기능하다, 작용하다; 기능, 작용			자연스럽게, 본래			
		운동, 움직임, 행동			모호하게 하다, 흐리게 하다			
		직감적인; 창자, 장, 배짱, 용기			윤곽, 개요; ~의 윤곽을 그리다			
		땀을 흘리다; 땀			이런 방식으로, 이렇게 해서			

Voca Test

❶ voca	❷ text	❸ [/]	❹ _____	❺ quiz 1	❻ quiz 2	❼ quiz 3	❽ quiz 4	❾ quiz 5
		혼자, 혼자 힘으로			인기, 평판, 대중성			
		붙이다, 첨부하다, 애착을 갖게 하다			생산[제조]하다, 초래하다; 농산물			
		진동, 흔들림			확실하게 하다, 보장하다			
		속이다, 이용하다, 물려주다			요구하다, 필요로 하다; 요구, 수요			
		나무로 된, 목재의			상태, 지위, 신분			
		패널, 토론자단			추정하다, (태도 등을) 취하다, 맡다			
		초기의, 본래의, 독창적인; 원형, 원작			완전히, 충분히			
38		경계(선), 한계, 범위			필요로 하다, 요구하다			
		휴대용의, 휴대가 쉬운; 휴대용 기기			구매, 구입; 구매[구입]하다			
		책임; 해야 할 일			바꾸다, 전환하다; 스위치, 개폐기			
		갈라진, 별개의; 분리하다, 갈라지다	40		판단하다, 심사하다; 판사, 심판			
		최소화하다, 축소하다			~에 근거하여			
		(~의 비율을) 차지하다, 설명하다			보통, 대개, 전반적으로			
		~을 하다, 지휘하다, (전기 등을) 전도하다; 행동			조사하다, 연구하다			
		~을 돌보다, 보살피다			판단, 판결, 견해			
		알아채다, 주목하다; 공지, 안내문, 주목			경기, 시합, 호적수; 경쟁시키다, 어울리다			
		융통성이 있는, 유연한, 탄력적인			기대, 요구, 예상, 가망			
		할 수 있게 하다, ~을 가능하게 하다			(외과 의사의) 수술복			
		구별, 차이, 특징, 뛰어남, 우수(성)			예외(사항), 제외			
		작동 중인, 작용하여			일련의			
		지속적으로, 끊임없이			(신문 등의) 기사, 글, 조항, 물품			
		수익, 귀환, 반환; 돌아오다			탐구하다, 탐험하다			
39		서로 보완하는, 보충하는			반응, 반작용, 반발			
		생산물, 상품, 산물			확립된, 입증된, 정착한, 상비의			
		소비하다, 섭취하다, 먹다			약간, 조금			

(.hwp) (.pdf) → www.englishmygod.com

Voca Test

| ❶ voca | ❷ text | ❸ [/] | ❹ _____ | ❺ quiz 1 | ❻ quiz 2 | ❼ quiz 3 | ❽ quiz 4 | ❾ quiz 5 |

		일, 사건, 문제			화석 연료
		고개를 숙이다, 절하다, 굴종하다			목초지
		특별함, 고유성			표면, 외관; 표면의; 겉으로 드러나다
		평점, 등급, 평가			(짐을) 싣다, (사람을) 태우다; 하중, 짐, 부담
		강연하다			중간[중도]의, 불완전한
		제안하다, 암시하다, 시사하다			배달하다, 전하다, 출산하다
41 ~42		일탈	43 ~45		사원, 신전
		주장[요구]하다, 차지하다; 요구, 주장			숭배하다, 예배하다; 숭배, 예배
		생산, 산출물, 연출, 제작, 상연			배열, 배치
		온실, 건조실			숙박 (시설), 적응, 편의
		배출(물), 배출량, 발산			돌보다
		줄이다, 낮추다, 감소하다			신청자, 지원자
		불타는, 화급한, 중대한			겪다, 경험[통과]하다, 자세히 조사[검토]하다
		교통, 운송, 교통수단			제공하다, 제안하다; 제공, 제안
		연료; 연료를 가하다, 부채질하다			~을 돌보다, 좋아하다
		운송, 수송; 운반[수송]하다			가르치다, 교육시키다
		낭비적인, 비경제적인, 소모성의			혼란을 느끼는
		멀리서			묻다, 매장하다
		~에 따라			(작은) 길, 진로, 보도, 경로
		탄소			~에 걸려 넘어지다
		발생시키다, 만들어내다, (감정을) 일으키다			제거하다, 없애다, 옮기다
		빻다, 두드리다; (단위) 파운드, 동물 수용소			의무, 임무, 근무, 관세, 세금
		~에 비해, ~와 비교하여			
		높이다, 올리다, 기르다, 제기하다; 인상			
		먹이를 주다, 먹이다; 먹이			

2023 고1 9월 모의고사

18 목적

❶ Dear Professor Sanchez, My name is Ellis Wight, and I'm the director of the Alexandria Science Museum.

Sanchez 교수님께, 제 이름은 Ellis Wight이고 Alexandria 과학 박물관의 관장입니다.

❷ We are holding a Chemistry Fair for local middle school students on Saturday, October 28.

저희는 10월 28일 토요일에 지역 중학교 학생을 위한 화학 박람회를 개최합니다.

❸ The goal of the fair is to encourage them to be interested in science through guided experiments.

이 박람회의 목적은 안내적 실험을 통해 학생들이 과학에 관한 관심을 갖도록 장려하는 것입니다.

❹ We are looking for college students who can help with the experiments during the event.

저희는 행사 기간 동안 실험을 도와줄 수 있는 대학생을 모집하고자 합니다.

❺ I am contacting you to ask you to recommend some students from the chemistry department at your college who you think are qualified for this job.

저는 이 일에 적합하다고 생각되는 귀교의 화학과 학생 몇 명을 추천해 달라는 요청을 드리고자 연락드렸습니다.

❻ With their help, I'm sure the participants will have a great experience.

저는 그 학생들의 도움으로 참가자들이 훌륭한 경험을 하게 될 것이라 확신합니다.

❼ I look forward to hearing from you soon.

빠른 시일 내에 당신으로부터 연락이 오기를 기대하겠습니다.

❽ Sincerely, Ellis Wight

진심을 담아, Ellis Wight

19 심경

❶ Gregg and I had been rock climbing since sunrise and had had no problems.

Gregg와 나는 일출 이후에 암벽 등반을 해왔고 아무런 문제가 없었다.

❷ So we took a risk. "Look, the first bolt is right there. I can definitely climb out to it. Piece of cake," I persuaded Gregg, minutes before I found myself pinned.

그래서 우리는 위험을 감수했다. "봐, 첫 번째 볼트가 바로 저기에 있어. 나는 분명히 거기까지 올라갈 수 있어. 식은 죽 먹기야."라고 나는 Gregg를 설득했고, 얼마 지나지 않아 나는 내가 꼼짝 못 하게 되었다는 것을 알게 되었다.

❸ It wasn't a piece of cake. The rock was deceptively barren of handholds.

그것은 식은 죽 먹기가 아니었다. 그 바위는 믿을 수 없게도 손으로 잡을 곳이 없었다.

❹ I clumsily moved back and forth across the cliff face and ended up with nowhere to go...but down.

나는 서툴게 절벽 면을 이리저리 가로질러 보았지만 갈 곳이... 결국 아래쪽밖에는 없었다.

❺ The bolt that would save my life, if I could get to it, was about two feet above my reach.

만약 내가 거기까지 갈 수 있다면, 내 목숨을 구해줄 볼트는 손이 닿을 수 있는 곳에서 약 2피트 위에 있었다.

❻ My arms trembled from exhaustion.

내 팔은 극도의 피로로 떨렸다.

❼ I looked at Gregg.

나는 Gregg를 쳐다보았다.

❽ My body froze with fright from my neck down to my toes.

내 몸은 목에서부터 발끝까지 공포로 얼어붙었다. 우리 사이에 밧줄이 묶여 있었다.

❾ Our rope was tied between us. If I fell, he would fall with me.

내가 떨어지면, 그도 나와 함께 떨어질 것이다.

20 요지

❶ We are always teaching our children something by our words and our actions.

우리는 항상 우리 자녀에게 말과 행동으로 무언가를 가르치고 있다.

❷ They learn from seeing.

그들은 보는 것으로부터 배운다.

❸ They learn from hearing and from *overhearing*.

그들은 듣거나 '우연히 듣는 것'으로부터 배운다.

❹ Children share the values of their parents about the most important things in life.

아이들은 인생에서 가장 중요한 것에 대해 그들 부모의 가치를 공유한다.

❺ Our priorities and principles and our examples of good behavior can teach our children to take the high road when other roads look tempting.

우리의 우선순위와 원칙 그리고 훌륭한 행동에 대한 본보기는 우리 자녀에게 다른 길이 유혹적으로 보일 때 올바른 길로 가도록 가르칠 수 있다.

❻ Remember that children do not learn the values that make up strong character simply by being *told* about them.

아이들은 확고한 인격을 구성하는 가치를 단순히 그것에 대해 '들음'으로써 배우지 않는다는 것을 기억하라.

❼ They learn by seeing the people around them *act* on and *uphold* those values in their daily lives.

그들은 그들 주변 사람들이 그들의 일상생활에서 그러한 가치를 좇아 '행동'하고 '유지'하는 것을 봄으로써 배운다.

❽ Therefore show your child good examples of life by your action.

그러므로 여러분의 자녀에게 여러분의 행동으로 삶의 모범을 보여라.

❾ In our daily lives, we can show our children that we respect others.

우리 일상생활에서, 우리는 우리 자녀에게 우리가 타인을 존중하는 것을 보여줄 수 있다.

❿ We can show them our compassion and concern when others are suffering, and our own self-discipline, courage and honesty as we make difficult decisions.

우리는 그들에게 타인이 괴로워할 때 우리의 연민과 걱정을, 그리고 우리가 어려운 결정을 할 때 우리 자신의 자제력, 용기 그리고 정직을 보여줄 수 있다.

21 주장

❶ Most people have no doubt heard this question: If a tree falls in the forest and there is no one there to hear it fall, does it make a sound? The correct answer is no.

대부분의 사람들은 틀림없이 이 질문을 들어 봤을 것이다. : 만약 숲에서 나무가 쓰러지고 그것이 쓰러지는 것을 들을 사람이 거기에 없다면, 소리가 나는 것일까? 정답은 '아니요'이다..

❷ Sound is more than pressure waves, and indeed there can be no sound without a hearer.

소리는 압력파 이상이며, 정말로 듣는 사람 없이는 소리가 있을 수 없다.

❸ And similarly, scientific communication is a two-way process.

마찬가지로, 과학적 커뮤니케이션은 양방향 프로세스이다.

❹ Just as a signal of any kind is useless unless it is perceived, a published scientific paper (signal) is useless unless it is both received *and* understood by its intended audience.

어떠한 종류의 신호든 그것이 감지되지 않으면 쓸모가 없는 것처럼, 출판된 과학 논문(신호)은 그것이 의도된 독자에 의해 수신 '그리고' 이해가 둘 다 되지 않으면 쓸모가 없다.

❺ Thus we can restate the axiom of science as follows: A scientific experiment is not complete until the results have been published *and understood*.

따라서 우리는 과학의 자명한 이치를 다음과 같이 재진술할 수 있다. : 과학 실험은 결과가 출판되고 '그리고 이해될' 때까지 완성되지 않는다.

❻ Publication is no more than pressure waves unless the published paper is understood.

출판된 논문이 이해되지 않으면 출판은 압력파에 지나지 않는다.

❼ Too many scientific papers fall silently in the woods.

너무 많은 과학 논문이 소리 없이 숲속에서 쓰러진다.

22 의미

❶ We all negotiate every day, whether we realise it or not.

우리가 그것을 알든지 모르든지 간에, 우리 모두는 매일 협상한다.

❷ Yet few people ever learn *how* to negotiate.

하지만 이제까지 '어떻게' 협상하는지를 배운 사람은 거의 없다.

❸ Those who do usually learn the traditional, win-lose negotiating style rather than an approach that is likely to result in a win-win agreement.

(협상 방식을) 배우는 사람들은 대개 양측에 유리한 합의를 도출할 가능성이 있는 접근법보다는 전통적인, 한쪽에만 유리한 협상 방식을 배운다.

❹ This old-school, adversarial approach may be useful in a one-off negotiation where you will probably not deal with that person again.

이 구식의 적대적인 접근법은 아마도 여러분이 그 사람을 다시 상대하지 않을 일회성 협상에서 유용할지도 모른다.

❺ However, such transactions are becoming increasingly rare, because most of us deal with the same people repeatedly — our spouses and children, our friends and colleagues, our customers and clients.

그러나, 우리 대부분은 배우자와 자녀, 친구와 동료, 고객과 의뢰인같이 동일한 사람들을 반복적으로 상대하기 때문에, 이러한 거래는 점점 더 드물어지고 있다.

❻ In view of this, it's essential to achieve successful results for ourselves and maintain a healthy relationship with our negotiating partners at the same time.

이러한 관점에서, 우리 자신을 위해 성공적인 결과를 얻어내는 동시에 협상 파트너들과 건전한 관계를 유지하는 것이 중요하다.

❼ In today's interdependent world of business partnerships and long-term relationships, a win-win outcome is fast becoming the *only* acceptable result.

오늘날 비즈니스 파트너십과 장기적 관계의 상호 의존적인 세계에서, 양측에 유리한 성과는 '유일하게' 받아들일 수 있는 결과가 빠르게 되어가고 있다.

23 주제

❶ The interaction of workers from different cultural backgrounds with the host population might increase productivity due to positive externalities like knowledge spillovers.

다른 문화적 배경으로부터의 노동자들과 현지 주민의 상호 작용은 지식 파급과 같은 긍정적인 외부 효과로 인해 생산성을 증가시킬 수 있다.

❷ This is only an advantage up to a certain degree.

이것은 어느 정도까지만 장점이다.

❸ When the variety of backgrounds is too large, fractionalization may cause excessive transaction costs for communication, which may lower productivity.

배경의 다양성이 너무 클 경우, 분열은 의사소통에 대한 과도한 거래 비용을 초래하는데, 이는 생산성을 저하시킬 수 있다.

❹ Diversity not only impacts the labour market, but may also affect the quality of life in a location.

다양성은 노동 시장에 영향을 줄 뿐만 아니라 한 지역의 삶의 질에도 영향을 미칠 수 있다.

❺ A tolerant native population may value a multicultural city or region because of an increase in the range of available goods and services.

관용적인 원주민은 이용 가능한 재화와 용역 범위의 증가로 인해 다문화 도시나 지역을 가치 있게 여길 수 있다.

❻ On the other hand, diversity could be perceived as an unattractive feature if natives perceive it as a distortion of what they consider to be their national identity.

반면에, 원주민들이 다양성을 그들의 국가 정체성이라고 생각하는 것에 대한 왜곡으로 인식한다면 다양성은 매력적이지 않은 특징으로 인식될 수 있다.

❼ They might even discriminate against other ethnic groups and they might fear that social conflicts between different foreign nationalities are imported into their own neighbourhood.

그들은 심지어 다른 민족 집단을 차별할 수도 있고 그들은 다른 외국 국적들 간의 사회적 갈등이 그들 인근으로 유입되는 것을 두려워할 수도 있다.

24 제목

❶ We think we are shaping our buildings.

우리는 우리가 건물을 형성하고 있다고 생각한다.

❷ But really, our buildings and development are also shaping us.

그러나 실제로 우리의 건물과 개발도 또한 우리를 형성하고 있다.

❸ One of the best examples of this is the oldest-known construction: the ornately carved rings of standing stones at Göbekli Tepe in Turkey.

이것의 가장 좋은 예 중 하나는 가장 오래된 것으로 알려진 건축물인 튀르키예의 Göbekli Tepe에 있는 화려하게 조각된 입석의 고리이다.

❹ Before these ancestors got the idea to erect standing stones some 12,000 years ago, they were hunter-gatherers.

이 조상들이 약 12,000년 전에 입석을 세우는 아이디어를 얻기 전에 그들은 수렵 채집인이었다.

❺ It appears that the erection of the multiple rings of megalithic stones took so long, and so many successive generations, that these innovators were forced to settle down to complete the construction works.

거석으로 된 여러 개의 고리를 세우는 데 오랜 시간이 걸렸고 많은 잇따른 세대를 거쳤어야 해서 이 혁신가들은 건설 작업을 완료하기 위해 정착해야만 했던 것으로 보이다.

❻ In the process, they became the first farming society on Earth.

그 과정에서, 그들은 지구상 최초의 농업 사회가 되었다.

❼ This is an early example of a society constructing something that ends up radically remaking the society itself.

이것은 결국 사회 자체를 근본적으로 재구성하는 무언가를 건설하는 사회의 초기 예이다.

❽ Things are not so different in our own time.

우리 시대에도 상황이 그렇게 다르지 않다.

26 일치

❶ American jazz pianist Bill Evans was born in New Jersey in 1929.

미국인 재즈 피아니스트 Bill Evans는 뉴저지에서 1929년에 태어났다.

❷ His early training was in classical music.

그의 초기 교육은 클래식 음악이었다.

❸ At the age of six, he began receiving piano lessons, later adding flute and violin.

6세에 그는 피아노 수업을 받기 시작해서, 나중에 플루트와 바이올린을 더했다.

❹ He earned bachelor's degrees in piano and music education from Southeastern Louisiana College in 1950.

그는 1950년에 Southeastern Louisiana 대학에서 피아노와 음악 교육에서 학사 학위를 취득했다.

❺ He went on to serve in the army from 1951 to 1954 and played flute in the Fifth Army Band.

그는 1951에서 1954년까지 군 복무를 하며 제5군악대에서 플루트를 연주했다.

❻ After serving in the military, he studied composition at the Mannes School of Music in New York.

군 복무 이후 그는 뉴욕에 있는 Mannes School of Music에서 작곡을 공부했다.

❼ Composer George Russell admired his playing and hired Evans to record and perform his compositions.

작곡가 George Russell은 그의 연주에 감탄하여 자신의 곡을 녹음하고 연주하도록 하기 위해 Evans를 고용했다.

❽ Evans became famous for recordings made from the late-1950s through the 1960s.

Evans는 1950년대 후반부터 1960년대 동안에 만들어진 음반으로 유명해졌다.

❾ He won his first Grammy Award in 1964 for his album *Conversations with Myself*.

그는 자신의 앨범 Conversations with Myself로 1964년에 자신의 첫 번째 그래미상을 수상했다.

❿ Evans' expressive piano works and his unique harmonic approach inspired a whole generation of musicians.

Evans의 표현이 풍부한 피아노 작품과 그의 독특한 화성적 접근은 전 세대의 음악가들에게 영감을 주었다.

29 어법

❶ There is a reason the title "Monday Morning Quarterback" exists.

'Monday Morning Quarterback'이라는 이름이 존재하는 이유가 있다.

❷ Just read the comments on social media from fans discussing the weekend's games, and you quickly see how many people believe they could play, coach, and manage sport teams more successfully than those on the field.

주말 경기에 대해 토론하는 팬들의 소셜 미디어의 댓글만 읽어봐도 여러분은 자신이 경기장에 있는 사람들보다 더 성공적으로 경기를 뛰고, 감독하고, 스포츠팀을 관리할 수 있다고 얼마나 많은 사람들이 믿는지 금방 알 수 있다.

❸ This goes for the boardroom as well.

이것은 이사회실에서도 마찬가지이다.

❹ Students and professionals with years of training and specialized degrees in sport business may also find themselves being given advice on how to do their jobs from friends, family, or even total strangers without any expertise.

스포츠 사업에서 수년간의 훈련을 받고 전문적인 학위를 가진 학생들과 전문가들 또한 친구들, 가족, 혹은 전문 지식이 전혀 없는 심지어 완전히 낯선 사람들로부터 어떻게 자신의 일을 해야 하는지에 대한 충고를 듣고 있는 자신을 발견할지도 모른다.

❺ Executives in sport management have decades of knowledge and experience in their respective fields.

스포츠 경영 임원진들은 자신의 각 분야에서 수십 년의 지식과 경험을 가지고 있다.

❻ However, many of them face criticism from fans and community members telling them how to run their business.

하지만, 그들 중 많은 사람들이 그들에게 그들의 사업 운영 방식을 알려주는 팬들과 지역 사회 구성원들로부터의 비난에 직면한다.

❼ Very few people tell their doctor how to perform surgery or their accountant how to prepare their taxes, but many people provide feedback on how sport organizations should be managed.

자신의 의사에게 수술하는 방법을 알려주거나 자신의 회계사에게 자신의 세금을 준비하는 방법을 알려주는 사람은 거의 없지만, 많은 사람들이 스포츠 조직이 어떻게 관리되어야 하는지에 대한 피드백은 제공한다..

32 빈칸

❶ The famous primatologist Frans de Waal, of Emory University, says humans downplay similarities between us and other animals as a way of maintaining our spot at the top of our imaginary ladder.

Emory 대학의 유명한 영장류학자 Frans de Waal은 인간은 상상 속 사다리의 꼭대기에서 우리의 위치를 유지하는 방법으로 우리와 다른 동물들 사이의 유사성을 경시한다고 말한다.

❷ Scientists, de Waal points out, can be some of the worst offenders — employing technical language to distance the other animals from us.

de Waal은 과학자들이 우리와 다른 동물들 사이에 거리를 두기 위해 기술적인 언어를 사용하는 최악의 죄를 범하는 자들 중 일부일 수 있다고 지적한다.

❸ They call "kissing" in chimps "mouth-to-mouth contact"; they call "friends" between primates "favorite affiliation partners"; they interpret evidence showing that crows and chimps can make tools as being somehow qualitatively different from the kind of toolmaking said to define humanity.

그들은 침팬지의 '키스'를 '입과 입의 접촉'이라고 부르고, 영장류 사이의 '친구'를 '좋아하는 제휴 파트너'라고 부르며, 그들은 까마귀와 침팬지가 도구를 만들 수 있다는 것을 보여주는 증거를 인류를 정의한다고 하는 종류의 도구 제작과는 아무래도 질적으로 다르다고 해석한다.

❹ If an animal can beat us at a cognitive task — like how certain bird species can remember the precise locations of thousands of seeds — they write it off as instinct, not intelligence.

만약 동물이, 특정 종의 새들이 수천 개의 씨앗의 정확한 위치를 기억할 수 있는 방식처럼, 인지적인 과업에서 우리를 이길 수 있다면, 그들은 그것을 지능이 아니라 본능으로 치부한다.

❺ This and so many more tricks of language are what de Waal has termed "linguistic castration."

이것과 더 많은 언어적 수법은 de Waal이 '언어적 거세'라고 명명한 것이다.

❻ The way we use our tongues to disempower animals, the way we invent words to maintain our spot at the top.

우리가 동물로부터 힘을 빼앗기 위해 우리의 언어를 사용하는 방식이며, 우리가 꼭대기에서 우리의 위치를 유지하기 위해 단어들을 만드는 방식이다.

33 빈칸

❶ A key to engagement and achievement is providing students with relevant texts they will be interested in.

참여와 성취의 핵심은 학생들에게 그들이 관심 있어 할 적절한 글을 제공하는 것이다.

❷ My scholarly work and my teaching have been deeply influenced by the work of Rosalie Fink.

나의 학문적인 연구와 나의 수업은 Rosalie Fink의 연구에 깊이 영향을 받아왔다.

❸ She interviewed twelve adults who were highly successful in their work, including a physicist, a biochemist, and a company CEO.

그녀는 물리학자, 생화학자 그리고 회사의 최고 경영자를 포함해 그들의 직업에서 매우 성공한 열두 명의 성인들과 면담했다.

❹ All of them had dyslexia and had had significant problems with reading throughout their school years.

그들 모두가 난독증이 있었고 그들의 학령기 내내 읽기에 상당한 문제를 겪어 왔다.

❺ While she expected to find that they had avoided reading and discovered ways to bypass it or compensate with other strategies for learning, she found the opposite.

그녀는 그들이 학습에 있어 읽기를 피했고 그것을 우회하거나 다른 전략들로 보완할 방법을 발견했을 것이라고 알아낼 것을 예상했으나, 정반대를 알아냈다.

❻ "To my surprise, I found that these dyslexics were enthusiastic readers… they rarely avoided reading. On the contrary, they sought out books."

"놀랍게도, 나는 난독증이 있는 이런 사람들이 열성적인 독자인 것을… 그들이 좀처럼 읽기를 피하지 않는 것을 알아냈다. 이에 반하여, 그들은 책을 찾았다."

❼ The pattern Fink discovered was that all of her subjects had been passionate in some personal interest.

Fink가 발견한 패턴은 그녀의 실험대상자 모두가 어떤 개인적인 관심사에 열정적이었다는 것이었다.

❽ The areas of interest included religion, math, business, science, history, and biography.

관심 분야는 종교, 수학, 상업, 과학, 역사 그리고 생물학을 포함했다.

❾ What mattered was that they read voraciously to find out more.

중요한 것은 그들이 더 많이 알아내기 위해 탐욕스럽게 읽었다는 것이다.

(.hwp) (.pdf) ➜ www.englishmygod.com

34 빈칸

❶ For many people, *ability* refers to intellectual competence, so they want everything they do to reflect how smart they are — writing a brilliant legal brief, getting the highest grade on a test, writing elegant computer code, saying something exceptionally wise or witty in a conversation.

많은 사람들에게 '능력'은 지적 능력을 의미하기 때문에 그들은 자신이 하는 모든 것이 자신이 얼마나 똑똑한지를 보여주기를 원한다. 예컨대, 훌륭한 법률 보고서를 작성하는 것, 시험에서 최고의 성적을 받는 것, 정연한 컴퓨터 코드를 작성하는 것, 대화에서 비범하게 현명하거나 재치 있는 말을 하는 것이다.

❷ You could also define ability in terms of a particular skill or talent, such as how well one plays the piano, learns a language, or serves a tennis ball.

여러분은 또한 피아노를 얼마나 잘 치는지, 언어를 얼마나 잘 배우는지, 테니스공을 얼마나 잘 서브하는지와 같은 특정한 기술이나 재능의 관점에서 능력을 정의할 수도 있다.

❸ Some people focus on their ability to be attractive, entertaining, up on the latest trends, or to have the newest gadgets.

어떤 사람들은 매력적이고, 재미있고, 최신 유행에 맞추거나, 최신 기기를 가질 수 있는 그들의 능력에 초점을 맞춘다.

❹ However ability may be defined, a problem occurs when it is the sole determinant of one's self-worth.

능력이 어떻게 정의되든지, 그것이 자신의 가치를 결정하는 유일한 결정 요소일 때 문제가 발생한다.

❺ The performance becomes the only measure of the person; nothing else is taken into account.

수행이 그 사람의 '유일한' 척도가 되며, 다른 것은 고려되지 않는다.

❻ An outstanding performance means an outstanding person; an average performance means an average person. Period.

뛰어난 수행은 뛰어난 사람을 의미하고, 평범한 수행은 평범한 사람을 의미한다. 끝.

35 무관

❶ Sensory nerves have specialized endings in the tissues that pick up a particular sensation.

감각 신경은 특정 감각을 포착하는 특화된 말단을 조직에 가지고 있다.

❷ If, for example, you step on a sharp object such as a pin, nerve endings in the skin will transmit the pain sensation up your leg, up and along the spinal cord to the brain.

예를 들어, 만약 여러분이 핀과 같이 날카로운 물체를 밟는다면, 피부의 신경 말단이 통증 감각을 여러분의 다리 위로, 그리고 척수를 따라 위로 뇌까지 전달할 것이다.

❸ While the pain itself is unpleasant, it is in fact acting as a protective mechanism for the foot.

통증 자체는 불쾌하지만, 사실은 발을 보호하는 메커니즘으로 작용하고 있다.

❹ Within the brain, nerves will connect to the area that controls speech, so that you may well shout 'ouch' or something rather less polite.

뇌 안에서, 신경은 언어를 통제하는 부분에 연결될 것이고, 그래서 여러분은 '아야' 또는 다소 덜 공손한 무언가를 외칠 것이다.

❺ They will also connect to motor nerves that travel back down the spinal cord, and to the muscles in your leg that now contract quickly to lift your foot away from the painful object.

그것들은 또한 척수를 타고 다시 내려오는 운동 신경에 연결될 것이고, 그리고 이제 재빨리 수축하여 고통을 주는 물체로부터 발을 떼어 들어 올리게 하는 여러분의 다리 근육에 연결될 것이다.

❻ Sensory and motor nerves control almost all functions in the body — from the beating of the heart to the movement of the gut, sweating and just about everything else.

감각 신경과 운동 신경은 심장의 박동에서부터 장 운동, 발한과 그 밖에 모든 것에 이르기까지 신체의 거의 모든 기능을 통제한다.

36 순서

❶ Maybe you've heard this joke: "How do you eat an elephant?" The answer is "one bite at a time."

아마 여러분은 이 농담을 들어본 적이 있을 것이다. : "코끼리를 어떻게 먹는가?" 정답은 '한 번에 한 입'이다.

❷ So, how do you "build" the Earth? That's simple, too: one atom at a time.

그렇다면, 여러분은 어떻게 지구를 '건설'하는가? 그것은 또한 간단하다. : 한 번에 하나의 원자이다.

❸ Atoms are the basic building blocks of crystals, and since all rocks are made up of crystals, the more you know about atoms, the better.

원자는 결정의 기본 구성 요소이고, 모든 암석은 결정으로 이루어져 있기 때문에, 여러분은 원자에 대해 더 많이 알수록 더 좋다.

❹ Crystals come in a variety of shapes that scientists call *habits*.

결정은 과학자들이 '습성'이라고 부르는 다양한 모양으로 나온다.

❺ Common crystal habits include squares, triangles, and six-sided hexagons.

일반적인 결정 습성은 사각형, 삼각형, 육면의 육각형을 포함한다.

❻ Usually crystals form when liquids cool, such as when you create ice cubes.

보통 여러분이 얼음을 만들 때와 같이 액체가 차가워질 때 결정이 형성된다.

❼ Many times, crystals form in ways that do not allow for perfect shapes.

많은 경우, 결정은 완벽한 모양을 허용하지 않는 방식으로 형성된다.

❽ If conditions are too cold, too hot, or there isn't enough source material, they can form strange, twisted shapes.

조건이 너무 차갑거나, 너무 뜨겁거나, 혹은 원천 물질이 충분하지 않으면 이상하고 뒤틀린 모양을 형성할 수 있다.

❾ But when conditions are right, we see beautiful displays. Usually, this involves a slow, steady environment where the individual atoms have plenty of time to join and fit perfectly into what's known as the *crystal lattice*.

하지만 조건이 맞을 때, 우리는 아름다운 배열을 본다. 보통, 이것은 개별적인 원자들이 결합하고 '결정격자'라고 알려진 것에 완벽하게 들어맞는 충분한 시간을 가지는 느리고 안정적인 환경을 수반한다.

❿ This is the basic structure of atoms that is seen time after time.

이것은 반복하여 보이는 원자의 기본적인 구조이다.

37 순서

❶ When you pluck a guitar string it moves back and forth hundreds of times every second.

여러분이 기타 줄을 뜯을 때 그것은 매초 수백 번 이리저리 움직인다.

❷ Naturally, this movement is so fast that you cannot see it — you just see the blurred outline of the moving string.

당연히, 이 움직임은 너무 빨라서 여러분이 그것을 볼 수 없다. 여러분은 그저 움직이는 줄의 흐릿한 윤곽만 본다.

❸ Strings vibrating in this way on their own make hardly any noise because strings are very thin and don't push much air about.

이렇게 스스로 진동하는 줄들은 거의 소리가 나지 않는데, 이는 줄이 매우 가늘어 많은 공기를 밀어내지 못하기 때문이다.

❹ But if you attach a string to a big hollow box (like a guitar body), then the vibration is amplified and the note is heard loud and clear.

하지만 여러분이 (기타 몸통 같은) 커다란 속이 빈 상자에 줄을 달면, 그 진동은 증폭되어 그 음이 크고 선명하게 들린다.

❺ The vibration of the string is passed on to the wooden panels of the guitar body, which vibrate back and forth at the same rate as the string.

그 줄의 진동은 기타 몸통의 나무판으로 전달되어 줄과 같은 속도로 이리저리 떨린다.

❻ The vibration of the wood creates more powerful waves in the air pressure, which travel away from the guitar.

그 나무의 진동은 공기의 압력에 더 강력한 파동을 만들어 내어 기타로부터 멀리 퍼진다.

❼ When the waves reach your eardrums they flex in and out the same number of times a second as the original string.

그 파동이 여러분의 고막에 도달할 때 원래의 줄과 초당 동일한 횟수로 굽이쳐 들어가고 나온다.

38 삽입

❶ Boundaries between work and home are blurring as portable digital technology makes it increasingly possible to work anywhere, anytime.

　휴대용 디지털 기술이 언제, 어디서나 작업하는 것을 점차 가능하게 함에 따라 직장과 가정의 경계가 흐릿해지고 있다.

❷ Individuals differ in how they like to manage their time to meet work and outside responsibilities.

　사람들은 직장과 외부의 책임을 수행하기 위해 자신의 시간을 관리하기를 바라는 방식에 차이가 있다.

❸ Some people prefer to separate or segment roles so that boundary crossings are minimized.

　어떤 사람들은 경계 교차 지점이 최소화되도록 역할을 분리하거나 분할하는 것을 선호한다.

❹ For example, these people might keep separate email accounts for work and family and try to conduct work at the workplace and take care of family matters only during breaks and non-work time.

　예를 들어, 이러한 사람들은 직장과 가정을 위한 별개의 이메일 계정을 유지하고 직장에서 일을 수행하고 휴식 시간과 일을 하지 않는 시간 동안에만 가정사를 처리하려고 할지도 모른다.

❺ We've even noticed more of these "segmenters" carrying two phones — one for work and one for personal use.

　우리는 더 많은 이러한 '분할자들'이 하나는 업무용이고 하나는 개인용인 두 개의 전화기를 가지고 다니고 있음을 심지어 알게 되었다.

❻ Flexible schedules work well for these individuals because they enable greater distinction between time at work and time in other roles.

　유연근로시간제는 이런 사람들에게 잘 적용되는데, 직장에서의 시간과 다른 역할에서의 시간 간에 더 큰 구별을 가능하게 하기 때문이다.

❼ Other individuals prefer integrating work and family roles all day long.

　다른 사람들은 하루 종일 직장과 가정의 역할을 통합하는 것을 선호한다.

❽ This might entail constantly trading text messages with children from the office, or monitoring emails at home and on vacation, rather than returning to work to find hundreds of messages in their inbox.

　이것은 직장으로 돌아가서 받은 편지함에서 수백 개의 메시지를 발견하는 것 대신 사무실에서 아이들과 문자 메시지를 지속적으로 주고받거나 집에서 그리고 휴가 중에 이메일을 확인하는 것을 수반할지도 모른다.

39 삽입

❶ A "complementary good" is a product that is often consumed alongside another product.

'보완재'는 종종 다른 제품과 함께 소비되는 제품이다.

❷ For example, popcorn is a complementary good to a movie, while a travel pillow is a complementary good for a long plane journey.

예를 들어, 팝콘은 영화에 대한 보완재인 한편, 여행 베개는 긴 비행기 여행에 대한 보완재이다.

❸ When the popularity of one product increases, the sales of its complementary good also increase.

한 제품의 인기가 높아지면 그것의 보완재 판매량도 늘어난다.

❹ By producing goods that complement other products that are already (or about to be) popular, you can ensure a steady stream of demand for your product.

여러분은 이미 인기가 있는 (또는 곧 있을) 다른 제품을 보완하는 제품을 생산함으로써 여러분의 제품에 대한 꾸준한 수요 흐름을 보장할 수 있다.

❺ Some products enjoy perfect complementary status — they *have* to be consumed together, such as a lamp and a lightbulb.

일부 제품들은 완벽한 보완적 상태를 누리고 있고, 그것들은 램프와 전구와 같이 함께 소비'되어야' 한다.

❻ However, do not assume that a product is perfectly complementary, as customers may not be completely locked in to the product.

그러나 고객들이 그 제품에 완전히 고정되어 있지 않을 수 있으므로, 어떤 제품이 완벽하게 보완적이라고 가정하지 마라.

❼ For example, although motorists may seem required to purchase gasoline to run their cars, they can switch to electric cars.

예를 들어, 비록 운전자들이 자신의 차를 운전하기 위해 휘발유를 구매할 필요가 있는 것처럼 보일지라도, 그들은 전기 자동차로 바꿀 수 있다.

40 요약

❶ It's not news to anyone that we judge others based on their clothes.

우리가 다른 사람들을 그들의 의복을 보고 판단하는 것은 누구에게도 새로운 일이 아니다.

❷ In general, studies that investigate these judgments find that people prefer clothing that matches expectations — surgeons in scrubs, little boys in blue — with one notable exception.

일반적으로, 이러한 판단을 조사하는 연구는 사람들이 수술복을 입은 외과 의사, 파란 옷을 입은 남자아이와 같이 예상에 맞는 의복이되 하나의 눈에 띄는 예외가 있는 것을 선호한다는 것을 발견한다.

❸ A series of studies published in an article in June 2014 in the *Journal of Consumer Research* explored observers' reactions to people who broke established norms only slightly.

Journal of Consumer Research의 2014년 9월 기사에 실린 일련의 연구는 확립된 규범을 아주 약간 어긴 사람들에 대한 관찰자들의 반응을 탐구했다.

❹ In one scenario, a man at a black-tie affair was viewed as having higher status and competence when wearing a red bow tie.

한 시나리오에서는, 정장 차림의 행사에서 한 남자가 빨간 나비 넥타이를 맸을 때 더 높은 지위와 능력을 가진 것으로 보여졌다.

❺ The researchers also found that valuing uniqueness increased audience members' ratings of the status and competence of a professor who wore red sneakers while giving a lecture.

연구자들은 독특함을 중시하는 것이 강의를 하는 동안 빨간 운동화를 신은 교수의 지위와 역량에 대한 청중들의 평가를 높였다는 것을 또한 발견했다.

❻ The results suggest that people judge these slight deviations from the norm as positive because they suggest that the individual is powerful enough to risk the social costs of such behaviors.

그 결과들은 사람들이 규범으로부터 이러한 약간의 일탈들을 긍정적으로 판단한다는 것을 시사하는데, 왜냐하면 그것들은 그 사람이 그러한 행동으로 인한 사회적 비용을 감수할 만큼 충분히 강하다는 것을 시사하기 때문이다.

41~42 제목, 어휘

❶ Claims that local food production cut greenhouse gas emissions by reducing the burning of transportation fuel are usually not well founded.

로컬푸드 생산이 운송 연료의 연소를 줄임으로써 온실가스 배출을 줄였다는 주장들은 대개 근거가 충분하지 않다.

❷ Transport is the source of only 11 percent of greenhouse gas emissions within the food sector, so reducing the distance that food travels after it leaves the farm is far less important than reducing wasteful energy use on the farm.

운송은 식품 부문 내에서 온실가스 배출의 11퍼센트만을 차지하는 원천이기에, 식품이 농장을 떠난 후 이동하는 거리를 줄이는 것은 농장에서 낭비되는 에너지 사용을 줄이는 것보다 훨씬 덜 중요하다.

❸ Food coming from a distance can actually be better for the climate, depending on how it was grown.

먼 곳에서 오는 식품은 그것이 어떻게 재배되었느냐에 따라 실제로 기후에 더 좋을 수 있다.

❹ For example, field-grown tomatoes shipped from Mexico in the winter months will have a smaller carbon footprint than local winter tomatoes grown in a greenhouse.

예를 들어, 겨울에 멕시코로부터 수송된 밭에서 재배된 토마토는 온실에서 재배된 현지의 겨울 토마토보다 탄소 발자국이 더 적을 것이다.

❺ In the United Kingdom, lamb meat that travels 11,000 miles from New Zealand generates only one-quarter the carbon emissions per pound compared to British lamb because farmers in the United Kingdom raise their animals on feed (which must be produced using fossil fuels) rather than on clover pastureland.

영국에서는, 영국의 농부들이 클로버 목초지에서가 아닌 (화석 연료를 사용하여 생산되어야 하는) 사료로 자신의 동물들을 기르기 때문에 뉴질랜드에서 11,000마일을 이동하는 양고기는 영국의 양고기에 비해 파운드당 탄소 배출량의 1분의 일만 발생시킨다.

❻ When food does travel, what matters most is not the distance traveled but the travel mode (surface versus air), and most of all the load size.

식품이 이동할 때, 가장 중요한 것은 이동 거리가 아니라 이동 방식(지상 대 공중), 그리고 무엇보다 적재량의 규모이다.

❼ Bulk loads of food can travel halfway around the world by ocean freight with a smaller carbon footprint, per pound delivered, than foods traveling just a short distance but in much smaller loads.

대량의 적재된 식품은 단지 단거리를 이동하지만 훨씬 더 적은 적재량인 식품에 비해 배달된 파운드당 탄소 발자국이 더 적은 해상 화물 운송으로 세계의 절반을 이동할 수 있다.

❽ For example, 18-wheelers carry much larger loads than pickup trucks so they can move food 100 times as far while burning only one-third as much gas per pound of food delivered.

예를 들어, 18륜 대형트럭은 픽업트럭보다 훨씬 더 많은 적재량을 운반하기에 배달된 식품 파운드당 3분의 일의 연료만 연소하면서 100배 멀리 식품을 이동시킬 수 있다.

(.hwp) (.pdf) → www.englishmygod.com

43~45 순서, 지칭, 세부 내용

❶ Long ago, an old man built a grand temple at the center of his village. People traveled to worship at the temple.

옛날, 한 노인이 마을 중심부에 큰 사원을 지었다. 사람들이 사원에서 예배를 드리기 위해 멀리서 왔다.

❷ So the old man made arrangements for food and accommodation inside the temple itself.

그래서 노인은 사원 안에 음식과 숙소를 준비했다.

❸ He needed someone who could look after the temple, so he put up a notice: Manager needed. Seeing the notice, many people went to the old man.

그는 사원을 관리할 수 있는 사람이 필요했고, 그래서 그는 '관리자 구함'이라는 공고를 붙였다. 공고를 보고 많은 사람들이 노인을 찾아갔다.

❹ But he returned all the applicants after interviews, telling them, "I need a qualified person for this work."

그러나 그는 면접 후에 그들에게 "나는 이 일에 자격을 갖춘 사람이 필요합니다."라고 말하며, 모든 지원자들을 돌려보냈다.

❺ The old man would sit on the roof of his house every morning, watching people go through the temple doors. One day, he saw a young man come to the temple.

노인은 사람들이 사원의 문을 통과하는 것을 지켜보며 매일 아침 그의 집 지붕에 앉아 있곤 했다. 어느 날 그는 한 젊은이가 사원으로 오는 것을 보았다.

❻ When that young man left the temple, the old man called him and asked, "Will you take care of this temple?" The young man was surprised by the offer and replied, "I have no experience caring for a temple. I'm not even educated."

젊은이가 사원을 나설 때, 노인이 그를 불러 "이 사원의 관리를 맡아 주겠소?"라고 질문했다. 젊은이는 그 제안에 놀라서 "저는 사원을 관리한 경험이 없고, 심지어 교육도 받지 못했습니다."라고 대답했다.

❼ The old man smiled and said, "I don't want any educated man. I want a qualified person." Confused, the young man asked, "But why do you consider me a qualified person?"

노인은 웃으며 "나는 교육을 받은 사람이 필요한 게 아니오. 나는 자격 있는 사람을 원하오."라고 말했다. 당황하여, 젊은이는 "그런데 당신은 왜 저를 자격이 있는 사람이라고 여기시나요?"라고 물었다.

❽ The old man replied, "I buried a brick on the path to the temple. I watched for many days as people tripped over that brick. No one thought to remove it. But you dug up that brick."

노인은 대답했다. "나는 사원으로 통하는 길에 벽돌 한 개를 묻었소. 나는 여러 날 동안 사람들이 그 벽돌에 발이 걸려 넘어지는 것을 지켜보았소. 아무도 그것을 치울 생각을 하지 않았소. 하지만 당신은 그 벽돌을 파냈소."

❾ The young man said, "I haven't done anything great. It's the duty of every human being to think about others. I only did my duty."

젊은이는 "저는 대단한 일을 한 것이 아닙니다. 타인을 생각하는 것은 모든 인간의 의무입니다. 저는 제 의무를 다했을 뿐입니다."라고 말했다.

❿ The old man smiled and said, "Only people who know their duty and perform it are qualified people."

노인은 미소를 지으며 "자신의 의무를 알고 그 의무를 수행하는 사람만이 자격이 있는 사람이오."라고 말했다.

2023 고1 9월 모의고사 ❶ 회차 : 점 / 200점

❶ voca   ❷ text   ❸ [/]   ❹ ____   ❺ quiz 1   ❻ quiz 2   ❼ quiz 3   ❽ quiz 4   ❾ quiz 5

18

Dear Professor Sanchez,
My name is Ellis Wight, and I'm the director of the Alexandria Science Museum. We are [**held / holding**]¹⁾ a Chemistry Fair for local middle school students [**on / in**]²⁾ Saturday, October 28. The goal of the fair is to encourage them [**being / to be**]³⁾ interested in science through [**guiding / guided**]⁴⁾ experiments. We are looking [**for / at**]⁵⁾ college students who can help with the experiments [**while / during**]⁶⁾ the event. I am contacting you to ask you to [**command / recommend**]⁷⁾ some students from the chemistry department at your college who you think are [**qualified / quantified**]⁸⁾ for this job. With their help, I'm sure the participants will have a great experience. I look forward to [**hear / hearing**]⁹⁾ from you soon.
Sincerely, Ellis Wight

Sanchez 교수님께,
제 이름은 Ellis Wight이고 Alexandria 과학 박물관의 관장입니다. 저희는 10월 28일 토요일에 지역 중학교 학생을 위한 화학 박람회를 개최합니다. 이 박람회의 목적은 안내적 실험을 통해 학생들이 과학에 관한 관심을 갖도록 장려하는 것입니다. 저희는 행사 기간 동안 실험을 도와줄 수 있는 대학생을 모집하고자 합니다. 저는 이 일에 적합하다고 생각되는 귀교의 화학과 학생 몇 명을 추천해 달라는 요청을 드리고자 연락드렸습니다. 저는 그 학생들의 도움으로 참가자들이 훌륭한 경험을 하게 될 것이라 확신합니다. 빠른 시일 내에 당신으로부터 연락이 오기를 기대하겠습니다.
진심을 담아, Ellis Wight

19

Gregg and I had been rock climbing since sunrise and had had no problems. So we took a risk. "Look, the first bolt is right there. I can [**definitely / infinitely**]¹⁰⁾ climb out to it. Piece of cake," I persuaded Gregg, minutes before I found myself [**pinned / pinning**]¹¹⁾. It wasn't a piece of cake. The rock was [**inceptively / deceptively**]¹²⁾ barren of handholds. I clumsily moved back and forth across the cliff face and ended up with nowhere to go...but down. The bolt that would save my life, if I could get to it, [**was / being**]¹³⁾ about two feet above my reach. My arms trembled from exhaustion. I looked [**at / for**]¹⁴⁾ Gregg. My body froze with fright from my neck down to my toes. Our rope [**tied / was tied**]¹⁵⁾ between us. If I fell, he would fall with me.

Gregg와 나는 일출 이후에 암벽 등반을 해왔고 아무런 문제가 없었다. 그래서 우리는 위험을 감수했다. "봐, 첫 번째 볼트가 바로 저기에 있어. 나는 분명히 거기까지 올라갈 수 있어. 식은 죽 먹기야."라고 나는 Gregg를 설득했고, 얼마 지나지 않아 나는 내가 꼼짝 못 하게 되었다는 것을 알게 되었다. 그것은 식은 죽 먹기가 아니었다. 그 바위는 믿을 수 없게도 손으로 잡을 곳이 없었다. 나는 서툴게 절벽 면을 이리저리 가로질러 보았지만 갈 곳이... 결국 아래쪽밖에는 없었다. 만약 내가 거기까지 갈 수 있다면, 내 목숨을 구해줄 볼트는 손이 닿을 수 있는 곳에서 약 2피트 위에 있었다. 내 팔은 극도의 피로로 떨렸다. 나는 Gregg를 쳐다보았다. 내 몸은 목에서부터 발끝까지 공포로 얼어붙었다. 우리 사이에 밧줄이 묶여 있었다. 내가 떨어지면, 그도 나와 함께 떨어질 것이다.

20

We are always teaching our children something by our words and our actions. They learn from seeing. They learn from hearing and from *overhearing*. Children share the values of their parents about the most important things in life. Our [**properties / priorities**]16) and [**principals / principles**]17) and our examples of good behavior can teach our children to take the high road when other roads look [**tempting / like tempting**]18). Remember [**that / what**]19) children do not learn the values that make up strong character simply by [**telling / being *told***]20) about them. They learn by seeing the people around them *act* on and *uphold* those values in their daily lives. [**Therefore / However**]21) show your child good examples of life by your action. In our daily lives, we can show our children **that** (무슨 that? _____)22) we respect others. We can show them our compassion and concern when others are suffering, and our own self-discipline, courage and honesty as we make difficult decisions.

우리는 항상 우리 자녀에게 말과 행동으로 무언가를 가르치고 있다. 그들은 보는 것으로부터 배운다. 그들은 듣거나 '우연히 듣는 것'으로부터 배운다. 아이들은 인생에서 가장 중요한 것에 대해 그들 부모의 가치를 공유한다. 우리의 우선순위와 원칙 그리고 훌륭한 행동에 대한 본보기는 우리 자녀에게 다른 길이 유혹적으로 보일 때 올바른 길로 가도록 가르칠 수 있다. 아이들은 확고한 인격을 구성하는 가치를 단순히 그것에 대해 '들음'으로써 배우지 않는다는 것을 기억하라. 그들은 그들 주변 사람들이 그들의 일상생활에서 그러한 가치를 좇아 '행동'하고 '유지'하는 것을 봄으로써 배운다. 그러므로 여러분의 자녀에게 여러분의 행동으로 삶의 모범을 보여라. 우리 일상생활에서, 우리는 우리 자녀에게 우리가 타인을 존중하는 것을 보여줄 수 있다. 우리는 그들에게 타인이 괴로워할 때 우리의 연민과 걱정을, 그리고 우리가 어려운 결정을 할 때 우리 자신의 자제력, 용기 그리고 정직을 보여줄 수 있다.

21

Most people have no doubt [**heard / hearing**]23) this question: If a tree falls in the forest and there is no one there to hear [**it / them**]24) fall, does it make a sound? The correct answer is no. Sound is more than pressure waves, and indeed there can be no sound without a hearer. And [**similarly / conversely**]25), scientific communication is a two-way process. Just as a signal of any kind is useless [**if / unless**]26) it is perceived, a published scientific paper (signal) is useless [**if / unless**]27) it is both received *and* understood by [**its / their**]28) intended audience. Thus we can restate the axiom of science as follows: A scientific experiment is not complete until the results have [**published / been published**]29) *and understood*. Publication is no more than pressure waves unless the published paper is understood. Too many scientific papers fall silently in the woods.

대부분의 사람들은 틀림없이 이 질문을 들어 봤을 것이다. 만약 숲에서 나무가 쓰러지고 그것이 쓰러지는 것을 들을 사람이 거기에 없다면, 소리가 나는 것일까? 정답은 '아니요'이다. 소리는 압력파 이상이며, 정말로 듣는 사람 없이는 소리가 있을 수 없다. 마찬가지로, 과학적 커뮤니케이션은 양방향 프로세스이다. 어떠한 종류의 신호든 그것이 감지되지 않으면 쓸모가 없는 것처럼, 출판된 과학 논문(신호)은 그것이 의도된 독자에 의해 수신 '그리고' 이해가 둘 다 되지 않으면 쓸모가 없다. 따라서 우리는 과학의 자명한 이치를 다음과 같이 재진술할 수 있다. 과학 실험은 결과가 출판되고 '그리고 이해될' 때까지 완성되지 않는다. 출판된 논문이 이해되지 않으면 출판은 압력파에 지나지 않는다. 너무 많은 과학 논문이 소리 없이 숲속에서 쓰러진다.

22

We all negotiate every day, [**if / whether**]30) we realise it or not. Yet [**few / a few**]31) people ever learn *how* to negotiate. Those who do usually learn the traditional, win-lose negotiating style rather than an approach that is likely to result [**in / from**]32) a win-win agreement. This old-school, [**advert / adversarial**]33) approach may be useful in a one-off negotiation where you will probably not deal with **that** (무슨 that? _____)34) person again. However, such [**transactions / transformations**]35) are becoming increasingly rare, because most of us deal with the same people repeatedly — our spouses and children, our friends and colleagues, our customers and clients. In view of this, it's essential to achieve [**successful / successive**]36) results for ourselves and maintain a healthy relationship with our negotiating partners at the same time. In today's [**independent / interdependent**]37) world of business partnerships and long-term relationships, a win-win outcome is fast becoming the *only* acceptable result.

우리가 그것을 알든지 모르든지 간에, 우리 모두는 매일 협상한다. 하지만 이제까지 '어떻게' 협상하는지를 배운 사람은 거의 없다. (협상 방식을) 배우는 사람들은 대개 양측에 유리한 합의를 도출할 가능성이 있는 접근법보다는 전통적인, 한쪽에만 유리한 협상 방식을 배운다. 이 구식의 적대적인 접근법은 아마도 여러분이 그 사람을 다시 상대하지 않을 일회성 협상에서 유용할지도 모른다. 그러나, 우리 대부분은 배우자와 자녀, 친구와 동료, 고객과 의뢰인같이 동일한 사람들을 반복적으로 상대하기 때문에, 이러한 거래는 점점 더 드물어지고 있다. 이러한 관점에서, 우리 자신을 위해 성공적인 결과를 얻어내는 동시에 협상 파트너들과 건전한 관계를 유지하는 것이 중요하다. 오늘날 비즈니스 파트너십과 장기적 관계의 상호 의존적인 세계에서, 양측에 유리한 성과는 '유일하게' 받아들일 수 있는 결과가 빠르게 되어가고 있다.

23

The interaction of workers from different cultural backgrounds with the host population might increase [**product / productivity**]38) due [**to / on**]39) positive externalities like knowledge spillovers. This is only an [**advantage / disadvantage**]40) up to a certain degree. When the variety of backgrounds [**is / are**]41) too large, fractionalization may cause [**exceptional / excessive**]42) transaction costs for communication, [**which / that**]43) may [**boost / lower**]44) productivity. Diversity not only impacts the labour market, but may also [**affect / affect on**]45) the quality of life in a location. A tolerant native population may value a multicultural city or region because of an increase in the range of available goods and services. On the other hand, diversity could be perceived as an [**attractive / unattractive**]46) feature if natives perceive **it** (무엇을 가리키는가? _____)47) as a distortion of [**that / what**]48) they consider to be their national identity. They might even discriminate against other ethnic groups and they might fear that social conflicts between different foreign nationalities are [**imported / exported**]49) into their own neighbourhood.

다른 문화적 배경으로부터의 노동자들과 현지 주민의 상호 작용은 지식 파급과 같은 긍정적인 외부 효과로 인해 생산성을 증가시킬 수 있다. 이것은 어느 정도까지만 장점이다. 배경의 다양성이 너무 클 경우, 분열은 의사소통에 대한 과도한 거래 비용을 초래하는데, 이는 생산성을 저하시킬 수 있다. 다양성은 노동 시장에 영향을 줄 뿐만 아니라 한 지역의 삶의 질에도 영향을 미칠 수 있다. 관용적인 원주민은 이용 가능한 재화와 용역 범위의 증가로 인해 다문화 도시나 지역을 가치 있게 여길 수 있다. 반면에, 원주민들이 다양성을 그들의 국가 정체성이라고 생각하는 것에 대한 왜곡으로 인식한다면 다양성은 매력적이지 않은 특징으로 인식될 수 있다. 그들은 심지어 다른 민족 집단을 차별할 수도 있고 그들은 다른 외국 국적들 간의 사회적 갈등이 그들 인근으로 유입되는 것을 두려워할 수도 있다.

24

We think we are shaping our buildings. But really, our buildings and development are also shaping us. One of the best examples of this is the oldest-known construction: the ornately carved rings of standing stones at Göbekli Tepe in Turkey. Before these ancestors got the idea to [**erect** / **elect**]50) standing stones some 12,000 years ago, [**which / they**]51) were hunter-gatherers. It [**appears** / **is appeared**]52) that the [**erection** / **election**]53) of the multiple rings of megalithic stones took so long, and so many [**successive** / **successful**]54) generations, [**that** / **which**]55) these innovators [**forced** / **were forced**]56) to settle down to complete the construction works. In the process, they became the first farming society on Earth. This is an early example of a society constructing something that ends up radically [**remaking** / **remade**]57) the society itself. Things are not so different in our own time.

우리는 우리가 건물을 형성하고 있다고 생각한다. 그러나 실제로 우리의 건물과 개발도 또한 우리를 형성하고 있다. 이것의 가장 좋은 예 중 하나는 가장 오래된 것으로 알려진 건축물인 튀르키예의 Göbekli Tepe에 있는 화려하게 조각된 입석의 고리이다. 이 조상들이 약 12,000년 전에 입석을 세우는 아이디어를 얻기 전에 그들은 수렵 채집인이었다. 거석으로 된 여러 개의 고리를 세우는 데 오랜 시간이 걸렸고 많은 잇따른 세대를 거쳤어야 해서 이 혁신가들은 건설 작업을 완료하기 위해 정착해야만 했던 것으로 보인다. 그 과정에서, 그들은 지구상 최초의 농업 사회가 되었다. 이것은 결국 사회 자체를 근본적으로 재구성하는 무언가를 건설하는 사회의 초기 예이다. 우리 시대에도 상황이 그렇게 다르지 않다.

26

American jazz pianist Bill Evans was born in New Jersey in 1929. His early training was in classical music. At the age of six, he began [**receiving** / **perceiving**]58) piano lessons, later [**added** / **adding**]59) flute and violin. He earned bachelor's degrees in piano and music education from Southeastern Louisiana College in 1950. He went on to serve in the army from 1951 to 1954 and [**play** / **played**]60) flute in the Fifth Army Band. After serving in the military, he studied [**composition** / **competition**]61) at the Mannes School of Music in New York. Composer George Russell admired his playing and hired Evans to record and perform **his** (누구? **George Russell**? **Bill Evans**?)62) compositions. Evans became famous for recordings made from the [**late** / **lately**]63) -1950s through the 1960s. He won his first Grammy Award in 1964 for his album *Conversations with Myself*. Evans' expressive piano works and his unique harmonic approach inspired a whole generation of musicians.

미국인 재즈 피아니스트 Bill Evans는 뉴저지에서 1929년에 태어났다. 그의 초기 교육은 클래식 음악이었다. 6세에 그는 피아노 수업을 받기 시작해서, 나중에 플루트와 바이올린을 더했다. 그는 1950년에 Southeastern Louisiana 대학에서 피아노와 음악 교육에서 학사 학위를 취득했다. 그는 1951에서 1954년까지 군 복무를 하며 제5군악대에서 플루트를 연주했다. 군 복무 이후 그는 뉴욕에 있는 Mannes School of Music에서 작곡을 공부했다. 작곡가 George Russell은 그의 연주에 감탄하여 자신의 곡을 녹음하고 연주하도록 하기 위해 Evans를 고용했다. Evans는 1950년대 후반부터 1960년대 동안에 만들어진 음반으로 유명해졌다. 그는 자신의 앨범 Conversations with Myself로 1964년에 자신의 첫 번째 그래미상을 수상했다. Evans의 표현이 풍부한 피아노 작품과 그의 독특한 화성적 접근은 전 세대의 음악가들에게 영감을 주었다.

29

There is a reason the title "Monday Morning Quarterback" [**exists / is existed**]⁶⁴⁾. Just read the comments on social media from fans [**discussing / discussing about**]⁶⁵⁾ the weekend's games, and you quickly see how many people believe they could play, coach, and manage sport teams more [**successfully / successively**]⁶⁶⁾ than [**that / those**]⁶⁷⁾ on the field. This goes for the boardroom as well. Students and professionals with years of training and [**specializing / specialized**]⁶⁸⁾ degrees in sport business may also find [**them / themselves**]⁶⁹⁾ [**giving / being given**]⁷⁰⁾ advice on how to do their jobs from friends, family, or even total strangers without any expertise. Executives in sport management have decades of knowledge and experience in their [**respective / respectable**]⁷¹⁾ fields. However, many of them face criticism from fans and community members [**tell / telling**]⁷²⁾ them (무엇을 가리키는가? _____)⁷³⁾ how to [**run / run into**]⁷⁴⁾ their business. Very few people tell their doctor how to perform surgery or their accountant how to prepare their taxes, but many people provide feedback on how sport organizations should be managed.

'Monday Morning Quarterback'이라는 이름이 존재하는 이유가 있다. 주말 경기에 대해 토론하는 팬들의 소셜 미디어의 댓글만 읽어봐도 여러분은 자신이 경기장에 있는 사람들보다 더 성공적으로 경기를 뛰고, 감독하고, 스포츠팀을 관리할 수 있다고 얼마나 많은 사람들이 믿는지 금방 알 수 있다. 이것은 이사회실에서도 마찬가지이다. 스포츠 사업에서 수년간의 훈련을 받고 전문적인 학위를 가진 학생들과 전문가들 또한 친구들, 가족, 혹은 전문 지식이 전혀 없는 심지어 완전히 낯선 사람들로부터 어떻게 자신의 일을 해야 하는지에 대한 충고를 듣고 있는 자신을 발견할지도 모른다. 스포츠 경영 임원진들은 자신의 각 분야에서 수십 년의 지식과 경험을 가지고 있다. 하지만, 그들 중 많은 사람들이 그들에게 그들의 사업 운영 방식을 알려주는 팬들과 지역 사회 구성원들로부터의 비난에 직면한다. 자신의 의사에게 수술하는 방법을 알려주거나 자신의 회계사에게 자신의 세금을 준비하는 방법을 알려주는 사람은 거의 없지만, 많은 사람들이 스포츠 조직이 어떻게 관리되어야 하는지에 대한 피드백은 제공한다.

30

While moving is difficult for everyone, it is particularly stressful for children. They lose their sense of security and may feel [**disoriented / disorienting**]⁷⁵⁾ when their routine is disrupted and all that is familiar is taken [**on / away**]⁷⁶⁾. Young children, ages 3-6, are particularly affected by a move. Their understanding at this stage is quite [**lateral / literal**]⁷⁷⁾, and [**it / which**]⁷⁸⁾ is difficult [**of / for**]⁷⁹⁾ them to imagine beforehand a new home and their new room. Young children may have worries such as "Will I still be me in the new place?" and "Will my toys and bed come with us?" It is important to establish a balance between [**vagueness / validating**]⁸⁰⁾ children's past experiences and [**focus / focusing**]⁸¹⁾ on helping them [**adjust / adjusting**]⁸²⁾ to the new place. Children need to have opportunities to share their backgrounds in a way that respects their past as an important part of who they are. This contributes to [**build / building**]⁸³⁾ a sense of community, [**it / which**]⁸⁴⁾ is essential for all children, especially those in transition.

이사는 모두에게 힘들지만, 아이들에게 특히 스트레스가 많은 일이다. 그들은 안심감을 잃고 그들의 일상이 무너지고 익숙한 모든 것이 사라질 때 혼란스러움을 느낄 수도 있다. 3세에서 6세 사이의 어린아이들은 이사에 특히 영향을 받는다. 이 시기에 그들의 이해력은 꽤 융통성이 없어서, 그들이 새로운 집과 자신의 새로운 방을 미리 상상하는 것은 쉽다(→ 어렵다). 어린아이들은 "내가 새로운 곳에서 여전히 나일까?"와 "내 장난감과 침대가 우리와 함께 갈까?"와 같은 걱정들을 가질지도 모른다. 아이들의 과거 경험을 인정하는 것과 그들이 새로운 곳에 적응하도록 돕는 데 집중하는 것 사이에 균형을 잡는 것이 중요하다. 아이들은 자신이 누구인지에 대한 중요한 부분으로서 자신의 과거를 존중하는 방식으로 자신의 배경을 공유할 기회를 가질 필요가 있다. 이것은 공동체 의식을 형성하는 데 기여하고, 이는 모든 아이들, 특히 변화를 겪는 아이들에게 가장 중요하다.

31

Many people are [**terrific / terrified**]85) to fly in airplanes. Often, this fear stems from a lack of control. The pilot is in control, not the passengers, and this lack of control [**installs / instills**]86) fear. Many potential passengers are so afraid they choose to drive great distances to get to a [**destination / determination**]87) instead of flying. But their decision to drive is based solely on emotion, not logic. Logic says that statistically, the odds of dying in a car crash [**is / are**]88) around 1 in 5,000, while the odds of dying in a plane crash [**is / are**]89) closer to 1 in 11 million. If you're going to take a risk, especially one that could possibly [**involve / evolve**]90) your well-being, wouldn't you want the odds in your favor? However, most people choose the option that will cause them the least amount of anxiety. [**Pay / Paying**]91) attention to the thoughts you have about taking the risk and make sure you're [**based / basing**]92) your decision on facts, not just feelings.

많은 사람들은 비행기를 타는 것을 두려워한다. 종종, 이 두려움은 통제력의 부족에서 비롯된다. 조종사는 통제를 하지만 승객은 그렇지 않으며, 이러한 통제력의 부족은 두려움을 스며들게 한다. 많은 잠재적인 승객들은 너무 두려워서 그들은 비행기를 타는 대신 목적지에 도착하기 위해 먼 거리를 운전하는 것을 선택한다. 그러나 운전을 하기로 한 그들의 결정은 논리가 아닌 오직 감정에 근거한다. 논리에 따르면 통계적으로 자동차 사고로 사망할 확률은 약 5,000분의 1이고, 반면 비행기 사고로 사망할 확률은 1,100만분의 1에 가깝다고 한다. 만약 여러분이 위험을 감수할 것이라면, 특히 여러분의 안녕을 혹시 포함할 수 있는 위험을 감수할 것이라면, 여러분에게 유리한 확률을 원하지 않겠는가? 그러나 대부분의 사람들은 그들에게 최소한의 불안감을 야기할 수 있는 선택을 한다. 위험을 감수하는 것에 대해 여러분이 가지고 있는 생각에 주의를 기울이고 여러분의 결정을 단지 감정이 아닌 사실에 근거하고 있는지 확인하라.

32

The famous primatologist Frans de Waal, of Emory University, [**says / saying**]93) humans downplay [**similarities / differences**]94) between us and other animals as a way of maintaining our spot at the top of our [**imaginary / imaginable**]95) ladder. Scientists, de Waal points out, can be some of the worst offenders — [**employing / deploying**]96) technical language to distance the other animals from us . They call "kissing" in chimps "mouth-to-mouth contact"; they call "friends" between primates "favorite [**affliction / affiliation**]97) partners"; they interpret evidence showing [**that / what**]98) crows and chimps can make tools as being somehow qualitatively different from the kind of toolmaking said to define humanity. If an animal can beat us at a cognitive task — like how certain bird species can remember the precise locations of thousands of seeds — they write [**it / them**]99) off as instinct, not intelligence. This and so many more tricks of language are what de Waal has [**termed / been termed**]100) "linguistic castration." The way we use our tongues to disempower animals, the way we invent words to maintain our spot at the top.

Emory 대학의 유명한 영장류학자 Frans de Waal은 인간은 상상 속 사다리의 꼭대기에서 우리의 위치를 유지하는 방법으로 우리와 다른 동물들 사이의 유사성을 경시한다고 말한다. de Waal은 과학자들이 우리와 다른 동물들 사이에 거리를 두기 위해 기술적인 언어를 사용하는 최악의 죄를 범하는 자들 중 일부일 수 있다고 지적한다. 그들은 침팬지의 '키스'를 '입과 입의 접촉'이라고 부르고, 영장류 사이의 '친구'를 '좋아하는 제휴 파트너'라고 부르며, 그들은 까마귀와 침팬지가 도구를 만들 수 있다는 것을 보여주는 증거를 인류를 정의한다고 하는 종류의 도구 제작과는 아무래도 질적으로 다르다고 해석한다. 만약 동물이, 특정 종의 새들이 수천 개의 씨앗의 정확한 위치를 기억할 수 있는 방식처럼, 인지적인 과업에서 우리를 이길 수 있다면, 그들은 그것을 지능이 아니라 본능으로 치부한다. 이것과 더 많은 언어적 수법은 de Waal이 '언어적 거세'라고 명명한 것이다. 우리가 동물로부터 힘을 빼앗기 위해 우리의 언어를 사용하는 방식이며, 우리가 꼭대기에서 우리의 위치를 유지하기 위해 단어들을 만드는 방식이다.

33

A key to engagement and achievement is providing students **[for / with]**101) relevant texts **(생략된 것은?** _____ **)**102) they will be interested in. My scholarly work and my teaching have been deeply influenced by the work of Rosalie Fink. She interviewed twelve adults who were **[high / highly]**103) successful in their work, including a physicist, a biochemist, and a company CEO. All of them had dyslexia and had had significant problems with reading throughout their school years. While she expected to find that they had avoided **[reading / to avoid]**104) and discovered ways to bypass it or compensate with other strategies for learning, she found the opposite. "To my surprise, I found that these dyslexics were enthusiastic readers...they rarely avoided **[reading / to read]**105) . On the contrary, they sought out books." The pattern Fink discovered was **[what / that]**106) all of her subjects had been passionate in some personal interest. The areas of interest included religion, math, business, science, history, and biography. What mattered was that they read **[intimately / voraciously]**107) to find out more.

참여와 성취의 핵심은 학생들에게 그들이 관심 있어 할 적절한 글을 제공하는 것이다. 나의 학문적인 연구와 나의 수업은 Rosalie Fink의 연구에 깊이 영향을 받아왔다. 그녀는 물리학자, 생화학자 그리고 회사의 최고 경영자를 포함해 그들의 직업에서 매우 성공한 열두 명의 성인들과 면담했다. 그들 모두가 난독증이 있었고 그들의 학령기 내내 읽기에 상당한 문제를 겪어 왔다. 그녀는 그들이 학습에 있어 읽기를 피했고 그것을 우회하거나 다른 전략들로 보완할 방법을 발견했을 것이라고 알아낼 것을 예상했으나, 정반대를 알아냈다. "놀랍게도, 나는 난독증이 있는 이런 사람들이 열성적인 독자인 것을... 그들이 좀처럼 읽기를 피하지 않는 것을 알아냈다. 이에 반하여, 그들은 책을 찾았다." Fink가 발견한 패턴은 그녀의 실험대상자 모두가 어떤 개인적인 관심사에 열정적이었다는 것이었다. 관심 분야는 종교, 수학, 상업, 과학, 역사 그리고 생물학을 포함했다. 중요한 것은 그들이 더 많이 알아내기 위해 탐욕스럽게 읽었다는 것이다.

34

For many people, *ability* refers to intellectual **[competence / competition]**108), so they want everything they do to reflect how **[they are smart / smart they are]**109) — writing a brilliant legal brief, getting the highest grade on a test, writing elegant computer code, saying something **[exceptionally / exponentially]**110) wise or witty in a conversation. You could also define ability in **[term / terms]**111) of a particular skill or talent, such as how well one plays the piano, **[learns / learning]**112) a language, or serves a tennis ball. Some people focus on their ability to be attractive, entertaining, up on the latest trends, or to have the newest gadgets. **[How / However]**113) ability may be **[defined / confined]**114), a problem occurs when it is the sole **[determinant / determination]**115) of one's self-worth. The performance becomes the only measure of the person; **[anything / nothing]**116) else is taken into account. An outstanding performance means an outstanding person; an average performance means an average person. Period.

많은 사람들에게 '능력'은 지적 능력을 의미하기 때문에 그들은 자신이 하는 모든 것이 자신이 얼마나 똑똑한지를 보여주기를 원한다. 예컨대, 훌륭한 법률 보고서를 작성하는 것, 시험에서 최고의 성적을 받는 것, 정연한 컴퓨터 코드를 작성하는 것, 대화에서 비범하게 현명하거나 재치 있는 말을 하는 것이다. 여러분은 또한 피아노를 얼마나 잘 치는지, 언어를 얼마나 잘 배우는지, 테니스공을 얼마나 잘 서브 하는지와 같은 특정한 기술이나 재능의 관점에서 능력을 정의할 수도 있다. 어떤 사람들은 매력적이고, 재미있고, 최신 유행에 맞추거나, 최신 기기를 가질 수 있는 그들의 능력에 초점을 맞춘다. 능력이 어떻게 정의되든지, 그것이 자신의 가치를 결정하는 유일한 결정 요소일 때 문제가 발생한다. 수행이 그 사람의 '유일한' 척도가 되며, 다른 것은 고려되지 않는다. 뛰어난 수행은 뛰어난 사람을 의미하고, 평범한 수행은 평범한 사람을 의미한다. 끝.

35

Sensory nerves have [**specialized** / **been specialized**]¹¹⁷⁾ endings in the tissues that pick up a particular sensation. If, for example, you step on a sharp object such as a pin, nerve endings in the skin will [**transmit** / **transform**]¹¹⁸⁾ the pain sensation up your leg, up and along the spinal cord to the brain. While the pain [**it** / **itself**]¹¹⁹⁾ is unpleasant, it is in fact acting as a protective mechanism for the foot. Within the brain, nerves will connect to the area that controls speech, so that you may [**well** / **as well**]¹²⁰⁾ shout 'ouch' or something rather [**more** / **less**]¹²¹⁾ polite. They will also connect to motor nerves that travel back down the spinal cord, and to the muscles in your leg that now [**contract** / **contracts**]¹²²⁾ quickly to lift your foot away from the painful object. Sensory and motor nerves control almost all functions in the body — from the beating of the heart to the movement of the gut, sweating and just about everything else.

감각 신경은 특정 감각을 포착하는 특화된 말단을 조직에 가지고 있다. 예를 들어, 만약 여러분이 핀과 같이 날카로운 물체를 밟는다면, 피부의 신경 말단이 통증 감각을 여러분의 다리 위로, 그리고 척수를 따라 위로 뇌까지 전달할 것이다. 통증 자체는 불쾌하지만, 사실은 발을 보호하는 메커니즘으로 작용하고 있다. (즉, 여러분은 그 통증에 익숙해져 통증을 피할 수 있는 능력이 감소한다.) 뇌 안에서, 신경은 언어를 통제하는 부분에 연결될 것이고, 그래서 여러분은 '아야' 또는 다소 덜 공손한 무언가를 외칠 것이다. 그것들은 또한 척수를 타고 다시 내려오는 운동 신경에 연결될 것이고, 그리고 이제 재빨리 수축하여 고통을 주는 물체로부터 발을 떼어 들어 올리게 하는 여러분의 다리 근육에 연결될 것이다. 감각 신경과 운동 신경은 심장의 박동에서부터 장 운동, 발한과 그 밖에 모든 것에 이르기까지 신체의 거의 모든 기능을 통제한다.

36

Maybe you've heard this joke: "How do you eat an elephant?" The answer is "one bite at a time." So, how do you "build" the Earth? That's simple, too: one atom at a time. Atoms are the basic building blocks of crystals, and since all rocks [**make** / **are made**]¹²³⁾ up of crystals, the [**much** / **more**]¹²⁴⁾ you know about atoms, the better. Crystals come in a [**variety** / **variation**]¹²⁵⁾ of shapes <u>that (무슨 that? _____)</u>¹²⁶⁾ scientists call *habits*. Common crystal habits [**conclude** / **include**]¹²⁷⁾ squares, triangles, and six-sided hexagons. Usually crystals form when liquids cool, such as when you create ice cubes. Many times, crystals form in ways that do not allow [**for** / **to**]¹²⁸⁾ perfect shapes. If conditions are too cold, too hot, or there isn't enough source material, they can form strange, [**twisted** / **twisting**]¹²⁹⁾ shapes. But when conditions are right, we see beautiful displays. Usually, this involves a slow, steady environment where the individual atoms have plenty of time to join and fit perfectly into what's known [**as** / **for**]¹³⁰⁾ the *crystal lattice*. This is the basic structure of atoms that [**is** / **are**]¹³¹⁾ seen time after time.

아마 여러분은 이 농담을 들어본 적이 있을 것이다. "코끼리를 어떻게 먹는가?" 정답은 '한 번에 한 입'이다. 그렇다면, 여러분은 어떻게 지구를 '건설'하는가? 그것은 또한 간단하다. 한 번에 하나의 원자이다. 원자는 결정의 기본 구성 요소이고, 모든 암석은 결정으로 이루어져 있기 때문에, 여러분은 원자에 대해 더 많이 알수록 더 좋다. 결정은 과학자들이 '습성'이라고 부르는 다양한 모양으로 나온다. 일반적인 결정 습성은 사각형, 삼각형, 육면의 육각형을 포함한다. 보통 여러분이 얼음을 만들 때와 같이 액체가 차가워질 때 결정이 형성된다. 많은 경우, 결정은 완벽한 모양을 허용하지 않는 방식으로 형성된다. 조건이 너무 차갑거나, 너무 뜨겁거나, 혹은 원천 물질이 충분하지 않으면 이상하고 뒤틀린 모양을 형성할 수 있다. 하지만 조건이 맞을 때, 우리는 아름다운 배열을 본다. 보통, 이것은 개별적인 원자들이 결합하고 '결정격자'라고 알려진 것에 완벽하게 들어맞는 충분한 시간을 가지는 느리고 안정적인 환경을 수반한다. 이것은 반복하여 보이는 원자의 기본적인 구조이다.

37

When you pluck a guitar string it moves back and forth hundreds of times every second. Naturally, this movement is so fast [**that / when**]132) you cannot see it — you just see the blurred outline of the moving string. Strings [**vibrated / vibrating**]133) in this way on their own [**make / makes**]134) [**hard / hardly**]135) any noise because strings are very thin and don't push [**much / many**]136) air about. But if you [**attach / attach to**]137) a string to a big hollow box (like a guitar body), then the vibration is amplified and the note is heard loud and clear. The vibration of the string [**passes / is passed**]138) on to the wooden panels of the guitar body, [**that / which**]139) vibrate back and forth at the same rate as the string. The vibration of the wood [**creates / creating**]140) more powerful waves in the air pressure, [**when / which**]141) travel away from the guitar. When the waves [**reach / reach at**]142) your eardrums they flex in and out the same number of times a second as the original string.

여러분이 기타 줄을 뜯을 때 그것은 매초 수백 번 이리저리 움직인다. 당연히, 이 움직임은 너무 빨라서 여러분이 그것을 볼 수 없다. 여러분은 그저 움직이는 줄의 흐릿한 윤곽만 본다. 이렇게 스스로 진동하는 줄들은 거의 소리가 나지 않는데, 이는 줄이 매우 가늘어 많은 공기를 밀어내지 못하기 때문이다. 하지만 여러분이 (기타 몸통 같은) 커다란 속이 빈 상자에 줄을 달면, 그 진동은 증폭되어 그 음이 크고 선명하게 들린다. 그 줄의 진동은 기타 몸통의 나무판으로 전달되어 줄과 같은 속도로 이리저리 떨린다. 그 나무의 진동은 공기의 압력에 더 강력한 파동을 만들어 내어 기타로부터 멀리 퍼진다. 그 파동이 여러분의 고막에 도달할 때 원래의 줄과 초당 동일한 횟수로 굽이쳐 들어가고 나온다.

38

Boundaries between work and home [**is / are**]143) blurring as portable digital technology [**makes / making**]144) **it** (무슨 it? _____)145) increasingly possible to work anywhere, anytime. Individuals differ in [**how / what**]146) they like to manage their time to meet work and outside responsibilities. Some people prefer to separate or segment roles so that boundary crossings are [**minimized / maximized**]147). For example, these people might keep separate email accounts for work and family and try to conduct work at the workplace and take care of family matters only [**during / while**]148) breaks and non-work time. We've even noticed more of these "segmenters" [**carried / carrying**]149) two phones — one for work and one for personal use. Flexible schedules work well for these individuals because they enable greater distinction between time at work and time in other roles. Other individuals prefer integrating work and family roles all day long. This might [**instill / entail**]150) constantly trading text messages with children from the office, or [**monitor / monitoring**]151) emails at home and on vacation, rather than returning to work to find hundreds of messages in their inbox.

휴대용 디지털 기술이 언제, 어디서나 작업하는 것을 점차 가능하게 함에 따라 직장과 가정의 경계가 흐릿해지고 있다. 사람들은 직장과 외부의 책임을 수행하기 위해 자신의 시간을 관리하기를 바라는 방식에 차이가 있다. 어떤 사람들은 경계 교차 지점이 최소화되도록 역할을 분리하거나 분할하는 것을 선호한다. 예를 들어, 이러한 사람들은 직장과 가정을 위한 별개의 이메일 계정을 유지하고 직장에서 일을 수행하고 휴식 시간과 일을 하지 않는 시간 동안에만 가정사를 처리하려고 할지도 모른다. 우리는 더 많은 이러한 '분할자들'이 하나는 업무용이고 하나는 개인용인 두 개의 전화기를 가지고 다니고 있음을 심지어 알게 되었다. 유연근로시간제는 이런 사람들에게 잘 적용되는데, 직장에서의 시간과 다른 역할에서의 시간 간에 더 큰 구별을 가능하게 하기 때문이다. 다른 사람들은 하루 종일 직장과 가정의 역할을 통합하는 것을 선호한다. 이것은 직장으로 돌아가서 받은 편지함에서 수백 개의 메시지를 발견하는 것 대신 사무실에서 아이들과 문자 메시지를 지속적으로 주고받거나 집에서 그리고 휴가 중에 이메일을 확인하는 것을 수반할지도 모른다.

39

A "complementary good" is a product that is often [**consumed / consuming**]152) alongside another product. For example, popcorn is a complementary good to a movie, while a travel pillow is a complementary good for a long plane journey. When the popularity of one product [**increases / decreases**]153), the sales of [**its / their**]154) complementary good also [**increase / decrease**]155). By producing goods that complement other products that are already (or about to be) popular, you can [**insure / ensure**]156) a steady stream of demand for your product. Some products enjoy perfect complementary status — they *have* to [**consume / be consumed**]157) together, such as a lamp and a lightbulb. [**Therefore / However**]158), do not assume that a product is perfectly complementary, as customers may not be completely locked in to the product. For example, although motorists may seem [**acquired / required**]159) to purchase gasoline to run [**its / their**]160) cars, they can switch [**x / to**]161) electric cars.

'보완재'는 종종 다른 제품과 함께 소비되는 제품이다. 예를 들어, 팝콘은 영화에 대한 보완재인 한편, 여행 베개는 긴 비행기 여행에 대한 보완재이다. 한 제품의 인기가 높아지면 그것의 보완재 판매량도 늘어난다. 여러분은 이미 인기가 있는 (또는 곧 있을) 다른 제품을 보완하는 제품을 생산함으로써 여러분의 제품에 대한 꾸준한 수요 흐름을 보장할 수 있다. 일부 제품들은 완벽한 보완적 상태를 누리고 있고, 그것들은 램프와 전구와 같이 함께 소비'되어야' 한다. 그러나 고객들이 그 제품에 완전히 고정되어 있지 않을 수 있으므로, 어떤 제품이 완벽하게 보완적이라고 가정하지 마라. 예를 들어, 비록 운전자들이 자신의 차를 운전하기 위해 휘발유를 구매할 필요가 있는 것처럼 보일지라도, 그들은 전기 자동차로 바꿀 수 있다.

40

It's not news to anyone that we judge others based on their clothes. In general, studies that investigate these judgments find that people prefer clothing that matches expectations — surgeons in scrubs, little boys in blue — with one notable [**exception / expectation**]162). A series of studies [**published / are published**]163) in an article in June 2014 in the *Journal of Consumer Research* [**explored / exploring**]164) observers' reactions to people who broke established norms only slightly. In one scenario, a man at a black-tie affair was viewed as [**having / to have**]165) higher status and [**competence / competition**]166) when [**wearing / to wear**]167) a red bow tie. The researchers also found that valuing uniqueness [**increased / decreased**]168) audience members' ratings of the status and competence of a professor who wore red sneakers [**while / during**]169) giving a lecture. The results suggest that people judge these slight [**dedications / deviations**]170) from the norm as positive because they suggest that the individual is [**enough powerful / powerful enough**]171) to risk the social costs of such behaviors.

우리가 다른 사람들을 그들의 의복을 보고 판단하는 것은 누구에게도 새로운 일이 아니다. 일반적으로, 이러한 판단을 조사하는 연구는 사람들이 수술복을 입은 외과 의사, 파란 옷을 입은 남자아이와 같이 예상에 맞는 의복이되 하나의 눈에 띄는 예외가 있는 것을 선호한다는 것을 발견한다. Journal of Consumer Research의 2014년 9월 기사에 실린 일련의 연구는 확립된 규범을 아주 약간 어긴 사람들에 대한 관찰자들의 반응을 탐구했다. 한 시나리오에서는, 정장 차림의 행사에서 한 남자가 빨간 나비 넥타이를 맸을 때 더 높은 지위와 능력을 가진 것으로 보여졌다. 연구자들은 독특함을 중시하는 것이 강의를 하는 동안 빨간 운동화를 신은 교수의 지위와 역량에 대한 청중들의 평가를 높였다는 것을 또한 발견했다. 그 결과들은 사람들이 규범으로부터 이러한 약간의 일탈들을 긍정적으로 판단한다는 것을 시사하는데, 왜냐하면 그것들은 그 사람이 그러한 행동으로 인한 사회적 비용을 감수할 만큼 충분히 강하다는 것을 시사하기 때문이다.

41~42

Claims that local food [**product / production**]172) cut greenhouse gas [**emissions / omissions**]173) by reducing the burning of [**transformation / transportation**]174) fuel [**is / are**]175) usually not well [**found / founded**]176). [**Transport / Transmit**]177) is the source of only 11 percent of greenhouse gas emissions within the food sector, so reducing the distance that food travels after it [**leaves / leaves for**]178) the farm is far less important than [**reduces / reducing**]179) wasteful energy use on the farm. Food coming from a distance can actually be better for the climate, depending on [**how / what**]180) it was grown. For example, field-grown tomatoes shipped from Mexico in the winter months will have a smaller carbon footprint than local winter tomatoes [**grown / growing**]181) in a greenhouse. In the United Kingdom, lamb meat that travels 11,000 miles from New Zealand generates only one-quarter the carbon [**emissions / omissions**]182) per pound [**compared / comparing**]183) to British lamb because farmers in the United Kingdom raise their animals on feed (which must be produced using fossil fuels) rather than on clover pastureland.

 When food does travel, what matters most is not the distance traveled but the travel mode (surface versus air), and most of all the load size. Bulk loads of food can travel halfway around the world by ocean [**flight / freight**]184) with a smaller carbon footprint, per pound [**delivered / delivering**]185), than foods traveling just a short distance but in much smaller loads. For example, 18-wheelers carry much larger loads than pickup trucks so they can move food 100 times as far [**during / while**]186) burning only one-third as much gas per pound of food delivered.

로컬푸드 생산이 운송 연료의 연소를 줄임으로써 온실가스 배출을 줄였다는 주장들은 대개 근거가 충분하지 않다. 운송은 식품 부문 내에서 온실가스 배출의 11퍼센트만을 차지하는 원천이기에, 식품이 농장을 떠난 후 이동하는 거리를 줄이는 것은 농장에서 낭비되는 에너지 사용을 줄이는 것보다 훨씬 덜 중요하다. 먼 곳에서 오는 식품은 그것이 어떻게 재배되었느냐에 따라 실제로 기후에 더 좋을 수 있다. 예를 들어, 겨울에 멕시코로부터 수송된 밭에서 재배된 토마토는 온실에서 재배된 현지의 겨울 토마토보다 탄소 발자국이 더 적을 것이다. 영국에서는, 영국의 농부들이 클로버 목초지에서가 아닌 (화석 연료를 사용하여 생산되어야 하는) 사료로 자신의 동물들을 기르기 때문에 뉴질랜드에서 11,000마일을 이동하는 양고기는 영국의 양고기에 비해 파운드당 탄소 배출량의 4분의 일만 발생시킨다.
 식품이 이동할 때, 가장 중요한 것은 이동 거리가 아니라 이동 방식(지상 대 공중), 그리고 무엇보다 적재량의 규모이다. 대량의 적재된 식품은 단지 단거리를 이동하지만 훨씬 더 적은 적재량인 식품에 비해 배달된 파운드당 탄소 발자국이 더 적은 해상 화물 운송으로 세계의 절반을 이동할 수 있다. 예를 들어, 18륜 대형트럭은 픽업트럭보다 훨씬 더 많은 적재량을 운반하기에 배달된 식품 파운드당 3분의 일의 연료만 연소하면서 100배 멀리 식품을 이동시킬 수 있다.

43~45

Long ago, an old man built a grand temple at the center of his village. People traveled to worship at the temple. So the old man made arrangements for food and [**accommodation / recommendation**]187) inside the temple itself. He needed someone who could look [**for / after**]188) the temple, so he put up a notice: Manager needed. [**Seen / Seeing**]189) the notice, many people went to the old man. But he returned all the [**applicants / appliances**]190) after interviews, telling them, "I need a [**quantified / qualified**]191) person for this work." The old man would sit on the roof of his house every morning, watching people [**go / to go**]192) through the temple doors. One day, he saw a young man [**come / to come**]193) to the temple. When [**that / those**]194) young man left the temple, the old man called him and asked, "Will you take care of this temple?" The young man was surprised by the offer and replied, "I have no experience [**caring / to care**]195) for a temple. I'm not even educated." The old man smiled and said, "I don't want any educated man. I want a qualified person." [**Confused / Confusing**]196), the young man asked, "But why do you consider me a qualified person?" The old man replied, "I buried a brick on the path to the temple. I watched for many days as people tripped over that brick. No one thought [**removing / to remove**]197) it. But you dug up that brick." The young man said, "I haven't done [**something / anything**]198) great. It's the duty of every human [**to be / being**]199) to think about others. I only did my duty." The old man smiled and said, "Only people who know their duty and perform it [**is / are**]200) qualified people."

옛날, 한 노인이 마을 중심부에 큰 사원을 지었다. 사람들이 사원에서 예배를 드리기 위해 멀리서 왔다. 그래서 노인은 사원 안에 음식과 숙소를 준비했다. 그는 사원을 관리할 수 있는 사람이 필요했고, 그래서 그는 '관리자 구함'이라는 공고를 붙였다. 공고를 보고 많은 사람들이 노인을 찾아갔다. 그러나 그는 면접 후에 그들에게 "나는 이 일에 자격을 갖춘 사람이 필요합니다."라고 말하며, 모든 지원자들을 돌려 보냈다. 노인은 사람들이 사원의 문을 통과하는 것을 지켜보며 매일 아침 그의 집 지붕에 앉아 있곤 했다. 어느 날 그는 한 젊은이가 사원으로 오는 것을 보았다. 젊은이가 사원을 나설 때, 노인이 그를 불러 "이 사원의 관리를 맡아 주겠소?"라고 질문했다. 젊은이는 그 제안에 놀라서 "저는 사원을 관리한 경험이 없고, 심지어 교육도 받지 못했습니다."라고 대답했다. 노인은 웃으며 "나는 교육을 받은 사람이 필요한 게 아니오. 나는 자격 있는 사람을 원하오."라고 말했다. 당황하여, 젊은이는 "그런데 당신은 왜 저를 자격이 있는 사람이라고 여기시나요?"라고 물었다. 노인은 대답했다. "나는 사원으로 통하는 길에 벽돌 한 개를 묻었소. 나는 여러 날 동안 사람들이 그 벽돌에 발이 걸려 넘어지는 것을 지켜보았소. 아무도 그것을 치울 생각을 하지 않았소. 하지만 당신은 그 벽돌을 파냈소." 젊은이는 "저는 대단한 일을 한 것이 아닙니다. 타인을 생각하는 것은 모든 인간의 의무입니다. 저는 제 의무를 다했을 뿐입니다."라고 말했다. 노인은 미소를 지으며 "자신의 의무를 알고 그 의무를 수행하는 사람만이 자격이 있는 사람이오."라고 말했다.

18

Dear Professor Sanchez,

My name is Ellis Wight, and I'm the director of the Alexandria Science Museum. We are [**held** / **holding**]1) a Chemistry Fair for local middle school students [**on** / **in**]2) Saturday, October 28. The goal of the fair is to encourage them [**being** / **to be**]3) interested in science through [**guiding** / **guided**]4) experiments. We are looking [**for** / **at**]5) college students who can help with the experiments [**while** / **during**]6) the event. I am contacting you to ask you to [**command** / **recommend**]7) some students from the chemistry department at your college who you think are [**qualified** / **quantified**]8) for this job. With their help, I'm sure the participants will have a great experience. I look forward to [**hear** / **hearing**]9) from you soon.

Sincerely, Ellis Wight

19

Gregg and I had been rock climbing since sunrise and had had no problems. So we took a risk. "Look, the first bolt is right there. I can [**definitely** / **infinitely**]10) climb out to it. Piece of cake," I persuaded Gregg, minutes before I found myself [**pinned** / **pinning**]11). It wasn't a piece of cake. The rock was [**inceptively** / **deceptively**]12) barren of handholds. I clumsily moved back and forth across the cliff face and ended up with nowhere to go...but down. The bolt that would save my life, if I could get to it, [**was** / **being**]13) about two feet above my reach. My arms trembled from exhaustion. I looked [**at** / **for**]14) Gregg. My body froze with fright from my neck down to my toes. Our rope [**tied** / **was tied**]15) between us. If I fell, he would fall with me.

20

We are always teaching our children something by our words and our actions. They learn from seeing. They learn from hearing and from *overhearing*. Children share the values of their parents about the most important things in life. Our [**properties** / **priorities**]16) and [**principals** / **principles**]17) and our examples of good behavior can teach our children to take the high road when other roads look [**tempting** / **like tempting**]18). Remember [**that** / **what**]19) children do not learn the values that make up strong character simply by [**telling** / **being** *told*]20) about them. They learn by seeing the people around them *act* on and *uphold* those values in their daily lives. [**Therefore** / **However**]21) show your child good examples of life by your action. In our daily lives, we can show our children **that** (무슨 that? _____)22) we respect others. We can show them our compassion and concern when others are suffering, and our own self-discipline, courage and honesty as we make difficult decisions.

21

Most people have no doubt [**heard / hearing**]23) this question: If a tree falls in the forest and there is no one there to hear [**it / them**]24) fall, does it make a sound? The correct answer is no. Sound is more than pressure waves, and indeed there can be no sound without a hearer. And [**similarly / conversely**]25), scientific communication is a two-way process. Just as a signal of any kind is useless [**if / unless**]26) it is perceived, a published scientific paper (signal) is useless [**if / unless**]27) it is both received *and* understood by [**its / their**]28) intended audience. Thus we can restate the axiom of science as follows: A scientific experiment is not complete until the results have [**published / been published**]29) *and understood*. Publication is no more than pressure waves unless the published paper is understood. Too many scientific papers fall silently in the woods.

22

We all negotiate every day, [**if / whether**]30) we realise it or not. Yet [**few / a few**]31) people ever learn *how* to negotiate. Those who do usually learn the traditional, win-lose negotiating style rather than an approach that is likely to result [**in / from**]32) a win-win agreement. This old-school, [**advertent / adversarial**]33) approach may be useful in a one-off negotiation where you will probably not deal with **that** (무슨 that? _____)34) person again. However, such [**transactions / transformations**]35) are becoming increasingly rare, because most of us deal with the same people repeatedly — our spouses and children, our friends and colleagues, our customers and clients. In view of this, it's essential to achieve [**successful / successive**]36) results for ourselves and maintain a healthy relationship with our negotiating partners at the same time. In today's [**independent / interdependent**]37) world of business partnerships and long-term relationships, a win-win outcome is fast becoming the *only* acceptable result.

23

The interaction of workers from different cultural backgrounds with the host population might increase [**product / productivity**]38) due [**to / on**]39) positive externalities like knowledge spillovers. This is only an [**advantage / disadvantage**]40) up to a certain degree. When the variety of backgrounds [**is / are**]41) too large, fractionalization may cause [**exceptional / excessive**]42) transaction costs for communication, [**which / that**]43) may [**boost / lower**]44) productivity. Diversity not only impacts the labour market, but may also [**affect / affect on**]45) the quality of life in a location. A tolerant native population may value a multicultural city or region because of an increase in the range of available goods and services. On the other hand, diversity could be perceived as an [**attractive / unattractive**]46) feature if natives perceive **it** (무엇을 가리키는가? _____)47) as a distortion of [**that / what**]48) they consider to be their national identity. They might even discriminate against other ethnic groups and they might fear that social conflicts between different foreign nationalities are [**imported / exported**]49) into their own neighbourhood.

24

We think we are shaping our buildings. But really, our buildings and development are also shaping us. One of the best examples of this is the oldest-known construction: the ornately carved rings of standing stones at Göbekli Tepe in Turkey. Before these ancestors got the idea to [**erect / elect**]50) standing stones some 12,000 years ago, [**which / they**]51) were hunter-gatherers. It [**appears / is appeared**]52) that the [**erection / election**]53) of the multiple rings of megalithic stones took so long, and so many [**successive / successful**]54) generations, [**that / which**]55) these innovators [**forced / were forced**]56) to settle down to complete the construction works. In the process, they became the first farming society on Earth. This is an early example of a society constructing something that ends up radically [**remaking / remade**]57) the society itself. Things are not so different in our own time.

26

American jazz pianist Bill Evans was born in New Jersey in 1929. His early training was in classical music. At the age of six, he began [**receiving / perceiving**]58) piano lessons, later [**added / adding**]59) flute and violin. He earned bachelor's degrees in piano and music education from Southeastern Louisiana College in 1950. He went on to serve in the army from 1951 to 1954 and [**play / played**]60) flute in the Fifth Army Band. After serving in the military, he studied [**composition / competition**]61) at the Mannes School of Music in New York. Composer George Russell admired his playing and hired Evans to record and perform **his** (누구? George Russell? Bill Evans?)62) compositions. Evans became famous for recordings made from the [**late / lately**]63) -1950s through the 1960s. He won his first Grammy Award in 1964 for his album *Conversations with Myself.* Evans' expressive piano works and his unique harmonic approach inspired a whole generation of musicians.

29

There is a reason the title "Monday Morning Quarterback" [**exists / is existed**]64). Just read the comments on social media from fans [**discussing / discussing about**]65) the weekend's games, and you quickly see how many people believe they could play, coach, and manage sport teams more [**successfully / successively**]66) than [**that / those**]67) on the field. This goes for the boardroom as well. Students and professionals with years of training and [**specializing / specialized**]68) degrees in sport business may also find [**them / themselves**]69) [**giving / being given**]70) advice on how to do their jobs from friends, family, or even total strangers without any expertise. Executives in sport management have decades of knowledge and experience in their [**respective / respectable**]71) fields. However, many of them face criticism from fans and community members [**tell / telling**]72) **them** (무엇을 가리키는가? _____)73) how to [**run / run into**]74) their business. Very few people tell their doctor how to perform surgery or their accountant how to prepare their taxes, but many people provide feedback on how sport organizations should be managed.

30

While moving is difficult for everyone, it is particularly stressful for children. They lose their sense of security and may feel [**disoriented / disorienting**]75) when their routine is disrupted and all that is familiar is taken [**on / away**]76). Young children, ages 3-6, are particularly affected by a move. Their understanding at this stage is quite [**lateral / literal**]77), and [**it / which**]78) is difficult [**of / for**]79) them to imagine beforehand a new home and their new room. Young children may have worries such as "Will I still be me in the new place?" and "Will my toys and bed come with us?" It is important to establish a balance between [**vagueness / validating**]80) children's past experiences and [**focus / focusing**]81) on helping them [**adjust / adjusting**]82) to the new place. Children need to have opportunities to share their backgrounds in a way that respects their past as an important part of who they are. This contributes to [**build / building**]83) a sense of community, [**it / which**]84) is essential for all children, especially those in transition.

31

Many people are [**terrific / terrified**]85) to fly in airplanes. Often, this fear stems from a lack of control. The pilot is in control, not the passengers, and this lack of control [**installs / instills**]86) fear. Many potential passengers are so afraid they choose to drive great distances to get to a [**destination / determination**]87) instead of flying. But their decision to drive is based solely on emotion, not logic. Logic says that statistically, the odds of dying in a car crash [**is / are**]88) around 1 in 5,000, while the odds of dying in a plane crash [**is / are**]89) closer to 1 in 11 million. If you're going to take a risk, especially one that could possibly [**involve / evolve**]90) your well-being, wouldn't you want the odds in your favor? However, most people choose the option that will cause them the least amount of anxiety. [**Pay / Paying**]91) attention to the thoughts you have about taking the risk and make sure you're [**based / basing**]92) your decision on facts, not just feelings.

32

The famous primatologist Frans de Waal, of Emory University, [**says / saying**]93) humans downplay [**similarities / differences**]94) between us and other animals as a way of maintaining our spot at the top of our [**imaginary / imaginable**]95) ladder. Scientists, de Waal points out, can be some of the worst offenders — [**employing / deploying**]96) technical language to distance the other animals from us . They call "kissing" in chimps "mouth-to-mouth contact"; they call "friends" between primates "favorite [**affliction / affiliation**]97) partners"; they interpret evidence showing [**that / what**]98) crows and chimps can make tools as being somehow qualitatively different from the kind of toolmaking said to define humanity. If an animal can beat us at a cognitive task — like how certain bird species can remember the precise locations of thousands of seeds — they write [**it / them**]99) off as instinct, not intelligence. This and so many more tricks of language are what de Waal has [**termed / been termed**]100) "linguistic castration." The way we use our tongues to disempower animals, the way we invent words to maintain our spot at the top.

33

A key to engagement and achievement is providing students [**for / with**]101) relevant texts **(생략된 것은?** _____)102) they will be interested in. My scholarly work and my teaching have been deeply influenced by the work of Rosalie Fink. She interviewed twelve adults who were [**high / highly**]103) successful in their work, including a physicist, a biochemist, and a company CEO. All of them had dyslexia and had had significant problems with reading throughout their school years. While she expected to find that they had avoided [**reading / to avoid**]104) and discovered ways to bypass it or compensate with other strategies for learning, she found the opposite. "To my surprise, I found that these dyslexics were enthusiastic readers...they rarely avoided [**reading / to read** 105) . On the contrary, they sought out books." The pattern Fink discovered was [**what / that**]106) all of her subjects had been passionate in some personal interest. The areas of interest included religion, math, business, science, history, and biography. What mattered was that they read [**intimately / voraciously**]107) to find out more.

34

For many people, *ability* refers to intellectual [**competence / competition**]108), so they want everything they do to reflect how [**they are smart / smart they are**]109) — writing a brilliant legal brief, getting the highest grade on a test, writing elegant computer code, saying something [**exceptionally / exponentially**]110) wise or witty in a conversation. You could also define ability in [**term / terms**]111) of a particular skill or talent, such as how well one plays the piano, [**learns / learning**]112) a language, or serves a tennis ball. Some people focus on their ability to be attractive, entertaining, up on the latest trends, or to have the newest gadgets. [**How / However**]113) ability may be [**defined / confined**]114), a problem occurs when it is the sole [**determinant / determination**]115) of one's self-worth. The performance becomes the only measure of the person; [**anything / nothing**]116) else is taken into account. An outstanding performance means an outstanding person; an average performance means an average person. Period.

35

Sensory nerves have [**specialized / been specialized**]117) endings in the tissues that pick up a particular sensation. If, for example, you step on a sharp object such as a pin, nerve endings in the skin will [**transmit / transform**]118) the pain sensation up your leg, up and along the spinal cord to the brain. While the pain [**it / itself**]119) is unpleasant, it is in fact acting as a protective mechanism for the foot. Within the brain, nerves will connect to the area that controls speech, so that you may [**well / as well**]120) shout 'ouch' or something rather [**more / less**]121) polite. They will also connect to motor nerves that travel back down the spinal cord, and to the muscles in your leg that now [**contract / contracts**]122) quickly to lift your foot away from the painful object. Sensory and motor nerves control almost all functions in the body — from the beating of the heart to the movement of the gut, sweating and just about everything else.

36

Maybe you've heard this joke: "How do you eat an elephant?" The answer is "one bite at a time." So, how do you "build" the Earth? That's simple, too: one atom at a time. Atoms are the basic building blocks of crystals, and since all rocks [**make / are made**]123) up of crystals, the [**much / more**]124) you know about atoms, the better. Crystals come in a [**variety / variation**]125) of shapes <u>that</u> (무슨 that? _____)126) scientists call *habits*. Common crystal habits [**conclude / include**]127) squares, triangles, and six-sided hexagons. Usually crystals form when liquids cool, such as when you create ice cubes. Many times, crystals form in ways that do not allow [**for / to**]128) perfect shapes. If conditions are too cold, too hot, or there isn't enough source material, they can form strange, [**twisted / twisting**]129) shapes. But when conditions are right, we see beautiful displays. Usually, this involves a slow, steady environment where the individual atoms have plenty of time to join and fit perfectly into what's known [**as / for**]130) the *crystal lattice*. This is the basic structure of atoms that [**is / are**]131) seen time after time.

37

When you pluck a guitar string it moves back and forth hundreds of times every second. Naturally, this movement is so fast [**that / when**]132) you cannot see it — you just see the blurred outline of the moving string. Strings [**vibrated / vibrating**]133) in this way on their own [**make / makes**]134) [**hard / hardly**]135) any noise because strings are very thin and don't push [**much / many**]136) air about. But if you [**attach / attach to**]137) a string to a big hollow box (like a guitar body), then the vibration is amplified and the note is heard loud and clear. The vibration of the string [**passes / is passed**]138) on to the wooden panels of the guitar body, [**that / which**]139) vibrate back and forth at the same rate as the string. The vibration of the wood [**creates / creating**]140) more powerful waves in the air pressure, [**when / which**]141) travel away from the guitar. When the waves [**reach / reach at**]142) your eardrums they flex in and out the same number of times a second as the original string.

38

Boundaries between work and home [**is / are**]143) blurring as portable digital technology [**makes / making**]144) <u>it</u> (무슨 it? _____)145) increasingly possible to work anywhere, anytime. Individuals differ in [**how / what**]146) they like to manage their time to meet work and outside responsibilities. Some people prefer to separate or segment roles so that boundary crossings are [**minimized / maximized**]147). For example, these people might keep separate email accounts for work and family and try to conduct work at the workplace and take care of family matters only [**during / while**]148) breaks and non-work time. We've even noticed more of these "segmenters" [**carried / carrying**]149) two phones — one for work and one for personal use. Flexible schedules work well for these individuals because they enable greater distinction between time at work and time in other roles. Other individuals prefer integrating work and family roles all day long. This might [**instill / entail**]150) constantly trading text messages with children from the office, or [**monitor / monitoring**]151) emails at home and on vacation, rather than returning to work to find hundreds of messages in their inbox.

39

A "complementary good" is a product that is often [**consumed / consuming**]152) alongside another product. For example, popcorn is a complementary good to a movie, while a travel pillow is a complementary good for a long plane journey. When the popularity of one product [**increases / decreases**]153), the sales of [**its / their**]154) complementary good also [**increase / decrease**]155). By producing goods that complement other products that are already (or about to be) popular, you can [**insure / ensure**]156) a steady stream of demand for your product. Some products enjoy perfect complementary status — they *have* to [**consume / be consumed**]157) together, such as a lamp and a lightbulb. [**Therefore / However**]158), do not assume that a product is perfectly complementary, as customers may not be completely locked in to the product. For example, although motorists may seem [**acquired / required**]159) to purchase gasoline to run [**its / their**]160) cars, they can switch [**x / to**]161) electric cars.

40

It's not news to anyone that we judge others based on their clothes. In general, studies that investigate these judgments find that people prefer clothing that matches expectations — surgeons in scrubs, little boys in blue — with one notable [**exception / expectation**]162). A series of studies [**published / are published**]163) in an article in June 2014 in the *Journal of Consumer Research* [**explored / exploring**]164) observers' reactions to people who broke established norms only slightly. In one scenario, a man at a black-tie affair was viewed as [**having / to have**]165) higher status and [**competence / competition**]166) when [**wearing / to wear**]167) a red bow tie. The researchers also found that valuing uniqueness [**increased / decreased**]168) audience members' ratings of the status and competence of a professor who wore red sneakers [**while / during**]169) giving a lecture. The results suggest that people judge these slight [**dedications / deviations**]170) from the norm as positive because they suggest that the individual is [**enough powerful / powerful enough**]171) to risk the social costs of such behaviors.

41~42

Claims that local food [**product / production**]172) cut greenhouse gas [**emissions / omissions**]173) by reducing the burning of [**transformation / transportation**]174) fuel [**is / are**]175) usually not well [**found / founded**]176). [**Transport / Transmit**]177) is the source of only 11 percent of greenhouse gas emissions within the food sector, so reducing the distance that food travels after it [**leaves / leaves for**]178) the farm is far less important than [**reduces / reducing**]179) wasteful energy use on the farm. Food coming from a distance can actually be better for the climate, depending on [**how / what**]180) it was grown. For example, field-grown tomatoes shipped from Mexico in the winter months will have a smaller carbon footprint than local winter tomatoes [**grown / growing**]181) in a greenhouse. In the United Kingdom, lamb meat that travels 11,000 miles from New Zealand generates only one-quarter the carbon [**emissions / omissions**]182) per pound [**compared / comparing**]183) to British lamb because farmers in the United Kingdom raise their animals on feed (which must be produced using fossil fuels) rather than on clover pastureland.

(.hwp) (.pdf) ➔ www.englishmygod.com

When food does travel, what matters most is not the distance traveled but the travel mode (surface versus air), and most of all the load size. Bulk loads of food can travel halfway around the world by ocean [**flight / freight**]184) with a smaller carbon footprint, per pound [**delivered / delivering**]185), than foods traveling just a short distance but in much smaller loads. For example, 18-wheelers carry much larger loads than pickup trucks so they can move food 100 times as far [**during / while**]186) burning only one-third as much gas per pound of food delivered.

43~45

Long ago, an old man built a grand temple at the center of his village. People traveled to worship at the temple. So the old man made arrangements for food and [**accommodation / recommendation**]187) inside the temple itself. He needed someone who could look [**for / after**]188) the temple, so he put up a notice: Manager needed. [**Seen / Seeing**]189) the notice, many people went to the old man. But he returned all the [**applicants / appliances**]190) after interviews, telling them, "I need a [**quantified / qualified**]191) person for this work." The old man would sit on the roof of his house every morning, watching people [**go / to go**]192) through the temple doors. One day, he saw a young man [**come / to come**]193) to the temple. When [**that / those**]194) young man left the temple, the old man called him and asked, "Will you take care of this temple?" The young man was surprised by the offer and replied, "I have no experience [**caring / to care**]195) for a temple. I'm not even educated." The old man smiled and said, "I don't want any educated man. I want a qualified person." [**Confused / Confusing**]196), the young man asked, "But why do you consider me a qualified person?" The old man replied, "I buried a brick on the path to the temple. I watched for many days as people tripped over that brick. No one thought [**removing / to remove**]197) it. But you dug up that brick." The young man said, "I haven't done [**something / anything**]198) great. It's the duty of every human [**to be / being**]199) to think about others. I only did my duty." The old man smiled and said, "Only people who know their duty and perform it [**is / are**]200) qualified people."

2023 고1 9월 모의고사 　　　❶ 회차 ：　　　 점 / 300점

❶ voca　　❷ text　　❸ [/]　　❹ ____　　❺ quiz 1　　❻ quiz 2　　❼ quiz 3　　❽ quiz 4　　❾ quiz 5

18

Dear Professor Sanchez,

My name is Ellis Wight, and I'm the **d**_____ 1) of the Alexandria Science Museum. We are **h**_____ 2) a Chemistry Fair for **l**_____ 3) middle school students on Saturday, October 28. The **g**_____ 4) of the fair is to **e**_____ 5) them to be interested in science through guided experiments. We are looking for college students who can help with the experiments during the event. I am **c**_____ 6) you to ask you to **r**_____ 7) some students from the chemistry **d**_____ 8) at your college who you think are **q**_____ 9) for this job. With their help, I'm sure the **p**_____ 10) will have a great experience. I look forward to hearing from you soon.

Sincerely, Ellis Wight

Sanchez 교수님께,

제 이름은 Ellis Wight이고 Alexandria 과학 박물관의 관장입니다. 저희는 10월 28일 토요일에 지역 중학교 학생을 위한 화학 박람회를 개최합니다. 이 박람회의 목적은 안내적 실험을 통해 학생들이 과학에 관한 관심을 갖도록 장려하는 것입니다. 저희는 행사 기간 동안 실험을 도와줄 수 있는 대학생을 모집하고자 합니다. 저는 이 일에 적합하다고 생각되는 귀교의 화학과 학생 몇 명을 추천해 달라는 요청을 드리고자 연락드렸습니다. 저는 그 학생들의 도움으로 참가자들이 훌륭한 경험을 하게 될 것이라 확신합니다. 빠른 시일 내에 당신으로부터 연락이 오기를 기대하겠습니다.

진심을 담아, Ellis Wight

19

Gregg and I had been rock climbing **s**_____ 11) sunrise and had had no problems. So we took a **r**_____ 12) "Look, the first bolt is right there. I can **d**_____ 13) climb out to it. Piece of cake," I **p**_____ 14) Gregg, minutes before I found myself **p**_____ 15) It wasn't a piece of cake. The rock was **d**_____ 16) barren of handholds. I **c**_____ 17) moved back and forth across the **c**_____ 18) face and ended up with nowhere to go...but down. The bolt that would save my life, if I could get to it, was about two feet above my **r**_____ 19) . My arms **t**_____ 20) from **e**_____ 21) I looked at Gregg. My body froze with fright from my neck down to my toes. Our rope was **t**_____ 22) between us. If I fell, he would fall with me.

Gregg와 나는 일출 이후에 암벽 등반을 해왔고 아무런 문제가 없었다. 그래서 우리는 위험을 감수했다. "봐, 첫 번째 볼트가 바로 저기에 있어. 나는 분명히 거기까지 올라갈 수 있어. 식은 죽 먹기야."라고 나는 Gregg를 설득했고, 얼마 지나지 않아 나는 내가 꼼짝 못 하게 되었다는 것을 알게 되었다. 그것은 식은 죽 먹기가 아니었다. 그 바위는 믿을 수 없게도 손으로 잡을 곳이 없었다. 나는 서툴게 절벽 면을 이리저리 가로질러 보았지만 갈 곳이... 결국 아래쪽밖에는 없었다. 만약 내가 거기까지 갈 수 있다면, 내 목숨을 구해줄 볼트는 손이 닿을 수 있는 곳에서 약 2피트 위에 있었다. 내 팔은 극도의 피로로 떨렸다. 나는 Gregg를 쳐다보았다. 내 몸은 목에서부터 발끝까지 공포로 얼어붙었다. 우리 사이에 밧줄이 묶여 있었다. 내가 떨어지면, 그도 나와 함께 떨어질 것이다.

(.hwp) (.pdf) → www.englishmygod.com

20

We are always teaching our children something by our words and our actions. They learn from seeing. They learn from hearing and from o_____23) . Children share the values of their parents about the most important things in life. Our p_____24) and p_____25) and our examples of good behavior can teach our children to take the high road when other roads look t_____26) Remember that children do not learn the values that make up strong c_____27) simply by being t_____28) about them. They learn by seeing the people around them a_____29) on and u_____30) those values in their d_____31) lives. Therefore show your child good examples of life by your action. In our daily lives, we can show our children that we r_____32) others. We can show them our c_____33) and c_____34) when others are s_____35) and our own self-discipline, courage and h_____36) as we make difficult decisions.

우리는 항상 우리 자녀에게 말과 행동으로 무언가를 가르치고 있다. 그들은 보는 것으로부터 배운다. 그들은 듣거나 '우연히 듣는 것'으로부터 배운다. 아이들은 인생에서 가장 중요한 것에 대해 그들 부모의 가치를 공유한다. 우리의 우선순위와 원칙 그리고 훌륭한 행동에 대한 본보기는 우리 자녀에게 다른 길이 유혹적으로 보일 때 올바른 길로 가도록 가르칠 수 있다. 아이들은 확고한 인격을 구성하는 가치를 단순히 그것에 대해 '들음'으로써 배우지 않는다는 것을 기억하라. 그들은 그들 주변 사람들이 그들의 일상생활에서 그러한 가치를 좇아 '행동'하고 '유지'하는 것을 봄으로써 배운다. 그러므로 여러분의 자녀에게 여러분의 행동으로 삶의 모범을 보여라. 우리 일상생활에서, 우리는 우리 자녀에게 우리가 타인을 존중하는 것을 보여줄 수 있다. 우리는 그들에게 타인이 괴로워할 때 우리의 연민과 걱정을, 그리고 우리가 어려운 결정을 할 때 우리 자신의 자제력, 용기 그리고 정직을 보여줄 수 있다.

21

Most people have no d_____37) heard this question: If a tree falls in the forest and there is no one there to hear it fall, does it make a sound? The correct answer is no. Sound is more than p_____38) waves, and indeed there can be no sound without a hearer. And similarly, s_____39) communication is a two-way process. Just as a s_____40) of any kind is useless unless it is p_____41) a published scientific p_____42) (signal) is useless unless it is both received *and* understood by its i_____43) audience. Thus we can r_____44) the a_____45) of science as follows: A scientific experiment is not c_____46) until the results have been published *and understood*. P_____47) is no more than pressure waves unless the published paper is understood. Too many scientific papers fall s_____48) in the woods.

대부분의 사람들은 틀림없이 이 질문을 들어 봤을 것이다. 만약 숲에서 나무가 쓰러지고 그것이 쓰러지는 것을 들을 사람이 거기에 없다면, 소리가 나는 것일까? 정답은 '아니요'이다. 소리는 압력파 이상이며, 정말로 듣는 사람 없이는 소리가 있을 수 없다. 마찬가지로, 과학적 커뮤니케이션은 양방향 프로세스이다. 어떠한 종류의 신호든 그것이 감지되지 않으면 쓸모가 없는 것처럼, 출판된 과학 논문(신호)은 그것이 의도된 독자에 의해 수신 '그리고' 이해가 둘 다 되지 않으면 쓸모가 없다. 따라서 우리는 과학의 자명한 이치를 다음과 같이 재진술할 수 있다. 과학 실험은 결과가 출판되고 '그리고 이해될' 때까지 완성되지 않는다. 출판된 논문이 이해되지 않으면 출판은 압력파에 지나지 않는다. 너무 많은 과학 논문이 소리 없이 숲속에서 쓰러진다.

22

We all n_____⁴⁹⁾ every day, whether we realize it or not. Yet few people ever learn _____⁵⁰⁾ to negotiate. Those who do usually l_____⁵¹⁾ the t_____⁵²⁾ win-lose negotiating style rather than an approach that is likely to result in a win-win agreement. This old-school, a_____⁵³⁾ approach may be useful in a o_____⁵⁴⁾ negotiation where you will probably not deal with that person again. However, such t_____⁵⁵⁾ are becoming i_____⁵⁶⁾ rare, because most of us deal with the same people repeatedly — our spouses and children, our friends and c_____⁵⁷⁾ our customers and c_____⁵⁸⁾ In view of this, it's e_____⁵⁹⁾ to achieve successful results for ourselves and m_____⁶⁰⁾ a healthy relationship with our negotiating partners at the same time. In today's i_____⁶¹⁾ world of business partnerships and l_____⁶²⁾ relationships, a win-win o_____⁶³⁾ is fast becoming the *only* acceptable result.

우리가 그것을 알든지 모르든지 간에, 우리 모두는 매일 협상한다. 하지만 이제까지 '어떻게' 협상하는지를 배운 사람은 거의 없다. (협상 방식을) 배우는 사람들은 대개 양측에 유리한 합의를 도출할 가능성이 있는 접근법보다는 전통적인, 한쪽에만 유리한 협상 방식을 배운다. 이 구식의 적대적인 접근법은 아마도 여러분이 그 사람을 다시 상대하지 않을 일회성 협상에서 유용할지도 모른다. 그러나, 우리 대부분은 배우자와 자녀, 친구와 동료, 고객과 의뢰인같이 동일한 사람들을 반복적으로 상대하기 때문에, 이러한 거래는 점점 더 드물어지고 있다. 이러한 관점에서, 우리 자신을 위해 성공적인 결과를 얻어내는 동시에 협상 파트너들과 건전한 관계를 유지하는 것이 중요하다. 오늘날 비즈니스 파트너십과 장기적 관계의 상호 의존적인 세계에서, 양측에 유리한 성과는 '유일하게' 받아들일 수 있는 결과가 빠르게 되어 가고 있다.

23

The i_____⁶⁴⁾ of workers from different cultural backgrounds with the host population might increase p_____⁶⁵⁾ due to positive e_____⁶⁶⁾ like knowledge s_____⁶⁷⁾ . This is only an advantage up to a certain degree. When the variety of backgrounds is too large, f_____⁶⁸⁾ may cause e_____⁶⁹⁾ transaction costs for communication, which may l_____⁷⁰⁾ productivity. D_____⁷¹⁾ not only impacts the l_____⁷²⁾ market, but may also affect the quality of life in a location. A t_____⁷³⁾ native population may value a m_____⁷⁴⁾ city or region because of an i_____⁷⁵⁾ in the range of available goods and services. On the other hand, d_____⁷⁶⁾ could be perceived as an u_____⁷⁷⁾ f_____⁷⁸⁾ if natives perceive it as a d_____⁷⁹⁾ of what they consider to be their n_____⁸⁰⁾ identity. They might even d_____⁸¹⁾ against other ethnic groups and they might fear that social c_____⁸²⁾ between different foreign n_____⁸³⁾ are i_____⁸⁴⁾ into their own neighbourhood.

다른 문화적 배경으로부터의 노동자들과 현지 주민의 상호 작용은 지식 파급과 같은 긍정적인 외부 효과로 인해 생산성을 증가시킬 수 있다. 이것은 어느 정도까지만 장점이다. 배경의 다양성이 너무 클 경우, 분열은 의사소통에 대한 과도한 거래 비용을 초래하는데, 이는 생산성을 저하시킬 수 있다. 다양성은 노동 시장에 영향을 줄 뿐만 아니라 한 지역의 삶의 질에도 영향을 미칠 수 있다. 관용적인 원주민은 이용 가능한 재화와 용역 범위의 증가로 인해 다문화 도시나 지역을 가치 있게 여길 수 있다. 반면에, 원주민들이 다양성을 그들의 국가 정체성이라고 생각하는 것에 대한 왜곡으로 인식한다면 다양성은 매력적이지 않은 특징으로 인식될 수 있다. 그들은 심지어 다른 민족 집단을 차별할 수도 있고 그들은 다른 외국 국적들 간의 사회적 갈등이 그들 인근으로 유입되는 것을 두려워할 수도 있다.

24

We think we are s_____85) our buildings. But really, our buildings and development are also shaping us. One of the best examples of this is the oldest-known c_____86) the o_____87) carved rings of standing stones at Göbekli Tepe in Turkey. Before these a_____88) got the idea to e_____89) standing stones some 12,000 years ago, they were hunter-gatherers. It appears that the e_____90) of the m_____91) rings of megalithic stones took so long, and so many s_____92) generations, _____93) these i_____94) were forced to s_____95) down to complete the construction works. In the process, they became the first f_____96) society on Earth. This is an early example of a society c_____97) something that ends up r_____98) r_____99) the society itself. Things are not so different in our own time.

우리는 우리가 건물을 형성하고 있다고 생각한다. 그러나 실제로 우리의 건물과 개발도 또한 우리를 형성하고 있다. 이것의 가장 좋은 예 중 하나는 가장 오래된 것으로 알려진 건축물인 튀르키예의 Göbekli Tepe에 있는 화려하게 조각된 입석의 고리이다. 이 조상들이 약 12,000년 전에 입석을 세우는 아이디어를 얻기 전에 그들은 수렵 채집인이었다. 거석으로 된 여러 개의 고리를 세우는 데 오랜 시간이 걸렸고 많은 잇따른 세대를 거쳤어야 해서 이 혁신가들은 건설 작업을 완료하기 위해 정착해야만 했던 것으로 보인다. 그 과정에서, 그들은 지구상 최초의 농업 사회가 되었다. 이것은 결국 사회 자체를 근본적으로 재구성하는 무언가를 건설하는 사회의 초기 예이다. 우리 시대 에도 상황이 그렇게 다르지 않다.

26

American jazz pianist Bill Evans was born in New Jersey in 1929. His early training was in classical music. At the age of six, he began r_____100) piano lessons, later adding flute and violin. He earned bachelor's d_____101) in piano and music education from Southeastern Louisiana College in 1950. He went on to serve in the army from 1951 to 1954 and played flute in the Fifth Army Band. After s_____102) in the m_____103) he studied c_____104) at the Mannes School of Music in New York. Composer George Russell a_____105) his playing and hired Evans to record and p_____106) his compositions. Evans became famous _____107) recordings m_____108) from the late-1950s through the 1960s. He won his first Grammy Award in 1964 for his album *Conversations with Myself.* Evans' e_____109) piano works and his unique h_____110) approach i_____111) a whole g_____112) of musicians.

미국인 재즈 피아니스트 Bill Evans는 뉴저지에서 1929년에 태어났다. 그의 초기 교육은 클래식 음악이었다. 6세에 그는 피아노 수업을 받기 시작해서, 나중에 플루트와 바이올린을 더했다. 그는 1950년에 Southeastern Louisiana 대학에서 피아노와 음악 교육에서 학사 학위를 취득했다. 그는 1951에서 1954년까지 군 복무를 하며 제5군악대에서 플루트를 연주했다. 군 복무 이후 그는 뉴욕에 있는 Mannes School of Music에서 작곡을 공부했다. 작곡가 George Russell은 그의 연주에 감탄하여 자신의 곡을 녹음하고 연주하도록 하기 위해 Evans를 고용했다. Evans는 1950년대 후반부터 1960년대 동안에 만들어진 음반으로 유명해졌다. 그는 자신의 앨범 Conversations with Myself로 1964년에 자신의 첫 번째 그래미상을 수상했다. Evans의 표현이 풍부한 피아노 작품과 그의 독특한 화성적 접근은 전 세대의 음악가들에게 영감을 주었다.

29

There is a reason the title "Monday Morning Quarterback" exists. Just read the **c**_____113) on social media from fans **d**_____114) the weekend's games, and you quickly see how many people believe they could play, coach, and **m**_____115) sport teams more **s**_____116) than those on the field. This goes for the **b**_____117) as well. Students and professionals with years of training and **s**_____118) degrees in sport business may also find themselves **b**_____119) given advice on how to do their jobs from friends, family, or even total strangers without any **e**_____120) . **E**_____121) in sport management have **d**_____122) of knowledge and experience in their **r**_____123) fields. However, many of them **f**_____124) **c**_____125) from fans and community members telling them how to run their business. Very **f**_____126) people tell their doctor how to perform surgery or their **a**_____127) how to prepare their taxes, _____128) many people provide feedback on how sport **o**_____129) should be **m**_____130) .

'Monday Morning Quarterback'이라는 이름이 존재하는 이유가 있다. 주말 경기에 대해 토론하는 팬들의 소셜 미디어의 댓글만 읽어봐도 여러분은 자신이 경기장에 있는 사람들보다 더 성공적으로 경기를 뛰고, 감독하고, 스포츠팀을 관리할 수 있다고 얼마나 많은 사람들이 믿는지 금방 알 수 있다. 이것은 이사회실에서도 마찬가지이다. 스포츠 사업에서 수년간의 훈련을 받고 전문적인 학위를 가진 학생들과 전문가들 또한 친구들, 가족, 혹은 전문 지식이 전혀 없는 심지어 완전히 낯선 사람들로부터 어떻게 자신의 일을 해야 하는지에 대한 충고를 듣고 있는 자신을 발견할지도 모른다. 스포츠 경영 임원진들은 자신의 각 분야에서 수십 년의 지식과 경험을 가지고 있다. 하지만, 그들 중 많은 사람들이 그들에게 그들의 사업 운영 방식을 알려주는 팬들과 지역 사회 구성원들로부터의 비난에 직면한다. 자신의 의사에게 수술하는 방법을 알려주거나 자신의 회계사에게 자신의 세금을 준비하는 방법을 알려주는 사람은 거의 없지만, 많은 사람들이 스포츠 조직이 어떻게 관리되어야 하는지에 대한 피드백은 제공한다.

30

While moving is difficult for everyone, it is **p**_____131) stressful for children. They lose their sense of security and may feel **d**_____132) when their routine is **d**_____133) and all that is familiar is taken away. Young children, ages 3-6, are particularly affected by a move. Their understanding at this stage is quite **l**_____134) and it is difficult for them to imagine **b**_____135) a new home and their new room. Young children may have worries such as "Will I still be me in the new place?" and "Will my toys and bed come with us?" It is important to **e**_____136) a balance between **v**_____137) children's past experiences and focusing on helping them adjust to the new place. Children need to have opportunities to share their **b**_____138) in a way that respects their past as an important part of who they are. This **c**_____139) to building a sense of community, which is **e**_____140) for all children, especially those in transition.

이사는 모두에게 힘들지만, 아이들에게 특히 스트레스가 많은 일이다. 그들은 안심감을 잃고 그들의 일상이 무너지고 익숙한 모든 것이 사라질 때 혼란스러움을 느낄 수도 있다. 3세에서 6세 사이의 어린아이들은 이사에 특히 영향을 받는다. 이 시기에 그들의 이해력은 꽤 융통성이 없어서, 그들이 새로운 집과 자신의 새로운 방을 미리 상상하는 것은 쉽다(→ 어렵다). 어린아이들은 "내가 새로운 곳에서 여전히 나일까?"와 "내 장난감과 침대가 우리와 함께 갈까?"와 같은 걱정들을 가질지도 모른다. 아이들의 과거 경험을 인정하는 것과 그들이 새로운 곳에 적응하도록 돕는 데 집중하는 것 사이에 균형을 잡는 것이 중요하다. 아이들은 자신이 누구인지에 대한 중요한 부분으로서 자신의 과거를 존중하는 방식으로 자신의 배경을 공유할 기회를 가질 필요가 있다. 이것은 공동체 의식을 형성하는 데 기여하고, 이는 모든 아이들, 특히 변화를 겪는 아이들에게 가장 중요하다.

31

Many people are terrified to fly in airplanes. Often, this fear **s_____**141) from a lack of control. The pilot is in control, not the **p_____**142) and this lack of control **i_____**143) fear. Many **p_____**144) passengers are so afraid they choose to drive great distances to get to a **d_____**145) instead of flying. But their decision to drive is based solely on emotion, not **l_____**146) Logic says that statistically, the **o_____**147) of dying in a car crash are around 1 in 5,000, while the odds of dying in a plane crash are closer to 1 in 11 million. If you're going to take a risk, especially one that could possibly **i_____**148) your well-being, wouldn't you want the odds in your favor? However, most people choose the option that will cause them the least amount of **a_____**149) Pay attention to the thoughts you have about taking the risk and make sure you're **b_____**150) your decision on facts, not just feelings.

많은 사람들은 비행기를 타는 것을 두려워한다. 종종, 이 두려움은 통제력의 부족에서 비롯된다. 조종사는 통제를 하지만 승객은 그렇지 않으며, 이러한 통제력의 부족은 두려움을 스며들게 한다. 많은 잠재적인 승객들은 너무 두려워서 그들은 비행기를 타는 대신 목적지에 도착하기 위해 먼 거리를 운전하는 것을 선택한다. 그러나 운전을 하기로 한 그들의 결정은 논리가 아닌 오직 감정에 근거한다. 논리에 따르면 통계적으로 자동차 사고로 사망할 확률은 약 5,000분의 1이고, 반면 비행기 사고로 사망할 확률은 1,100만분의 1에 가깝다고 한다. 만약 여러분이 위험을 감수할 것이라면, 특히 여러분의 안녕을 혹시 포함할 수 있는 위험을 감수할 것이라면, 여러분에게 유리한 확률을 원하지 않겠는가? 그러나 대부분의 사람들은 그들에게 최소한의 불안감을 야기할 수 있는 선택을 한다. 위험을 감수하는 것에 대해 여러분이 가지고 있는 생각에 주의를 기울이고 여러분의 결정을 단지 감정이 아닌 사실에 근거하고 있는지 확인하라.

32

The famous primatologist Frans de Waal, of Emory University, says humans **d_____**151) similarities between us and other animals as a way of **m_____**152) our spot at the top of our **i_____**153) ladder. Scientists, de Waal points out, can be some of the worst **o_____**154) — employing technical language to distance the other animals from us . They call "kissing" in chimps "mouth-to-mouth contact"; they call "friends" between **p_____**_155) "favorite affiliation partners"; they **i_____**156) evidence showing that **c_____**157) and chimps can make tools as being somehow qualitatively different from the kind of toolmaking said to define humanity. If an animal can beat us at a **c_____**158) task — like how certain bird species can remember the **p_____**159) locations of thousands of seeds — they write it off as instinct, not intelligence. This and so many more tricks of language are what de Waal has termed "linguistic castration." The way we use our tongues to **d_____**160) animals, the way we invent words to maintain our spot at the top.

Emory 대학의 유명한 영장류학자 Frans de Waal은 인간은 상상 속 사다리의 꼭대기에서 우리의 위치를 유지하는 방법으로 우리와 다른 동물들 사이의 유사성을 경시한다고 말한다. de Waal은 과학자들이 우리와 다른 동물들 사이에 거리를 두기 위해 기술적인 언어를 사용하는 최악의 죄를 범하는 자들 중 일부일 수 있다고 지적한다. 그들은 침팬지의 '키스'를 '입과 입의 접촉'이라고 부르고, 영장류 사이의 '친구'를 '좋아하는 제휴 파트너'라고 부르며, 그들은 까마귀와 침팬지가 도구를 만들 수 있다는 것을 보여주는 증거를 인류를 정의한다고 하는 종류의 도구 제작과는 아무래도 질적으로 다르다고 해석한다. 만약 동물이, 특정 종의 새들이 수천 개의 씨앗의 정확한 위치를 기억할 수 있는 방식처럼, 인지적인 과업에서 우리를 이길 수 있다면, 그들은 그것을 지능이 아니라 본능으로 치부한다. 이것과 더 많은 언어적 수법은 de Waal이 '언어적 거세'라고 명명한 것이다. 우리가 동물로부터 힘을 빼앗기 위해 우리의 언어를 사용하는 방식이며, 우리가 꼭대기에서 우리의 위치를 유지하기 위해 단어들을 만드는 방식이다.

33

A key to **e**_____ **161)** and **a**_____ **162)** is providing students with **r**_____ **163)** texts they will be interested in. My **s**_____ **164)** work and my teaching have been deeply **i**_____ **165)** by the work of Rosalie Fink. She interviewed twelve adults who were highly successful in their work, including a physicist, a biochemist, and a company CEO. All of them had **d**_____ **166)** and had had **s**_____ **167)** problems with reading throughout their school years. While she expected to find that they had avoided reading and discovered ways to **b**_____ **168)** it or **c**_____ **169)** with other strategies for learning, she found the opposite. "To my surprise, I found that these dyslexics were **e**_____ **170)** readers...they rarely avoided reading. On the contrary, they **s**_____ **171)** out books." The pattern Fink discovered was that all of her subjects had been **p**_____ **172)** in some personal interest. The areas of interest included religion, math, business, science, history, and biography. What mattered was that they read **v**_____ **173)** to find out more.

참여와 성취의 핵심은 학생들에게 그들이 관심 있어 할 적절한 글을 제공하는 것이다. 나의 학문적인 연구와 나의 수업은 Rosalie Fink의 연구에 깊이 영향을 받아왔다. 그녀는 물리학자, 생화학자 그리고 회사의 최고 경영자를 포함해 그들의 직업에서 매우 성공한 열두 명의 성인들과 면담했다. 그들 모두가 난독증이 있었고 그들의 학령기 내내 읽기에 상당한 문제를 겪어 왔다. 그녀는 그들이 학습에 있어 읽기를 피했고 그것을 우회하거나 다른 전략들로 보완할 방법을 발견했을 것이라고 알아낼 것을 예상했으나, 정반대를 알아냈다. "놀랍게도, 나는 난독증이 있는 이런 사람들이 열성적인 독자인 것을... 그들이 좀처럼 읽기를 피하지 않는 것을 알아냈다. 이에 반하여, 그들은 책을 찾았다." Fink가 발견한 패턴은 그녀의 실험대상자 모두가 어떤 개인적인 관심사에 열정적이었다는 것이었다. 관심 분야는 종교, 수학, 상업, 과학, 역사 그리고 생물학을 포함했다. 중요한 것은 그들이 더 많이 알아내기 위해 탐욕스럽게 읽었다는 것이다.

34

For many people, *ability* **r**_____ **174)** to intellectual **c**_____ **175)** so they want everything they do to **r**_____ **176)** how smart they are — writing a brilliant legal **b**_____ **177)** , getting the highest grade on a test, writing **e**_____ **178)** computer code, saying something **e**_____ **179)** wise or **w**_____ **180)** in a conversation. You could also **d**_____ **181)** ability in terms of a particular skill or talent, such as how well one plays the piano, learns a language, or serves a tennis ball. Some people focus on their ability to be **a**_____ **182)** **e**_____ **183)** , up on the **l**_____ **184)** trends, or to have the newest **g**_____ **185)** However ability may be **d**_____ **186)** a problem occurs when it is the sole **d**_____ **187)** of one's self-worth. The performance becomes the only **m**_____ **188)** of the person; nothing else is taken into **a**_____ **189)** . An **o**_____ **190)** performance means an outstanding person; an average performance means an average person. **P**_____ **191)**

많은 사람들에게 '능력'은 지적 능력을 의미하기 때문에 그들은 자신이 하는 모든 것이 자신이 얼마나 똑똑한지를 보여주기를 원한다. 예컨대, 훌륭한 법률 보고서를 작성하는 것, 시험에서 최고의 성적을 받는 것, 정연한 컴퓨터 코드를 작성하는 것, 대화에서 비범하게 현명하거나 재치 있는 말을 하는 것이다. 여러분은 또한 피아노를 얼마나 잘 치는지, 언어를 얼마나 잘 배우는지, 테니스공을 얼마나 잘 서브하는지와 같은 특정한 기술이나 재능의 관점에서 능력을 정의할 수도 있다. 어떤 사람들은 매력적이고, 재미있고, 최신 유행에 맞추거나, 최신 기기를 가질 수 있는 그들의 능력에 초점을 맞춘다. 능력이 어떻게 정의되든지, 그것이 자신의 가치를 결정하는 유일한 결정 요소일 때 문제가 발생한다. 수행이 그 사람의 '유일한' 척도가 되며, 다른 것은 고려되지 않는다. 뛰어난 수행은 뛰어난 사람을 의미하고, 평범한 수행은 평범한 사람을 의미한다. 끝.

(.hwp) (.pdf) ➜ www.englishmygod.com

35

S_____192) n_____193) have s_____194) endings in the t_____195) that pick up a particular s_____196) If, for example, you step on a sharp object such as a pin, nerve endings in the skin will t_____197) the pain s_____198) up your leg, up and along the s_____199) cord to the brain. While the pain itself is u_____200) it is in fact acting as a protective m_____201) for the foot. Within the brain, nerves will connect to the area that controls speech, so that you may well shout 'ouch' or something rather less p_____202) They will also connect to m_____203) nerves that travel back down the s_____204) cord, and to the muscles in your leg that now c_____205) quickly to lift your foot away from the painful object. Sensory and motor nerves c_____206) almost all f_____207) in the body — from the beating of the heart to the movement of the g_____208) sweating and just about everything else.

감각 신경은 특정 감각을 포착하는 특화된 말단을 조직에 가지고 있다. 예를 들어, 만약 여러분이 핀과 같이 날카로운 물체를 밟는다면, 피부의 신경 말단이 통증 감각을 여러분의 다리 위로, 그리고 척수를 따라 위로 뇌까지 전달할 것이다. 통증 자체는 불쾌하지만, 사실은 발을 보호하는 메커니즘으로 작용하고 있다. (즉, 여러분은 그 통증에 익숙해져 통증을 피할 수 있는 능력이 감소한다.) 뇌 안에서, 신경은 언어를 통제하는 부분에 연결될 것이고, 그래서 여러분은 '아야' 또는 다소 덜 공손한 무언가를 외칠 것이다. 그것들은 또한 척수를 타고 다시 내려오는 운동 신경에 연결될 것이고, 그리고 이제 재빨리 수축하여 고통을 주는 물체로부터 발을 떼어 들어 올리게 하는 여러분의 다리 근육에 연결될 것이다. 감각 신경과 운동 신경은 심장의 박동에서부터 장 운동, 발한과 그 밖에 모든 것에 이르기까지 신체의 거의 모든 기능을 통제한다.

36

Maybe you've heard this joke: "How do you eat an elephant?" The answer is "one bite at a time." So, how do you "build" the Earth? That's simple, too: one a_____209) at a time. Atoms are the basic building blocks of c_____210) and since all rocks are m_____211) up of crystals, the more you know about atoms, the better. Crystals come in a variety of shapes that scientists call *h_____212)* . Common crystal habits i_____213) squares, triangles, and six-sided h_____214) Usually crystals form when l_____215) cool, such as when you create ice cubes. Many times, crystals form in ways that do not allow for perfect shapes. If c_____216) are too cold, too hot, or there isn't enough s_____217) material, they can form strange, t_____218) shapes. But when conditions are right, we see beautiful d_____219). Usually, this involves a slow, s_____220) environment where the i_____221) atoms have plenty of time to join and f_____222) perfectly into what's known as the *crystal lattice*. This is the basic s_____223) of atoms that is seen time after time.

아마 여러분은 이 농담을 들어본 적이 있을 것이다. "코끼리를 어떻게 먹는가?" 정답은 '한 번에 한 입'이다. 그렇다면, 여러분은 어떻게 지구를 '건설'하는가? 그것은 또한 간단하다. 한 번에 하나의 원자이다. 원자는 결정의 기본 구성 요소이고, 모든 암석은 결정으로 이루어져 있기 때문에, 여러분은 원자에 대해 더 많이 알수록 더 좋다. 결정은 과학자들이 '습성'이라고 부르는 다양한 모양으로 나온다. 일반적인 결정 습성은 사각형, 삼각형, 육면의 육각형을 포함한다. 보통 여러분이 얼음을 만들 때와 같이 액체가 차가워질 때 결정이 형성된다. 많은 경우, 결정은 완벽한 모양을 허용하지 않는 방식으로 형성된다. 조건이 너무 차갑거나, 너무 뜨겁거나, 혹은 원천 물질이 충분하지 않으면 이상하고 뒤틀린 모양을 형성할 수 있다. 하지만 조건이 맞을 때, 우리는 아름다운 배열을 본다. 보통, 이것은 개별적인 원자들이 결합하고 '결정격자'라고 알려진 것에 완벽하게 들어맞는 충분한 시간을 가지는 느리고 안정적인 환경을 수반한다. 이것은 반복하여 보이는 원자의 기본적인 구조이다.

37

When you p_____224) a guitar string it moves back and forth hundreds of times every s_____225) . Naturally, this movement is so fast _____226) you cannot see it — you just see the b_____227) outline of the moving string. Strings v_____228) in this way on their own make h_____229) any noise because strings are very thin and don't push m_____230) air about. But if you a_____231) a string to a big h_____232) box (like a guitar body), then the v_____233) is a_____234) and the note is heard loud and clear. The v_____235) of the string is p_____236) on to the wooden panels of the guitar body, _____237) vibrate back and forth at the same rate as the string. The v_____238) of the wood creates more powerful w_____239) in the air pressure, _____240) travel away from the guitar. When the waves r_____241) your e_____242) they f_____243) in and out the same number of t_____244) a second as the o_____245) string.

여러분이 기타 줄을 뜯을 때 그것은 매초 수백 번 이리저리 움직인다. 당연히, 이 움직임은 너무 빨라서 여러분이 그것을 볼 수 없다. 여러분은 그저 움직이는 줄의 흐릿한 윤곽만 본다. 이렇게 스스로 진동하는 줄들은 거의 소리가 나지 않는데, 이는 줄이 매우 가늘어 많은 공기를 밀어내지 못하기 때문이다. 하지만 여러분이 (기타 몸통 같은) 커다란 속이 빈 상자에 줄을 달면, 그 진동은 증폭되어 그 음이 크고 선명하게 들린다. 그 줄의 진동은 기타 몸통의 나무판으로 전달되어 줄과 같은 속도로 이리저리 떨린다. 그 나무의 진동은 공기의 압력에 더 강력한 파동을 만들어 내어 기타로부터 멀리 퍼진다. 그 파동이 여러분의 고막에 도달할 때 원래의 줄과 초당 동일한 횟수로 굽이쳐 들어가고 나온다.

38

B_____246) between work and home are b_____247) as p_____248) digital technology makes it i_____249) possible to work anywhere, anytime. Individuals d_____250) in how they like to manage their time to m_____251) work and outside responsibilities. Some people p_____252) to s_____253) or s_____254) roles so that boundary c_____255) are m_____256) For example, these people might keep s_____257) email accounts for work and family and try to c_____258) work at the workplace and take care of family matters only during breaks and non-work time. We've even n_____259) more of these " s_____260) " carrying two phones — one for work and one for personal use. F_____261) schedules work well for these individuals because they enable g_____262) d_____263) between time at work and time in other roles. Other individuals prefer i_____264) work and family roles all day long. This might e_____265) constantly t_____266) text messages with children from the office, or m_____267) emails at home and on vacation, rather than r_____268) to work to find hundreds of messages in their inbox.

휴대용 디지털 기술이 언제, 어디서나 작업하는 것을 점차 가능하게 함에 따라 직장과 가정의 경계가 흐릿해지고 있다. 사람들은 직장과 외부의 책임을 수행하기 위해 자신의 시간을 관리하기를 바라는 방식에 차이가 있다. 어떤 사람들은 경계 교차 지점이 최소화되도록 역할을 분리하거나 분할하는 것을 선호한다. 예를 들어, 이러한 사람들은 직장과 가정을 위한 별개의 이메일 계정을 유지하고 직장에서 일을 수행하고 휴식 시간과 일을 하지 않는 시간 동안에만 가정사를 처리하려고 할지도 모른다. 우리는 더 많은 이러한 '분할자들'이 하나는 업무용이고 하나는 개인용인 두 개의 전화기를 가지고 다니고 있음을 심지어 알게 되었다. 유연근로시간제는 이런 사람들에게 잘 적용되는데, 직장에서의 시간과 다른 역할에서의 시간 간에 더 큰 구별을 가능하게 하기 때문이다. 다른 사람들은 하루 종일 직장과 가정의 역할을 통합하는 것을 선호한다. 이것은 직장으로 돌아가서 받은 편지함에서 수백 개의 메시지를 발견하는 것 대신 사무실에서 아이들과 문자 메시지를 지속적으로 주고받거나 집에서 그리고 휴가 중에 이메일을 확인하는 것을 수반할지도 모른다.

39

A "_____269) good" is a product that is often c_____270) a_____271) another product. For example, popcorn is a c_____272) good to a movie, while a travel p_____273) is a c_____274) good for a long plane j_____275) When the p_____276) of one product increases, the s_____277) of its complementary good also increase. By producing goods that complement other products that are already (or about to be) popular, you can e_____278) a s_____279) stream of demand for your product. Some products enjoy perfect complementary s_____280) — they *have* to be consumed together, such as a lamp and a l_____281). However, do not a_____282) that a product is perfectly c_____283) , as customers may not be completely l_____284) in to the product. For example, although m_____285) may seem required to p_____286) gasoline to run their cars, they can switch to e_____287) cars.

'보완재'는 종종 다른 제품과 함께 소비되는 제품이다. 예를 들어, 팝콘은 영화에 대한 보완재인 한편, 여행 베개는 긴 비행기 여행에 대한 보완재이다. 한 제품의 인기가 높아지면 그것의 보완재 판매량도 늘어난다. 여러분은 이미 인기가 있는 (또는 곧 있을) 다른 제품을 보완하는 제품을 생산함으로써 여러분의 제품에 대한 꾸준한 수요 흐름을 보장할 수 있다. 일부 제품들은 완벽한 보완적 상태를 누리고 있고, 그것들은 램프와 전구와 같이 함께 소비'되어야' 한다. 그러나 고객들이 그 제품에 완전히 고정되어 있지 않을 수 있으므로, 어떤 제품이 완벽하게 보완적이라고 가정하지 마라. 예를 들어, 비록 운전자들이 자신의 차를 운전하기 위해 휘발유를 구매할 필요가 있는 것처럼 보일지라도, 그들은 전기 자동차로 바꿀 수 있다.

40

It's not news to anyone that we j_____288) others based on their clothes. In general, studies that i_____289) these j_____290) find that people p_____291) clothing that matches e_____292) — surgeons in s_____293) little boys in blue — with one n_____294) e_____295) . A series of studies published in an article in June 2014 in the *Journal of Consumer Research* explored observers' reactions to people who b_____296) established n_____297) only slightly. In one scenario, a man at a black-tie a_____298) was viewed as having higher s_____299) and c_____300) when wearing a red bow tie. The researchers also found that v_____301) u_____302) increased audience members' ratings of the status and c_____303) of a professor who wore red sneakers while giving a l_____304) The results suggest that people j_____305) these slight d_____306) from the n_____307) as p_____308) because they suggest that the individual is powerful enough to r_____309) the social c_____310) of such behaviors.

우리가 다른 사람들을 그들의 의복을 보고 판단하는 것은 누구에게도 새로운 일이 아니다. 일반적으로, 이러한 판단을 조사하는 연구는 사람들이 수술복을 입은 외과 의사, 파란 옷을 입은 남자아이와 같이 예상에 맞는 의복이되 하나의 눈에 띄는 예외가 있는 것을 선호한다는 것을 발견한다. Journal of Consumer Research의 2014년 9월 기사에 실린 일련의 연구는 확립된 규범을 아주 약간 어긴 사람들에 대한 관찰자들의 반응을 탐구했다. 한 시나리오에서는, 정장 차림의 행사에서 한 남자가 빨간 나비 넥타이를 맸을 때 더 높은 지위와 능력을 가진 것으로 보여졌다. 연구자들은 독특함을 중시하는 것이 강의를 하는 동안 빨간 운동화를 신은 교수의 지위와 역량에 대한 청중들의 평가를 높였다는 것을 또한 발견했다. 그 결과들은 사람들이 규범으로부터 이러한 약간의 일탈들을 긍정적으로 판단한다는 것을 시사하는데, 왜냐하면 그것들은 그 사람이 그러한 행동으로 인한 사회적 비용을 감수할 만큼 충분히 강하다는 것을 시사하기 때문이다.

41~42

Claims that local food production cut g_____311) gas e_____312) by r_____313) the burning of t_____314) fuel are usually not well founded. Transport is the source of only 11 percent of greenhouse gas emissions within the food s_____315) so reducing the d_____316) that food travels after it leaves the farm is far less important than reducing w_____317) energy use on the farm. Food coming from a distance can actually be better for the c_____318) depending on how it was grown. For example, field-grown tomatoes s_____319) from Mexico in the winter months will have a smaller c_____320) f_____321) than local winter tomatoes grown in a greenhouse. In the United Kingdom, l_____322) meat that travels 11,000 miles from New Zealand g_____323) only one-quarter the carbon emissions per pound c_____324) to British lamb because farmers in the United Kingdom r_____325) their animals on feed (which must be produced using fossil fuels) rather than on clover p_____326)

  When food does travel, what m_____327) most is not the d_____328) traveled but the travel mode (_____329) versus a_____330)) and most of all the l_____331) size. B_____332) loads of food can travel h_____333) around the world by ocean f_____334) with a smaller carbon footprint, per pound delivered, than foods traveling just a short distance but in much smaller l_____335) . For example, 18-wheelers c_____336) much larger loads than pickup trucks so they can move food 100 times as far while b_____ _337) only one-third as much gas per pound of food delivered.

로컬푸드 생산이 운송 연료의 연소를 줄임으로써 온실가스 배출을 줄였다는 주장들은 대개 근거가 충분하지 않다. 운송은 식품 부문 내에서 온실가스 배출의 11퍼센트만을 차지하는 원천이기에, 식품이 농장을 떠난 후 이동하는 거리를 줄이는 것은 농장에서 낭비되는 에너지 사용을 줄이는 것보다 훨씬 덜 중요하다. 먼 곳에서 오는 식품은 그것이 어떻게 재배되었느냐에 따라 실제로 기후에 더 좋을 수 있다. 예를 들어, 겨울에 멕시코로부터 수송된 밭에서 재배된 토마토는 온실에서 재배된 현지의 겨울 토마토보다 탄소 발자국이 더 적을 것이다. 영국에서는, 영국의 농부들이 클로버 목초지에서가 아닌 (화석 연료를 사용하여 생산되어야 하는) 사료로 자신의 동물들을 기르기 때문에 뉴질랜드에서 11,000마일을 이동하는 양고기는 영국의 양고기에 비해 파운드당 탄소 배출량의 4분의 일만 발생시킨다.

  식품이 이동할 때, 가장 중요한 것은 이동 거리가 아니라 이동 방식(지상 대 공중), 그리고 무엇보다 적재량의 규모이다. 대량의 적재된 식품은 단지 단거리를 이동하지만 훨씬 더 적은 적재량인 식품에 비해 배달된 파운드당 탄소 발자국이 더 적은 해상 화물 운송으로 세계의 절반을 이동할 수 있다. 예를 들어, 18륜 대형트럭은 픽업트럭보다 훨씬 더 많은 적재량을 운반하기에 배달된 식품 파운드당 3분의 일의 연료만 연소하면서 100배 멀리 식품을 이동시킬 수 있다.

(.hwp) (.pdf) → www.englishmygod.com

43~45

Long ago, an old man built a grand **t**_____338) at the center of his village. People traveled to **w**_____

_339) at the temple. So the old man made **a**_____340) for food and **a**_____341) inside the temple itself.

He needed someone who could look after the temple, so he put up a notice: Manager needed. Seeing the notice,

many people went to the old man. But he returned all the **a**_____342) after interviews, telling them, "I need a

q_____343) person for this work." The old man would sit on the roof of his house every morning, watching

people go through the temple doors. One day, he saw a young man come to the temple. When that young man left

the temple, the old man called him and asked, "Will you take care of this temple?" The young man was surprised by

the **o**_____344) and **r**_____345) "I have no experience caring for a temple. I'm not even educated." The

old man smiled and said, "I don't want any educated man. I want a qualified person." **C**_____346) , the young

man asked, "But why do you **c**_____347) me a qualified person?" The old man replied, "I buried a brick on the

path to the temple. I watched for many days as people **t**_____348) over that brick. No one thought to

r_____349) it. But you dug up that brick." The young man said, "I haven't done anything great. It's the duty of

every human being to think about others. I only did my duty." The old man smiled and said, "Only people who

know their **d**_____350) and perform it are qualified people."

옛날, 한 노인이 마을 중심부에 큰 사원을 지었다. 사람들이 사원에서 예배를 드리기 위해 멀리서 왔다. 그래서 노인은 사원 안에 음식과 숙소를 준비했다. 그는 사원을 관리할 수 있는 사람이 필요했고, 그래서 그는 '관리자 구함'이라는 공고를 붙였다. 공고를 보고 많은 사람들이 노인을 찾아갔다. 그러나 그는 면접 후에 그들에게 "나는 이 일에 자격을 갖춘 사람이 필요합니다."라고 말하며, 모든 지원자들을 돌려 보냈다. 노인은 사람들이 사원의 문을 통과하는 것을 지켜보며 매일 아침 그의 집 지붕에 앉아 있곤 했다. 어느 날 그는 한 젊은이가 사원으로 오는 것을 보았다. 젊은이가 사원을 나설 때, 노인이 그를 불러 "이 사원의 관리를 맡아 주겠소?"라고 질문했다. 젊은이는 그 제안에 놀라서 "저는 사원을 관리한 경험이 없고, 심지어 교육도 받지 못했습니다."라고 대답했다. 노인은 웃으며 "나는 교육을 받은 사람이 필요한 게 아니오. 나는 자격 있는 사람을 원하오."라고 말했다. 당황하여, 젊은이는 "그런데 당신은 왜 저를 자격이 있는 사람이라고 여기시나요?"라고 물었다. 노인은 대답했다. "나는 사원으로 통하는 길에 벽돌 한 개를 묻었소. 나는 여러 날 동안 사람들이 그 벽돌에 발이 걸려 넘어지는 것을 지켜보았소. 아무도 그것을 치울 생각을 하지 않았소. 하지만 당신은 그 벽돌을 파냈소." 젊은이는 "저는 대단한 일을 한 것이 아닙니다. 타인을 생각하는 것은 모든 인간의 의무입니다. 저는 제 의무를 다했을 뿐입니다."라고 말했다. 노인은 미소를 지으며 "자신의 의무를 알고 그 의무를 수행하는 사람만이 자격이 있는 사람이오."라고 말했다.

2023 고1 9월 모의고사 ❷ 회차 : 점 / 300점

18

Dear Professor Sanchez,

My name is Ellis Wight, and I'm the d_____1) of the Alexandria Science Museum. We are h_____2) a Chemistry Fair for l_____3) middle school students on Saturday, October 28. The g_____4) of the fair is to e_____5) them to be interested in science through guided experiments. We are looking for college students who can help with the experiments during the event. I am c_____6) you to ask you to r_____7) some students from the chemistry d_____8) at your college who you think are q_____9) for this job. With their help, I'm sure the p_____10) will have a great experience. I look forward to hearing from you soon.

Sincerely, Ellis Wight

19

Gregg and I had been rock climbing s_____11) sunrise and had had no problems. So we took a r_____12) "Look, the first bolt is right there. I can d_____13) climb out to it. Piece of cake," I p_____14) Gregg, minutes before I found myself p_____15) It wasn't a piece of cake. The rock was d_____16) barren of handholds. I c_____17) moved back and forth across the c_____18) face and ended up with nowhere to go...but down. The bolt that would save my life, if I could get to it, was about two feet above my r_____19) . My arms t_____20) from e_____21) I looked at Gregg. My body froze with fright from my neck down to my toes. Our rope was t_____22) between us. If I fell, he would fall with me.

20

We are always teaching our children something by our words and our actions. They learn from seeing. They learn from hearing and from o_____23) . Children share the values of their parents about the most important things in life. Our p_____24) and p_____25) and our examples of good behavior can teach our children to take the high road when other roads look t_____26) Remember that children do not learn the values that make up strong c_____27) simply by being t_____28) about them. They learn by seeing the people around them a_____29) on and u_____30) those values in their d_____31) lives. Therefore show your child good examples of life by your action. In our daily lives, we can show our children that we r_____32) others. We can show them our c_____33) and c_____34) when others are s_____35) and our own self-discipline, courage and h_____36) as we make difficult decisions.

21

Most people have no **d**_____37) heard this question: If a tree falls in the forest and there is no one there to hear it fall, does it make a sound? The correct answer is no. Sound is more than **p**_____38) waves, and indeed there can be no sound without a hearer. And similarly, **s**_____39) communication is a two-way process. Just as a **s**_____40) of any kind is useless unless it is **p**_____41) a published scientific **p**_____42) (signal) is useless unless it is both received *and* understood by its **i**_____43) audience. Thus we can **r**_____44) the **a**_____45) of science as follows: A scientific experiment is not **c**_____46) until the results have been published *and understood.* **P**_____47) is no more than pressure waves unless the published paper is understood. Too many scientific papers fall **s**_____48) in the woods.

22

We all **n**_____49) every day, whether we realize it or not. Yet few people ever learn _____50) to negotiate. Those who do usually **l**_____51) the **t**_____52) win-lose negotiating style rather than an approach that is likely to result in a win-win agreement. This old-school, **a**_____53) approach may be useful in a **o**_____54) negotiation where you will probably not deal with that person again. However, such **t**_____55) are becoming **i**_____56) rare, because most of us deal with the same people repeatedly — our spouses and children, our friends and **c**_____57) our customers and **c**_____58) In view of this, it's **e**_____59) to achieve successful results for ourselves and **m**_____60) a healthy relationship with our negotiating partners at the same time. In today's **i**_____61) world of business partnerships and **l**_____62) relationships, a win-win **o**_____63) is fast becoming the *only* acceptable result.

23

The **i**_____64) of workers from different cultural backgrounds with the host population might increase **p**_____65) due to positive **e**_____66) like knowledge **s**_____67) . This is only an advantage up to a certain degree. When the variety of backgrounds is too large, **f**_____68) may cause **e**_____69) transaction costs for communication, which may **l**_____70) productivity. **D**_____71) not only impacts the **l**_____72) market, but may also affect the quality of life in a location. A **t**_____73) native population may value a **m**_____74) city or region because of an **i**_____75) in the range of available goods and services. On the other hand, **d**_____76) could be perceived as an **u**_____77) **f**_____78) if natives perceive it as a **d**_____79) of what they consider to be their **n**_____80) identity. They might even **d**_____81) against other ethnic groups and they might fear that social **c**_____82) between different foreign **n**_____83) are **i**_____84) into their own neighbourhood.

24

We think we are s_____85) our buildings. But really, our buildings and development are also shaping us. One of the best examples of this is the oldest-known c_____86) the o_____87) carved rings of standing stones at Göbekli Tepe in Turkey. Before these a_____88) got the idea to e_____89) standing stones some 12,000 years ago, they were hunter-gatherers. It appears that the e_____90) of the m_____91) rings of megalithic stones took so long, and so many s_____92) generations, _____93) these i_____94) were forced to s_____95) down to complete the construction works. In the process, they became the first f_____96) society on Earth. This is an early example of a society c_____97) something that ends up r_____98) r_____99) the society itself. Things are not so different in our own time.

26

American jazz pianist Bill Evans was born in New Jersey in 1929. His early training was in classical music. At the age of six, he began r_____100) piano lessons, later adding flute and violin. He earned bachelor's d_____101) in piano and music education from Southeastern Louisiana College in 1950. He went on to serve in the army from 1951 to 1954 and played flute in the Fifth Army Band. After s_____102) in the m_____103) he studied c_____104) at the Mannes School of Music in New York. Composer George Russell a_____105) his playing and hired Evans to record and p_____106) his compositions. Evans became famous _____107) recordings m_____108) from the late-1950s through the 1960s. He won his first Grammy Award in 1964 for his album *Conversations with Myself.* Evans' e_____109) piano works and his unique h_____110) approach i_____111) a whole g_____112) of musicians.

29

There is a reason the title "Monday Morning Quarterback" exists. Just read the c_____113) on social media from fans d_____114) the weekend's games, and you quickly see how many people believe they could play, coach, and m_____115) sport teams more s_____116) than those on the field. This goes for the b_____117) as well. Students and professionals with years of training and s_____118) degrees in sport business may also find themselves b_____119) given advice on how to do their jobs from friends, family, or even total strangers without any e_____120) . E_____121) in sport management have d_____122) of knowledge and experience in their r_____123) fields. However, many of them f_____124) c_____125) from fans and community members telling them how to run their business. Very f_____126) people tell their doctor how to perform surgery or their a_____127) how to prepare their taxes, _____128) many people provide feedback on how sport o_____129) should be m_____130) .

30

While moving is difficult for everyone, it is **p**_____ 131) stressful for children. They lose their sense of security and may feel **d**_____ 132) when their routine is **d**_____ 133) and all that is familiar is taken away. Young children, ages 3-6, are particularly affected by a move. Their understanding at this stage is quite **l**_____ 134) and it is difficult for them to imagine **b**_____ 135) a new home and their new room. Young children may have worries such as "Will I still be me in the new place?" and "Will my toys and bed come with us?" It is important to **e**_____ 136) a balance between **v**_____ 137) children's past experiences and focusing on helping them adjust to the new place. Children need to have opportunities to share their **b**_____ 138) in a way that respects their past as an important part of who they are. This **c**_____ 139) to building a sense of community, which is **e**_____ 140) for all children, especially those in transition.

31

Many people are terrified to fly in airplanes. Often, this fear **s**_____ 141) from a lack of control. The pilot is in control, not the **p**_____ 142) and this lack of control **i**_____ 143) fear. Many **p**_____ 144) passengers are so afraid they choose to drive great distances to get to a **d**_____ 145) instead of flying. But their decision to drive is based solely on emotion, not **l**_____ 146) Logic says that statistically, the **o**_____ 147) of dying in a car crash are around 1 in 5,000, while the odds of dying in a plane crash are closer to 1 in 11 million. If you're going to take a risk, especially one that could possibly **i**_____ 148) your well-being, wouldn't you want the odds in your favor? However, most people choose the option that will cause them the least amount of **a**_____ 149) Pay attention to the thoughts you have about taking the risk and make sure you're **b**_____ 150) your decision on facts, not just feelings.

32

The famous primatologist Frans de Waal, of Emory University, says humans **d**_____ 151) similarities between us and other animals as a way of **m**_____ 152) our spot at the top of our **i**_____ 153) ladder. Scientists, de Waal points out, can be some of the worst **o**_____ 154) — employing technical language to distance the other animals from us . They call "kissing" in chimps "mouth-to-mouth contact"; they call "friends" between **p**_____ _155) "favorite affiliation partners"; they **i**_____ 156) evidence showing that **c**_____ 157) and chimps can make tools as being somehow qualitatively different from the kind of toolmaking said to define humanity. If an animal can beat us at a **c**_____ 158) task — like how certain bird species can remember the **p**_____ 159) locations of thousands of seeds — they write it off as instinct, not intelligence. This and so many more tricks of language are what de Waal has termed "linguistic castration." The way we use our tongues to **d**_____ 160) animals, the way we invent words to maintain our spot at the top.

33

A key to **e**_____161) and **a**_____162) is providing students with **r**_____163) texts they will be interested in. My **s**_____164) work and my teaching have been deeply **i**_____165) by the work of Rosalie Fink. She interviewed twelve adults who were highly successful in their work, including a physicist, a biochemist, and a company CEO. All of them had **d**_____166) and had had **s**_____167) problems with reading throughout their school years. While she expected to find that they had avoided reading and discovered ways to **b**_____168) it or **c**_____169) with other strategies for learning, she found the opposite. "To my surprise, I found that these dyslexics were **e**_____170) readers...they rarely avoided reading. On the contrary, they **s**_____171) out books." The pattern Fink discovered was that all of her subjects had been **p**_____172) in some personal interest. The areas of interest included religion, math, business, science, history, and biography. What mattered was that they read **v**_____173) to find out more.

34

For many people, *ability* **r**_____174) to intellectual **c**_____175) so they want everything they do to **r**_____176) how smart they are — writing a brilliant legal **b**_____177) , getting the highest grade on a test, writing **e**_____178) computer code, saying something **e**_____179) wise or **w**_____180) in a conversation. You could also **d**_____181) ability in terms of a particular skill or talent, such as how well one plays the piano, learns a language, or serves a tennis ball. Some people focus on their ability to be **a**_____182) **e**_____183) , up on the **l**_____184) trends, or to have the newest **g**_____185) However ability may be **d**_____186) a problem occurs when it is the sole **d**_____187) of one's self-worth. The performance becomes the only **m**_____188) of the person; nothing else is taken into **a**_____189) . An **o**_____190) performance means an outstanding person; an average performance means an average person. **P**_____191)

35

S_____192) **n**_____193) have **s**_____194) endings in the **t**_____195) that pick up a particular **s**_____196) If, for example, you step on a sharp object such as a pin, nerve endings in the skin will **t**_____197) the pain **s**_____198) up your leg, up and along the **s**_____199) cord to the brain. While the pain itself is **u**_____200) it is in fact acting as a protective **m**_____201) for the foot. Within the brain, nerves will connect to the area that controls speech, so that you may well shout 'ouch' or something rather less **p**_____202) They will also connect to **m**_____203) nerves that travel back down the **s**_____204) cord, and to the muscles in your leg that now **c**_____205) quickly to lift your foot away from the painful object. Sensory and motor nerves **c**_____206) almost all **f**_____207) in the body — from the beating of the heart to the movement of the **g**_____208) sweating and just about everything else.

36

Maybe you've heard this joke: "How do you eat an elephant?" The answer is "one bite at a time." So, how do you "build" the Earth? That's simple, too: one **a**_____209) at a time. Atoms are the basic building blocks of **c**_____210) and since all rocks are **m**_____211) up of crystals, the more you know about atoms, the better. Crystals come in a variety of shapes that scientists call **h**_____212) . Common crystal habits **i**_____213) squares, triangles, and six-sided **h**_____214) Usually crystals form when **l**_____215) cool, such as when you create ice cubes. Many times, crystals form in ways that do not allow for perfect shapes. If **c**_____216) are too cold, too hot, or there isn't enough **s**_____217) material, they can form strange, **t**_____218) shapes. But when conditions are right, we see beautiful **d**_____219). Usually, this involves a slow, **s**_____220) environment where the **i**_____221) atoms have plenty of time to join and **f**_____222) perfectly into what's known as the *crystal lattice*. This is the basic **s**_____223) of atoms that is seen time after time.

37

When you **p**_____224) a guitar string it moves back and forth hundreds of times every **s**_____225) . Naturally, this movement is so fast _____226) you cannot see it — you just see the **b**_____227) outline of the moving string. Strings **v**_____228) in this way on their own make **h**_____229) any noise because strings are very thin and don't push **m**_____230) air about. But if you **a**_____231) a string to a big **h**_____232) box (like a guitar body), then the **v**_____233) is **a**_____234) and the note is heard loud and clear. The **v**_____235) of the string is **p**_____236) on to the wooden panels of the guitar body, _____237) vibrate back and forth at the same rate as the string. The **v**_____238) of the wood creates more powerful **w**_____239) in the air pressure, _____240) travel away from the guitar. When the waves **r**_____241) your **e**_____242) they **f**_____243) in and out the same number of **t**_____244) a second as the **o**_____245) string.

38

B_____246) between work and home are **b**_____247) as **p**_____248) digital technology makes it **i**_____249) possible to work anywhere, anytime. Individuals **d**_____250) in how they like to manage their time to **m**_____251) work and outside responsibilities. Some people **p**_____252) to **s**_____253) or **s**_____254) roles so that boundary **c**_____255) are **m**_____256) For example, these people might keep **s**_____257) email accounts for work and family and try to **c**_____258) work at the workplace and take care of family matters only during breaks and non-work time. We've even **n**_____259) more of these " **s**_____260) " carrying two phones — one for work and one for personal use. **F**_____261) schedules work well for these individuals because they enable **g**_____262) **d**_____263) between time at work and time in other roles. Other individuals prefer **i**_____264) work and family roles all day long. This might **e**_____265) constantly **t**_____266) text messages with children from the office, or **m**_____267) emails at home and on vacation, rather than **r**_____268) to work to find hundreds of messages in their inbox.

39

A "_____ 269) good" is a product that is often c_____ 270) a_____ 271) another product. For example, popcorn is a c_____ 272) good to a movie, while a travel p_____ 273) is a c_____ 274) good for a long plane j_____ 275) When the p_____ 276) of one product increases, the s_____ 277) of its complementary good also increase. By producing goods that complement other products that are already (or about to be) popular, you can e_____ 278) a s_____ 279) stream of demand for your product. Some products enjoy perfect complementary s_____ 280) — they *have* to be consumed together, such as a lamp and a l_____ 281). However, do not a_____ 282) that a product is perfectly c_____ 283) , as customers may not be completely l_____ 284) in to the product. For example, although m_____ 285) may seem required to p_____ 286) gasoline to run their cars, they can switch to e_____ 287) cars.

40

It's not news to anyone that we j_____ 288) others based on their clothes. In general, studies that i_____ 289) these j_____ 290) find that people p_____ 291) clothing that matches e_____ 292) — surgeons in s_____ 293) little boys in blue — with one n_____ 294) e_____ 295) . A series of studies published in an article in June 2014 in the *Journal of Consumer Research* explored observers' reactions to people who b_____ 296) established n_____ 297) only slightly. In one scenario, a man at a black-tie a_____ 298) was viewed as having higher s_____ 299) and c_____ 300) when wearing a red bow tie. The researchers also found that v_____ 301) u_____ 302) increased audience members' ratings of the status and c_____ 303) of a professor who wore red sneakers while giving a l_____ 304) The results suggest that people j_____ 305) these slight d_____ 306) from the n_____ 307) as p_____ 308) because they suggest that the individual is powerful enough to r_____ 309) the social c_____ 310) of such behaviors.

41~42

Claims that local food production cut g_____ 311) gas e_____ 312) by r_____ 313) the burning of t_____ 314) fuel are usually not well founded. Transport is the source of only 11 percent of greenhouse gas emissions within the food s_____ 315) so reducing the d_____ 316) that food travels after it leaves the farm is far less important than reducing w_____ 317) energy use on the farm. Food coming from a distance can actually be better for the c_____ 318) depending on how it was grown. For example, field-grown tomatoes s_____ 319) from Mexico in the winter months will have a smaller c_____ 320) f_____ 321) than local winter tomatoes grown in a greenhouse. In the United Kingdom, l_____ 322) meat that travels 11,000 miles from New Zealand g_____ 323) only one-quarter the carbon emissions per pound c_____ 324) to British lamb because farmers in the United Kingdom r_____ 325) their animals on feed (which must be produced using fossil fuels) rather than on clover p_____ 326)

When food does travel, what m_____ 327) most is not the d_____ 328) traveled but the travel mode

(_____329) versus a_____330)) and most of all the l_____331) size. B_____332) loads of food can travel h_____333) around the world by ocean f_____334) with a smaller carbon footprint, per pound delivered, than foods traveling just a short distance but in much smaller l_____335) . For example, 18-wheelers c_____336) much larger loads than pickup trucks so they can move food 100 times as far while b_____337) only one-third as much gas per pound of food delivered.

43~45

Long ago, an old man built a grand t_____338) at the center of his village. People traveled to w_____339) at the temple. So the old man made a_____340) for food and a_____341) inside the temple itself. He needed someone who could look after the temple, so he put up a notice: Manager needed. Seeing the notice, many people went to the old man. But he returned all the a_____342) after interviews, telling them, "I need a q_____343) person for this work." The old man would sit on the roof of his house every morning, watching people go through the temple doors. One day, he saw a young man come to the temple. When that young man left the temple, the old man called him and asked, "Will you take care of this temple?" The young man was surprised by the o_____344) and r_____345) "I have no experience caring for a temple. I'm not even educated." The old man smiled and said, "I don't want any educated man. I want a qualified person." C_____346) , the young man asked, "But why do you c_____347) me a qualified person?" The old man replied, "I buried a brick on the path to the temple. I watched for many days as people t_____348) over that brick. No one thought to r_____349) it. But you dug up that brick." The young man said, "I haven't done anything great. It's the duty of every human being to think about others. I only did my duty." The old man smiled and said, "Only people who know their d_____350) and perform it are qualified people."

2023 고1 9월 모의고사

❶ voca　　❷ text　　❸ [/]　　❹ ____　　⑤ quiz 1　　❻ quiz 2　　❼ quiz 3　　❽ quiz 4　　❾ quiz 5

☑ **다음 글을 읽고 물음에 답하시오.** (18)

> We are looking for college students who can help with the experiments during the event.

Dear Professor Sanchez, My name is Ellis Wight, and I'm the director of the Alexandria Science Museum.(①) We are holding a Chemistry Fair for local middle school students on Saturday, October 28.(②) The goal of the fair is to encourage them to be interested in science through guided experiments.(③) I am contacting you to ask you to recommend some students from the chemistry department at your college who you think are qualified for this job.(④) With their help, I'm sure the participants will have a great experience.(⑤) I look forward to hearing from you soon. Sincerely, Ellis Wight.

1. 1)글의 흐름으로 보아, 주어진 문장이 들어가기에 <u>가장 적절한</u> 곳은?

☑ **다음 글을 읽고 물음에 답하시오.** (19)

> I clumsily moved back and forth across the cliff face and ended up with nowhere to go...but down.

Gregg and I had been rock climbing since sunrise and had had no problems. So we took a risk.(①) "Look, the first bolt is right there. I can definitely climb out to it. Piece of cake", I persuaded Gregg, minutes before I found myself pinned. It wasn't a piece of cake.(②) The rock was deceptively barren of handholds.(③) The bolt that would save my life, if I could get to it, was about two feet above my reach. My arms trembled from exhaustion.(④) I looked at Gregg. My body froze with fright from my neck down to my toes.(⑤) Our rope was tied between us. If I fell, he would fall with me.

2. 2)글의 흐름으로 보아, 주어진 문장이 들어가기에 <u>가장 적절한</u> 곳은?

☑ **다음 글을 읽고 물음에 답하시오.** (20)

> Remember that children do not learn the values that make up strong character simply by being told about them. They learn by seeing the people around them act on and uphold those values in their daily lives.

We are always teaching our children something by our words and our actions.(①) They learn from seeing. They learn from hearing and from overhearing.(②) Children share the values of their parents about the most important things in life.(③) Our priorities and principles and our examples of good behavior can teach our children to take the high road when other roads look tempting.(④) Therefore show your child good examples of life by your action. In our daily lives, we can show our children that we respect others.(⑤) We can show them our compassion and concern when others are suffering, and our own self-discipline, courage and honesty as we make difficult decisions.

3. 3)글의 흐름으로 보아, 주어진 문장이 들어가기에 <u>가장 적절한</u> 곳은?

(.hwp) (.pdf) → www.englishmygod.com

☑ **다음 글을 읽고 물음에 답하시오.** (21)

> And similarly, scientific communication is a two-way process.

Most people have no doubt heard this question: If a tree falls in the forest and there is no one there to hear it fall, does it make a sound?(①) The correct answer is no.(②) Sound is more than pressure waves, and indeed there can be no sound without a hearer.(③) Just as a signal of any kind is useless unless it is perceived, a published scientific paper (signal) is useless unless it is both received and understood by its intended audience.(④) Thus we can restate the axiom of science as follows: A scientific experiment is not complete until the results have been published and understood.(⑤) Publication is no more than pressure waves unless the published paper is understood. Too many scientific papers fall silently in the woods.

4. 4)글의 흐름으로 보아, 주어진 문장이 들어가기에 **가장 적절한** 곳은?

☑ **다음 글을 읽고 물음에 답하시오.** (22)

> This old-school, adversarial approach may be useful in a one-off negotiation where you will probably not deal with that person again.

We all negotiate every day, whether we realise it or not.(①) Yet few people ever learn how to negotiate.(②) Those who do usually learn the traditional, win-lose negotiating style rather than an approach that is likely to result in a win-win agreement.(③) However, such transactions are becoming increasingly rare, because most of us deal with the same people repeatedly — our spouses and children, our friends and colleagues, our customers and clients.(④) In view of this, it's essential to achieve successful results for ourselves and maintain a healthy relationship with our negotiating partners at the same time.(⑤) In today's interdependent world of business partnerships and long-term relationships, a win-win outcome is fast becoming the only acceptable result.

5. 5)글의 흐름으로 보아, 주어진 문장이 들어가기에 **가장 적절한** 곳은?

☑ **다음 글을 읽고 물음에 답하시오.** (23)

> Diversity not only impacts the labour market, but may also affect the quality of life in a location.

The interaction of workers from different cultural backgrounds with the host population might increase productivity due to positive externalities like knowledge spillovers.(①) This is only an advantage up to a certain degree.(②) When the variety of backgrounds is too large, fractionalization may cause excessive transaction costs for communication, which may lower productivity.(③) A tolerant native population may value a multicultural city or region because of an increase in the range of available goods and services.(④) On the other hand, diversity could be perceived as an unattractive feature if natives perceive it as a distortion of what they consider to be their national identity.(⑤) They might even discriminate against other ethnic groups and they might fear that social conflicts between different foreign nationalities are imported into their own neighbourhood.

6. 6)글의 흐름으로 보아, 주어진 문장이 들어가기에 **가장 적절한** 곳은?

☑ **다음 글을 읽고 물음에 답하시오.** (24)

It appears that the erection of the multiple rings of megalithic stones took so long, and so many successive generations, that these innovators were forced to settle down to complete the construction works.

We think we are shaping our buildings. But really, our buildings and development are also shaping us.(①) One of the best examples of this is the oldest-known construction: the ornately carved rings of standing stones at Göbekli Tepe in Turkey.(②)　Before these ancestors got the idea to erect standing stones some 12,000 years ago, they were hunter-gatherers.(③)　In the process, they became the first farming society on Earth.(④)　This is an early example of a society constructing something that ends up radically remaking the society itself.(⑤)　Things are not so different in our own time.

7. 7)글의 흐름으로 보아, 주어진 문장이 들어가기에 <u>가장 적절한</u> 곳은?

☑ **다음 글을 읽고 물음에 답하시오.** (26)

Composer George Russell admired his playing and hired Evans to record and perform his compositions.

American jazz pianist Bill Evans was born in New Jersey in 1929. His early training was in classical music. At the age of six, he began receiving piano lessons, later adding flute and violin.(①)　He earned bachelor's degrees in piano and music education from Southeastern Louisiana College in 1950.(②)　He went on to serve in the army from 1951 to 1954 and played flute in the Fifth Army Band.(③)　After serving in the military, he studied composition at the Mannes School of Music in New York.(④)　Evans became famous for

recordings made from the late-1950s through the 1960s.(⑤)　He won his first Grammy Award in 1964 for his album Conversations with Myself. Evans' expressive piano works and his unique harmonic approach inspired a whole generation of musicians.

8. 8)글의 흐름으로 보아, 주어진 문장이 들어가기에 <u>가장 적절한</u> 곳은?

☑ **다음 글을 읽고 물음에 답하시오.** (29)

However, many of them face criticism from fans and community members telling them how to run their business.

There is a reason the title "Monday Morning Quarterback" exists.(①)　Just read the comments on social media from fans discussing the weekend's games, and you quickly see how many people believe they could play, coach, and manage sport teams more successfully than those on the field.(②)　This goes for the boardroom as well.(③)　Students and professionals with years of training and specialized degrees in sport business may also find themselves being given advice on how to do their jobs from friends, family, or even total strangers without any expertise.(④)　Executives in sport management have decades of knowledge and experience in their respective fields.(⑤)　Very few people tell their doctor how to perform surgery or their accountant how to prepare their taxes, but many people provide feedback on how sport organizations should be managed.

9. 9)글의 흐름으로 보아, 주어진 문장이 들어가기에 <u>가장 적절한</u> 곳은?

(.hwp) (.pdf) ➔ www.englishmygod.com

☑ **다음 글을 읽고 물음에 답하시오.** (30)

> Their understanding at this stage is quite literal, and it is difficult for them to imagine beforehand a new home and their new room.

While moving is difficult for everyone, it is particularly stressful for children. They lose their sense of security and may feel disoriented when their routine is disrupted and all that is familiar is taken away.(①) Young children, ages 3-6, are particularly affected by a move.(②) Young children may have worries such as "Will I still be me in the new place"? and "Will my toys and bed come with us"?(③) It is important to establish a balance between validating children's past experiences and focusing on helping them adjust to the new place.(④) Children need to have opportunities to share their backgrounds in a way that respects their past as an important part of who they are.(⑤) This contributes to building a sense of community, which is essential for all children, especially those in transition.

10. 10)글의 흐름으로 보아, 주어진 문장이 들어가기에 <u>가장 적절한</u> 곳은?

☑ **다음 글을 읽고 물음에 답하시오.** (31)

> But their decision to drive is based solely on emotion, not logic.

Many people are terrified to fly in airplanes. Often, this fear stems from a lack of control.(①) The pilot is in control, not the passengers, and this lack of control instills fear.(②) Many potential passengers are so afraid they choose to drive great distances to get to a destination instead of flying.(③) Logic says that statistically, the odds of dying in a car crash are around 1 in 5,000, while the odds of dying in a plane crash are closer to 1 in 11 million.(④) If you're going to take a risk, especially one that could possibly involve your well-being, wouldn't you want the odds in your favor? However, most people choose the option that will cause them the least amount of anxiety.(⑤) Pay attention to the thoughts you have about taking the risk and make sure you're basing your decision on facts, not just feelings.

11. 11)글의 흐름으로 보아, 주어진 문장이 들어가기에 <u>가장 적절한</u> 곳은?

☑ **다음 글을 읽고 물음에 답하시오.** (32)

> This and so many more tricks of language are what de Waal has termed "linguistic castration".

The famous primatologist Frans de Waal, of Emory University, says humans downplay similarities between us and other animals as a way of maintaining our spot at the top of our imaginary ladder.(①) Scientists, de Waal points out, can be some of the worst offenders — employing technical language to distance the other animals from us.(②) They call "kissing" in chimps "mouth-to-mouth contact"; they call "friends" between primates "favorite affiliation partners";(③) they interpret evidence showing that crows and chimps can make tools as being somehow qualitatively different from the kind of toolmaking said to define humanity.(④) If an animal can beat us at a cognitive task — like how certain bird species can remember the precise locations of thousands of seeds — they write it off as instinct, not intelligence.(⑤) The way we use our tongues to disempower animals, the way we invent words to maintain our spot at the top.

12. 12)글의 흐름으로 보아, 주어진 문장이 들어가기에 <u>가장 적절한</u> 곳은?

☑ **다음 글을 읽고 물음에 답하시오.** (33)

> While she expected to find that they had avoided reading and discovered ways to bypass it or compensate with other strategies for learning, she found the opposite.

A key to engagement and achievement is providing students with relevant texts they will be interested in.(①) My scholarly work and my teaching have been deeply influenced by the work of Rosalie Fink. She interviewed twelve adults who were highly successful in their work, including a physicist, a biochemist, and a company CEO.(②) All of them had dyslexia and had had significant problems with reading throughout their school years.(③) "To my surprise, I found that these dyslexics were enthusiastic readers...they rarely avoided reading.(④) On the contrary, they sought out books".(⑤) The pattern Fink discovered was that all of her subjects had been passionate in some personal interest. The areas of interest included religion, math, business, science, history, and biography. What mattered was that they read voraciously to find out more.

13. 13)글의 흐름으로 보아, 주어진 문장이 들어가기에 가장 적절한 곳은?

☑ **다음 글을 읽고 물음에 답하시오.** (33)

> While she expected to find that they had avoided reading and discovered ways to bypass it or compensate with other strategies for learning, she found the opposite.

A key to engagement and achievement is providing students with relevant texts they will be interested in.(①) My scholarly work and my teaching have been deeply influenced by the work of Rosalie Fink. She interviewed twelve adults who were highly successful in their work, including a physicist, a biochemist, and a company CEO.(②) All of them had dyslexia and had had significant problems with reading throughout their school years.(③) "To my surprise, I found that these dyslexics were enthusiastic readers...they rarely avoided reading. On the contrary, they sought out books". The pattern Fink discovered was that all of her subjects had been passionate in some personal interest.(④) The areas of interest included religion, math, business, science, history, and biography.(⑤) What mattered was that they read voraciously to find out more.

14. 14)글의 흐름으로 보아, 주어진 문장이 들어가기에 가장 적절한 곳은?

☑ **다음 글을 읽고 물음에 답하시오.** (34)

> However ability may be defined, a problem occurs when it is the sole determinant of one's self-worth.

For many people, ability refers to intellectual competence, so they want everything they do to reflect how smart they are.(①) Writing a brilliant legal brief, getting the highest grade on a test, writing elegant computer code, saying something exceptionally wise or witty in a conversation are some kinds.(②) You could also define ability in terms of a particular skill or talent, such as how well one plays the piano, learns a language, or serves a tennis ball.(③) Some people focus on their ability to be attractive, entertaining, up on the latest trends, or to have the newest gadgets.(④) The performance becomes the only measure of the person; nothing else is taken into account.(⑤) An outstanding performance means an outstanding person; an average performance means an average person. Period.

15. 15)글의 흐름으로 보아, 주어진 문장이 들어가기에 가장 적절한 곳은?

☑ **다음 글을 읽고 물음에 답하시오.** (35)

> While the pain itself is unpleasant, it is in fact acting as a protective mechanism for the foot.

Sensory nerves have specialized endings in the tissues that pick up a particular sensation.(①) If, for example, you step on a sharp object such as a pin, nerve endings in the skin will transmit the pain sensation up your leg, up and along the spinal cord to the brain.(②) Within the brain, nerves will connect to the area that controls speech, so that you may well shout 'ouch' or something rather less polite.(③) They will also connect to motor nerves that travel back down the spinal cord, and to the muscles in your leg that now contract quickly to lift your foot away from the painful object.(④) Sensory and motor nerves control almost all functions in the body.(⑤) They control from the beating of the heart to the movement of the gut, sweating and just about everything else.

16. 16)글의 흐름으로 보아, 주어진 문장이 들어가기에 <u>가장 적절한</u> 곳은?

☑ **다음 글을 읽고 물음에 답하시오.** (36)

> Usually crystals form when liquids cool, such as when you create ice cubes. Many times, crystals form in ways that do not allow for perfect shapes.

Maybe you've heard this joke: "How do you eat an elephant"? The answer is "one bite at a time". So, how do you "build" the Earth? That's simple, too: one atom at a time.(①) Atoms are the basic building blocks of crystals, and since all rocks are made up of crystals, the more you know about atoms, the better.(②) Crystals come in a variety of shapes that scientists call habits. Common crystal habits include squares, triangles, and six-sided hexagons.(③) If conditions are too cold, too hot, or there isn't enough source material, they can form strange, twisted shapes.(④) But when conditions are right, we see beautiful displays.(⑤) Usually, this involves a slow, steady environment where the individual atoms have plenty of time to join and fit perfectly into what's known as the crystal lattice. This is the basic structure of atoms that is seen time after time.

17. 17)글의 흐름으로 보아, 주어진 문장이 들어가기에 <u>가장 적절한</u> 곳은?

☑ **다음 글을 읽고 물음에 답하시오.** (37)

> The vibration of the string is passed on to the wooden panels of the guitar body, which vibrate back and forth at the same rate as the string.

When you pluck a guitar string it moves back and forth hundreds of times every second.(①) Naturally, this movement is so fast that you cannot see it — you just see the blurred outline of the moving string.(②) Strings vibrating in this way on their own make hardly any noise because strings are very thin and don't push much air about.(③) But if you attach a string to a big hollow box (like a guitar body), then the vibration is amplified and the note is heard loud and clear.(④) The vibration of the wood creates more powerful waves in the air pressure, which travel away from the guitar.(⑤) When the waves reach your eardrums they flex in and out the same number of times a second as the original string.

18. 18)글의 흐름으로 보아, 주어진 문장이 들어가기에 <u>가장 적절한</u> 곳은?

☑ **다음 글을 읽고 물음에 답하시오.** (38)

> For example, these people might keep separate email accounts for work and family and try to conduct work at the workplace and take care of family matters only during breaks and non-work time.

Boundaries between work and home are blurring as portable digital technology makes it increasingly possible to work anywhere, anytime. Individuals differ in how they like to manage their time to meet work and outside responsibilities.(①) Some people prefer to separate or segment roles so that boundary crossings are minimized.(②) We've even noticed more of these "segmenters" carrying two phones — one for work and one for personal use.(③) Flexible schedules work well for these individuals because they enable greater distinction between time at work and time in other roles.(④) Other individuals prefer integrating work and family roles all day long.(⑤) This might entail constantly trading text messages with children from the office, or monitoring emails at home and on vacation, rather than returning to work to find hundreds of messages in their inbox.

19. 19)글의 흐름으로 보아, 주어진 문장이 들어가기에 가장 적절한 곳은?

☑ **다음 글을 읽고 물음에 답하시오.** (39)

> Some products enjoy perfect complementary status — they have to be consumed together, such as a lamp and a lightbulb.

A "complementary good" is a product that is often consumed alongside another product.(①) For example, popcorn is a complementary good to a movie, while a travel pillow is a complementary good for a long plane journey.(②) When the popularity of one product increases, the sales of its complementary good also increase.(③) By producing goods that complement other products that are already (or about to be) popular, you can ensure a steady stream of demand for your product.(④) However, do not assume that a product is perfectly complementary, as customers may not be completely locked in to the product.(⑤) For example, although motorists may seem required to purchase gasoline to run their cars, they can switch to electric cars.

20. 20)글의 흐름으로 보아, 주어진 문장이 들어가기에 가장 적절한 곳은?

☑ **다음 글을 읽고 물음에 답하시오.** (40)

> In one scenario, a man at a black-tie affair was viewed as having higher status and competence when wearing a red bow tie.

It's not news to anyone that we judge others based on their clothes.(①) In general, studies that investigate these judgments find that people prefer clothing that matches expectations — surgeons in scrubs, little boys in blue — with one notable exception.(②) A series of studies published in an article in June 2014 in the Journal of Consumer Research explored observers' reactions to people who broke established norms only slightly.(③) The researchers also found that valuing uniqueness increased audience members' ratings of the status and competence of a professor who wore red sneakers while giving a lecture.(④) The results suggest that people judge these slight deviations from the norm as positive because they suggest that the individual is powerful enough to risk the social costs of such behaviors.(⑤)

21. 21)글의 흐름으로 보아, 주어진 문장이 들어가기에 가장 적절한 곳은?

☑ **다음 글을 읽고 물음에 답하시오.** (41, 42)

> In the United Kingdom, lamb meat that travels 11,000 miles from New Zealand generates only one-quarter the carbon emissions per pound compared to British lamb because farmers in the United Kingdom raise their animals on feed (which must be produced using fossil fuels) rather than on clover pastureland.

Claims that local food production cut greenhouse gas emissions by reducing the burning of transportation fuel are usually not well founded.(①)　Transport is the source of only 11 percent of greenhouse gas emissions within the food sector, so reducing the distance that food travels after it leaves the farm is far less important than reducing wasteful energy use on the farm.(②) Food coming from a distance can actually be better for the climate, depending on how it was grown. For example, field-grown tomatoes shipped from Mexico in the winter months will have a smaller carbon footprint than local winter tomatoes grown in a greenhouse.(③) When food does travel, what matters most is not the distance traveled but the travel mode (surface versus air), and most of all the load size.(④)　Bulk loads of food can travel halfway around the world by ocean freight with a smaller carbon footprint, per pound delivered, than foods traveling just a short distance but in much smaller loads.(⑤)　For example, 18-wheelers carry much larger loads than pickup trucks so they can move food 100 times as far while burning only one-third as much gas per pound of food delivered.

22. 22)글의 흐름으로 보아, 주어진 문장이 들어가기에 <u>가장 적절한</u> 곳은?

☑ **다음 글을 읽고 물음에 답하시오.** (43, 44, 45)

> But he returned all the applicants after interviews, telling them, "I need a qualified person for this work". The old man would sit on the roof of his house every morning, watching people go through the temple doors. One day, he saw a young man come to the temple.

Long ago, an old man built a grand temple at the center of his village. People traveled to worship at the temple.(①)　So the old man made arrangements for food and accommodation inside the temple itself. He needed someone who could look after the temple, so he put up a notice: Manager needed. Seeing the notice, many people went to the old man.(②)　When that young man left the temple, the old man called him and asked, "Will you take care of this temple"? The young man was surprised by the offer and replied, "I have no experience caring for a temple. I'm not even educated".(③)　The old man smiled and said, "I don't want any educated man. I want a qualified person". Confused, the young man asked, "But why do you consider me a qualified person"? The old man replied, "I buried a brick on the path to the temple.(④)　I watched for many days as people tripped over that brick. No one thought to remove it. But you dug up that brick". The young man said, "I haven't done anything great.(⑤)　It's the duty of every human being to think about others. I only did my duty". The old man smiled and said, "Only people who know their duty and perform it are qualified people".

23. 23)글의 흐름으로 보아, 주어진 문장이 들어가기에 <u>가장 적절한</u> 곳은?

☑ **다음 글을 읽고 물음에 답하시오.** ^(43, 44, 45)

When that young man left the temple, the old man called him and asked, "Will you take care of this temple"? The young man was surprised by the offer and replied, "I have no experience caring for a temple. I'm not even educated". The old man smiled and said, "I don't want any educated man.

Long ago, an old man built a grand temple at the center of his village. People traveled to worship at the temple. So the old man made arrangements for food and accommodation inside the temple itself.(①) He needed someone who could look after the temple, so he put up a notice: Manager needed. Seeing the notice, many people went to the old man. But he returned all the applicants after interviews, telling them, "I need a qualified person for this work".(②) The old man would sit on the roof of his house every morning, watching people go through the temple doors. One day, he saw a young man come to the temple.(③) I want a qualified person". Confused, the young man asked, "But why do you consider me a qualified person"? The old man replied, "I buried a brick on the path to the temple. I watched for many days as people tripped over that brick. No one thought to remove it.(④) But you dug up that brick". The young man said, "I haven't done anything great. It's the duty of every human being to think about others.(⑤) I only did my duty". The old man smiled and said, "Only people who know their duty and perform it are qualified people".

24. ²⁴⁾글의 흐름으로 보아, 주어진 문장이 들어가기에 <u>가장</u> <u>적절한</u> 곳은?

(.hwp) (.pdf) → www.englishmygod.com

1. 25) ¹⁸

Dear Professor Sanchez, My name is Ellis Wight, and I'm the director of the Alexandria Science Museum.

(A) Sincerely, Ellis Wight.

(B) With their help, I'm sure the participants will have a great experience.

(C) I look forward to hearing from you soon.

(D) We are holding a Chemistry Fair for local middle school students on Saturday, October 28. The goal of the fair is to encourage them to be interested in science through guided experiments.

(E) We are looking for college students who can help with the experiments during the event. I am contacting you to ask you to recommend some students from the chemistry department at your college who you think are qualified for this job.

2. 26) ¹⁹

Gregg and I had been rock climbing since sunrise and had had no problems.

(A) Piece of cake," I persuaded Gregg, minutes before I found myself pinned. It wasn't a piece of cake. The rock was deceptively barren of handholds.

(B) I looked at Gregg. My body froze with fright from my neck down to my toes.

(C) Our rope was tied between us. If I fell, he would fall with me.

(D) So we took a risk. "Look, the first bolt is right there. I can definitely climb out to it.

(E) I clumsily moved back and forth across the cliff face and ended up with nowhere to go...but down. The bolt that would save my life, if I could get to it, was about two feet above my reach. My arms trembled from exhaustion.

3. 27) ²⁰

We are always teaching our children something by our words and our actions.

(A) They learn by seeing the people around them act on and uphold those values in their daily lives. Therefore show your child good examples of life by your action.

(B) In our daily lives, we can show our children that we respect others. We can show them our compassion and concern when others are suffering, and our own self-discipline, courage and honesty as we make difficult decisions.

(C) Our priorities and principles and our examples of good behavior can teach our children to take the high road when other roads look tempting. Remember that children do not learn the values that make up strong character simply by being told about them.

(D) They learn from seeing. They learn from hearing and from overhearing. Children share the values of their parents about the most important things in life.

4. 28) 21

Most people have no doubt heard this question: If a tree falls in the forest and there is no one there to hear it fall, does it make a sound?

(A) The correct answer is no. Sound is more than pressure waves, and indeed there can be no sound without a hearer. And similarly, scientific communication is a two-way process.

(B) Publication is no more than pressure waves unless the published paper is understood.

(C) Just as a signal of any kind is useless unless it is perceived, a published scientific paper (signal) is useless unless it is both received and understood by its intended audience.

(D) Thus we can restate the axiom of science as follows: A scientific experiment is not complete until the results have been published and understood.

(E) Too many scientific papers fall silently in the woods.

5. 29) 22

We all negotiate every day, whether we realise it or not.

(A) This old-school, adversarial approach may be useful in a one-off negotiation where you will probably not deal with that person again. However, such transactions are becoming increasingly rare, because most of us deal with the same people repeatedly — our spouses and children, our friends and colleagues, our customers and clients.

(B) Yet few people ever learn how to negotiate. Those who do usually learn the traditional, win-lose negotiating style rather than an approach that is likely to result in a win-win agreement.

(C) In view of this, it's essential to achieve successful results for ourselves and maintain a healthy relationship with our negotiating partners at the same time. In today's interdependent world of business partnerships and long-term relationships, a win-win outcome is fast becoming the only acceptable result.

6. 30) 23

The interaction of workers from different cultural backgrounds with the host population might increase productivity due to positive externalities like knowledge spillovers.

(A) Diversity not only impacts the labour market, but may also affect the quality of life in a location.

(B) On the other hand, diversity could be perceived as an unattractive feature if natives perceive it as a distortion of what they consider to be their national identity.

(C) This is only an advantage up to a certain degree. When the variety of backgrounds is too large, fractionalization may cause excessive transaction costs for communication, which may lower productivity.

(D) A tolerant native population may value a multicultural city or region because of an increase in the range of available goods and services.

(E) They might even discriminate against other ethnic groups and they might fear that social conflicts between different foreign nationalities are imported into their own neighbourhood.

(.hwp) (.pdf) ➜ www.englishmygod.com

7. 31) 24

We think we are shaping our buildings.

(A) Before these ancestors got the idea to erect standing stones some 12,000 years ago, they were hunter-gatherers. It appears that the erection of the multiple rings of megalithic stones took so long, and so many successive generations, that these innovators were forced to settle down to complete the construction works.

(B) But really, our buildings and development are also shaping us. One of the best examples of this is the oldest-known construction: the ornately carved rings of standing stones at Göbekli Tepe in Turkey.

(C) In the process, they became the first farming society on Earth.

(D) This is an early example of a society constructing something that ends up radically remaking the society itself.

(E) Things are not so different in our own time.

8. 32) 26

American jazz pianist Bill Evans was born in New Jersey in 1929.

(A) He went on to serve in the army from 1951 to 1954 and played flute in the Fifth Army Band. After serving in the military, he studied composition at the Mannes School of Music in New York.

(B) Composer George Russell admired his playing and hired Evans to record and perform his compositions. Evans became famous for recordings made from the late-1950s through the 1960s.

(C) His early training was in classical music. At the age of six, he began receiving piano lessons, later adding flute and violin. He earned bachelor's degrees in piano and music education from Southeastern Louisiana College in 1950.

(D) He won his first Grammy Award in 1964 for his album Conversations with Myself. Evans' expressive piano works and his unique harmonic approach inspired a whole generation of musicians.

9. 33) 29

There is a reason the title "Monday Morning Quarterback" exists.

(A) Students and professionals with years of training and specialized degrees in sport business may also find themselves being given advice on how to do their jobs from friends, family, or even total strangers without any expertise. Executives in sport management have decades of knowledge and experience in their respective fields.

(B) However, many of them face criticism from fans and community members telling them how to run their business. Very few people tell their doctor how to perform surgery or their accountant how to prepare their taxes, but many people provide feedback on how sport organizations should be managed.

(C) Just read the comments on social media from fans discussing the weekend's games, and you quickly see how many people believe they could play, coach, and manage sport teams more successfully than those on the field. This goes for the boardroom as well.

10. 34) 30

While moving is difficult for everyone, it is particularly stressful for children.

(A) They lose their sense of security and may feel disoriented when their routine is disrupted and all that is familiar is taken away. Young children, ages 3-6, are particularly affected by a move. Their understanding at this stage is quite literal, and it is difficult for them to imagine beforehand a new home and their new room.

(B) Young children may have worries such as "Will I still be me in the new place?" and "Will my toys and bed come with us?" It is important to establish a balance between validating children's past experiences and focusing on helping them adjust to the new place.

(C) Children need to have opportunities to share their backgrounds in a way that respects their past as an important part of who they are. This contributes to building a sense of community, which is essential for all children, especially those in transition.

11. 35) 31

Many people are terrified to fly in airplanes.

(A) Often, this fear stems from a lack of control. The pilot is in control, not the passengers, and this lack of control instills fear.

(B) Pay attention to the thoughts you have about taking the risk and make sure you're basing your decision on facts, not just feelings.

(C) Logic says that statistically, the odds of dying in a car crash are around 1 in 5,000, while the odds of dying in a plane crash are closer to 1 in 11 million. If you're going to take a risk, especially one that could possibly involve your well-being, wouldn't you want the odds in your favor?

(D) Many potential passengers are so afraid they choose to drive great distances to get to a destination instead of flying. But their decision to drive is based solely on emotion, not logic.

(E) However, most people choose the option that will cause them the least amount of anxiety.

12. 36) 32

The famous primatologist Frans de Waal, of Emory University, says humans downplay similarities between us and other animals as a way of maintaining our spot at the top of our imaginary ladder.

(A) Scientists, de Waal points out, can be some of the worst offenders — employing technical language to distance the other animals from us . They call "kissing" in chimps "mouth-to-mouth contact"; they call "friends" between primates "favorite affiliation partners"; they interpret evidence showing that crows and chimps can make tools as being somehow qualitatively different from the kind of toolmaking said to define humanity.

(B) The way we use our tongues to disempower animals, the way we invent words to maintain our spot at the top.

(C) This and so many more tricks of language are what de Waal has termed "linguistic castration."

(D) If an animal can beat us at a cognitive task — like how certain bird species can remember the precise locations of thousands of seeds — they write it off as instinct, not intelligence.

(.hwp) (.pdf) ➔ www.englishmygod.com

13. 37) 33

A key to engagement and achievement is providing students with relevant texts they will be interested in.

(A) On the contrary, they sought out books." The pattern Fink discovered was that all of her subjects had been passionate in some personal interest.

(B) The areas of interest included religion, math, business, science, history, and biography. What mattered was that they read voraciously to find out more.

(C) While she expected to find that they had avoided reading and discovered ways to bypass it or compensate with other strategies for learning, she found the opposite. "To my surprise, I found that these dyslexics were enthusiastic readers...they rarely avoided reading.

(D) My scholarly work and my teaching have been deeply influenced by the work of Rosalie Fink. She interviewed twelve adults who were highly successful in their work, including a physicist, a biochemist, and a company CEO. All of them had dyslexia and had had significant problems with reading throughout their school years.

14. 38) 34

For many people, ability refers to intellectual competence, so they want everything they do to reflect how smart they are — writing a brilliant legal brief, getting the highest grade on a test, writing elegant computer code, saying something exceptionally wise or witty in a conversation.

(A) An outstanding performance means an outstanding person; an average performance means an average person.

(B) Period.

(C) However ability may be defined, a problem occurs when it is the sole determinant of one's self-worth. The performance becomes the only measure of the person; nothing else is taken into account.

(D) You could also define ability in terms of a particular skill or talent, such as how well one plays the piano, learns a language, or serves a tennis ball. Some people focus on their ability to be attractive, entertaining, up on the latest trends, or to have the newest gadgets.

15. 39) 35

Sensory nerves have specialized endings in the tissues that pick up a particular sensation.

(A) Sensory and motor nerves control almost all functions in the body — from the beating of the heart to the movement of the gut, sweating and just about everything else.

(B) If, for example, you step on a sharp object such as a pin, nerve endings in the skin will transmit the pain sensation up your leg, up and along the spinal cord to the brain. While the pain itself is unpleasant, it is in fact acting as a protective mechanism for the foot.

(C) They will also connect to motor nerves that travel back down the spinal cord, and to the muscles in your leg that now contract quickly to lift your foot away from the painful object.

(D) Within the brain, nerves will connect to the area that controls speech, so that you may well shout 'ouch' or something rather less polite.

16. 40) 36

Maybe you've heard this joke: "How do you eat an elephant?"

(A) Crystals come in a variety of shapes that scientists call habits. Common crystal habits include squares, triangles, and six-sided hexagons. Usually crystals form when liquids cool, such as when you create ice cubes. Many times, crystals form in ways that do not allow for perfect shapes.

(B) The answer is "one bite at a time." So, how do you "build" the Earth? That's simple, too: one atom at a time. Atoms are the basic building blocks of crystals, and since all rocks are made up of crystals, the more you know about atoms, the better.

(C) If conditions are too cold, too hot, or there isn't enough source material, they can form strange, twisted shapes. But when conditions are right, we see beautiful displays. Usually, this involves a slow, steady environment where the individual atoms have plenty of time to join and fit perfectly into what's known as the crystal lattice. This is the basic structure of atoms that is seen time after time.

17. 41) 37

When you pluck a guitar string it moves back and forth hundreds of times every second.

(A) The vibration of the wood creates more powerful waves in the air pressure, which travel away from the guitar.

(B) The vibration of the string is passed on to the wooden panels of the guitar body, which vibrate back and forth at the same rate as the string.

(C) When the waves reach your eardrums they flex in and out the same number of times a second as the original string.

(D) But if you attach a string to a big hollow box (like a guitar body), then the vibration is amplified and the note is heard loud and clear.

(E) Naturally, this movement is so fast that you cannot see it — you just see the blurred outline of the moving string. Strings vibrating in this way on their own make hardly any noise because strings are very thin and don't push much air about.

18. 42) 38

Boundaries between work and home are blurring as portable digital technology makes it increasingly possible to work anywhere, anytime.

(A) We've even noticed more of these "segmenters" carrying two phones — one for work and one for personal use. Flexible schedules work well for these individuals because they enable greater distinction between time at work and time in other roles.

(B) Other individuals prefer integrating work and family roles all day long. This might entail constantly trading text messages with children from the office, or monitoring emails at home and on vacation, rather than returning to work to find hundreds of messages in their inbox.

(C) Individuals differ in how they like to manage their time to meet work and outside responsibilities. Some people prefer to separate or segment roles so that boundary crossings are minimized. For example, these people might keep separate email accounts for work and family and try to conduct work at the workplace and take care of family matters only during breaks and non-work time.

(.hwp) (.pdf) ➔ www.englishmygod.com

19. 43) 39.

A "complementary good" is a product that is often consumed alongside another product.

(A) For example, popcorn is a complementary good to a movie, while a travel pillow is a complementary good for a long plane journey. When the popularity of one product increases, the sales of its complementary good also increase.

(B) For example, although motorists may seem required to purchase gasoline to run their cars, they can switch to electric cars.

(C) However, do not assume that a product is perfectly complementary, as customers may not be completely locked in to the product.

(D) By producing goods that complement other products that are already (or about to be) popular, you can ensure a steady stream of demand for your product. Some products enjoy perfect complementary status — they have to be consumed together, such as a lamp and a lightbulb.

20. 44) 40

It's not news to anyone that we judge others based on their clothes.

(A) In general, studies that investigate these judgments find that people prefer clothing that matches expectations — surgeons in scrubs, little boys in blue — with one notable exception. A series of studies published in an article in June 2014 in the Journal of Consumer Research explored observers' reactions to people who broke established norms only slightly.

(B) In one scenario, a man at a black-tie affair was viewed as having higher status and competence when wearing a red bow tie. The researchers also found that valuing uniqueness increased audience members' ratings of the status and competence of a professor who wore red sneakers while giving a lecture.

(C) The results suggest that people judge these slight deviations from the norm as positive because they suggest that the individual is powerful enough to risk the social costs of such behaviors.

21. 45) 41, 42

Claims that local food production cut greenhouse gas emissions by reducing the burning of transportation fuel are usually not well founded.

(A) Transport is the source of only 11 percent of greenhouse gas emissions within the food sector, so reducing the distance that food travels after it leaves the farm is far less important than reducing wasteful energy use on the farm. Food coming from a distance can actually be better for the climate, depending on how it was grown.

(B) When food does travel, what matters most is not the distance traveled but the travel mode (surface versus air), and most of all the load size. Bulk loads of food can travel halfway around the world by ocean freight with a smaller carbon footprint, per pound delivered, than foods traveling just a short distance but in much smaller loads.

(C) For example, 18-wheelers carry much larger loads than pickup trucks so they can move food 100 times as far while burning only one-third as much gas per pound of food delivered.

(D) For example, field-grown tomatoes shipped from Mexico in the winter months will have a smaller carbon footprint than local winter tomatoes grown in a greenhouse. In the United Kingdom, lamb meat that travels 11,000 miles from New Zealand generates only one-quarter the carbon emissions per pound compared to British lamb because farmers in the United Kingdom raise their animals on feed (which must be produced using fossil fuels) rather than on clover pastureland.

22. 46) 43, 44, 45

Long ago, an old man built a grand temple at the center of his village.

(A) One day, he saw a young man come to the temple. When that young man left the temple, the old man called him and asked, "Will you take care of this temple?" The young man was surprised by the offer and replied, "I have no experience caring for a temple. I'm not even educated." The old man smiled and said, "I don't want any educated man.

(B) But you dug up that brick." The young man said, "I haven't done anything great. It's the duty of every human being to think about others. I only did my duty." The old man smiled and said, "Only people who know their duty and perform it are qualified people."

(C) I want a qualified person." Confused, the young man asked, "But why do you consider me a qualified person?" The old man replied, "I buried a brick on the path to the temple. I watched for many days as people tripped over that brick. No one thought to remove it.

(D) People traveled to worship at the temple. So the old man made arrangements for food and accommodation inside the temple itself. He needed someone who could look after the temple, so he put up a notice: Manager needed. Seeing the notice, many people went to the old man. But he returned all the applicants after interviews, telling them, "I need a qualified person for this work." The old man would sit on the roof of his house every morning, watching people go through the temple doors.

(.hwp) (.pdf) ➜ www.englishmygod.com

2023 고1 9월 모의고사

❶ voca ❷ text ❸ [/] ❹ _____ ❺ quiz 1 ❻ quiz 2 ❼ quiz 3 ❽ quiz 4 ❾ quiz 5

1. 1)밑줄 친 ⓐ~ⓗ 중 어법, 혹은 문맥상 어휘의 사용이 어색한 것끼리 짝지어진 것을 고르시오. 18

Dear Professor Sanchez,

My name is Ellis Wight, and I'm the director of the Alexandria Science Museum. We are ⓐ **holding** a Chemistry Fair for local middle school students on Saturday, October 28. The goal of the fair is to encourage them ⓑ **being** interested in science through guided experiments. We are looking for college students who can help with the experiments ⓒ **during** the event. I am ⓓ **contacting** you to ask you to ⓔ **recommend** some students from the chemistry department at your college who you think ⓕ **are** ⓖ **quantified** for this job. With their help, I'm sure the participants will have a great experience. I look forward to ⓗ **hearing** from you soon.

Sincerely, Ellis Wight

① ⓐ, ⓖ ② ⓑ, ⓖ ③ ⓖ, ⓗ ④ ⓐ, ⓔ, ⓗ
⑤ ⓐ, ⓒ, ⓓ, ⓗ

2. 2)밑줄 친 ⓐ~ⓚ 중 어법, 혹은 문맥상 어휘의 사용이 어색한 것끼리 짝지어진 것을 고르시오. 19

Gregg and I had been rock climbing since sunrise and had had no problems. So we took a risk. "Look, the first bolt is right there. I can definitely ⓐ **climb** out to it. Piece of ⓑ **bread** ", I persuaded Gregg, minutes before I found ⓒ **myself** pinned. It wasn't a piece of ⓓ **bread** . The rock was ⓔ **deceptively** ⓕ **fertile** of handholds. I ⓖ **clumsily** moved back and forth ⓗ **cross** the cliff face and ended up with nowhere to go...but down. The bolt that would save my life, if I could get to it, was about two feet above my reach. My arms ⓘ **trembled** from exhaustion. I looked at Gregg. My body froze with ⓙ **fright** from my neck down to my toes. Our rope was tied between us. If I fell, he ⓚ **would fall** with me.

① ⓐ, ⓕ, ⓗ ② ⓑ, ⓕ, ⓘ ③ ⓓ, ⓗ, ⓙ ④ ⓑ, ⓓ, ⓕ, ⓗ ⑤ ⓑ, ⓖ, ⓗ, ⓚ

3. 3)밑줄 친 ⓐ~ⓜ 중 어법, 혹은 문맥상 어휘의 사용이 어색한 것끼리 짝지어진 것을 고르시오. 20

We are always teaching our children something by our words and our actions. They learn from seeing. They learn from hearing and from overhearing. Children ⓐ **deny** the values of their parents about the most important things in life. Our priorities and principles and our examples of good behavior can teach our children ⓑ **took** the ⓒ **high** road when other roads look ⓓ **temptation** . Remember ⓔ **that** children do not learn the values that ⓕ **make** up strong character simply by ⓖ **being told** about them. They learn by seeing the people around them ⓗ **act** on and ⓘ **uphold** those values in their daily lives. Therefore show your child good examples of life by your ⓙ **action** . In our daily lives, we can show our children ⓚ **that** we respect others. We can show them our compassion and concern ⓛ **that** others are suffering, and our own ⓜ **self-discipline** , courage and honesty as we make difficult decisions.

① ⓔ, ⓛ, ⓜ ② ⓐ, ⓑ, ⓓ, ⓛ ③ ⓐ, ⓙ, ⓚ, ⓛ
④ ⓔ, ⓙ, ⓛ, ⓜ ⑤ ⓖ, ⓚ, ⓛ, ⓜ

보듬영어

4. ⁴⁾밑줄 친 ⓐ~ⓛ 중 어법, 혹은 문맥상 어휘의 사용이 어색한 것끼리 짝지어진 것을 고르시오. ²¹

Most people have no doubt ⓐ **heard** this question: If a tree falls in the forest and there is no one there to hear it fall, ⓑ **does** it make a sound? The correct answer is ⓒ **no** . Sound is more than pressure waves, and indeed there can be no sound ⓓ **with** a hearer. And similarly, scientific communication is a ⓔ **two-way** process. Just as a signal of any kind is ⓕ **useful** unless it is perceived, a published scientific paper (signal) is useless ⓖ **unless** it is both received and ⓗ **understands** by its ⓘ **intended** audience. Thus we can restate the axiom of science as follows: A scientific experiment is ⓙ **complete** until the results have ⓚ **been published** and understood. Publication is no more than pressure waves unless the published paper is understood. Too many scientific papers fall ⓛ **silently** in the woods.

① ⓑ, ⓘ, ⓙ   ② ⓓ, ⓖ, ⓘ   ③ ⓕ, ⓙ, ⓚ
④ ⓒ, ⓓ, ⓖ, ⓙ   ⑤ ⓓ, ⓕ, ⓗ, ⓙ

5. ⁵⁾밑줄 친 ⓐ~ⓟ 중 어법, 혹은 문맥상 어휘의 사용이 어색한 것끼리 짝지어진 것을 고르시오. ²²

We all negotiate every day, ⓐ **whether** we realise it or not. Yet ⓑ **little** people ever learn how to negotiate. Those who ⓒ **do** usually ⓓ **learn** the traditional, win-lose negotiating style rather than an approach that is likely to result ⓔ **from** a win-win agreement. This old-school, ⓕ **adversarial** approach may be useful in a one-off negotiation ⓖ **which** you will probably not deal with ⓗ **that** person again. However, such ⓘ **transactions** are becoming increasingly ⓙ **rare** , because most of us deal with the ⓚ **same** people repeatedly — our spouses and children, our friends and colleagues, our customers and clients. In view of this, it's essential to achieve ⓛ

successful results for ourselves and maintain a ⓜ **healthy** relationship with our negotiating partners at the same time. In today's ⓝ **interdependent** world of business partnerships and long-term relationships, a win-win ⓞ **income** is fast becoming the only ⓟ **acceptable** result.

① ⓑ, ⓔ, ⓛ   ② ⓓ, ⓔ, ⓙ   ③ ⓔ, ⓛ, ⓞ
④ ⓖ, ⓗ, ⓞ   ⑤ ⓑ, ⓔ, ⓖ, ⓞ

6. ⁶⁾밑줄 친 ⓐ~ⓡ 중 어법, 혹은 문맥상 어휘의 사용이 어색한 것끼리 짝지어진 것을 고르시오. ²³

The ⓐ **interaction** of workers from different cultural backgrounds with the host ⓑ **population** might ⓒ **increase** productivity due ⓓ **to** positive ⓔ **externalities** like knowledge spillovers. This is only an advantage up to a certain degree. When the variety of backgrounds ⓕ **are** too large, ⓖ **fractionalization** may cause excessive transaction costs for communication, ⓗ **which** may ⓘ **lower** productivity. ⓙ **Diversity** not only impacts the labour market, but may also ⓚ **affect** the quality of life in a location. A ⓛ **tolerant** native population may ⓜ **desert** a multicultural city or region because of an increase in the range of available goods and services. On the other hand, diversity could be ⓝ **perceived** as an unattractive feature if natives ⓞ **receive** it as a ⓟ **distortion** of what they consider to be their national ⓠ **identity** . They might even discriminate against other ethnic groups and they might fear that social conflicts between different foreign nationalities are ⓡ **exported** into their own neighbourhood.

① ⓕ, ⓖ, ⓡ   ② ⓜ, ⓝ, ⓡ   ③ ⓐ, ⓙ, ⓝ, ⓡ
④ ⓓ, ⓘ, ⓜ, ⓡ   ⑤ ⓕ, ⓜ, ⓞ, ⓡ

7. 7)밑줄 친 ⓐ~ⓜ 중 어법, 혹은 문맥상 어휘의 사용이 어색한 것끼리 짝지어진 것을 고르시오. 24

We think we are shaping our buildings. But really, our buildings and development are also shaping us. One of the best ⓐ **examples** of this is the oldest-known construction: the ornately ⓑ **carved** rings of standing stones at Göbekli Tepe in Turkey. Before these ancestors got the idea to ⓒ **erect** standing stones some 12,000 years ago, they were hunter-gatherers. It appears ⓓ **which** the ⓔ **erection** of the multiple rings of megalithic stones took so long, and so many ⓕ **successive** generations, ⓖ **that** these innovators were forced ⓗ **to settle** down to ⓘ **complete** the construction works. In the ⓙ **process** , they became the first farming society on Earth. This is an early example of a society ⓚ **constructing** something that ends up radically ⓛ **remaking** the society itself. Things are not so ⓜ **similar** in our own time.

① ⓓ, ⓜ   ② ⓐ, ⓚ, ⓜ   ③ ⓒ, ⓕ, ⓗ
④ ⓔ, ⓕ, ⓘ   ⑤ ⓐ, ⓔ, ⓕ, ⓚ

8. 8)밑줄 친 ⓐ~ⓖ 중 어법, 혹은 문맥상 어휘의 사용이 어색한 것끼리 짝지어진 것을 고르시오. 26

American jazz pianist Bill Evans was born in New Jersey in 1929. His early training was in classical music. At the age of six, he began receiving piano lessons, later ⓐ **adding** flute and violin. He earned bachelor's degrees in piano and music education from Southeastern Louisiana College in 1950. He went on to serve in the army from 1951 to 1954 and played flute in the Fifth Army Band. After ⓑ **serving** in the military, he studied ⓒ **disposition** at the Mannes School of Music in New York. Composer George Russell ⓓ **administered** his playing and hired

Evans to record and ⓔ **perform** his compositions. Evans became famous for recordings ⓕ **are made** from the late-1950s through the 1960s. He won his first Grammy Award in 1964 for his album Conversations with Myself. Evans' expressive piano works and his unique harmonic approach ⓖ **inspired** a whole generation of musicians.

① ⓐ, ⓑ   ② ⓐ, ⓓ, ⓖ   ③ ⓐ, ⓔ, ⓕ
④ ⓒ, ⓓ, ⓕ   ⑤ ⓐ, ⓑ, ⓔ, ⓖ

9. 9)밑줄 친 ⓐ~ⓙ 중 어법, 혹은 문맥상 어휘의 사용이 어색한 것끼리 짝지어진 것을 고르시오. 29

There is a reason the title "Monday Morning Quarterback" ⓐ **exists** . Just read the comments on social media from fans ⓑ **discussing** the weekend's games, and you quickly see how many people believe they could play, coach, and manage sport teams ⓒ **more** successfully than those on the field. This goes for the boardroom as well. Students and professionals with years of training and specialized degrees in sport business may also find ⓓ **themselves** ⓔ **being given** ⓕ **advise** on how to do their jobs from friends, family, or even total strangers without any ⓖ **expertise** . Executives in sport management have decades of knowledge and experience in their ⓗ **respective** fields. However, many of them face ⓘ **approval** from fans and community members telling them how to run their business. Very ⓙ **a few** people tell their doctor how to perform surgery or their accountant how to prepare their taxes, but many people provide feedback on how sport organizations should be managed.

① ⓒ, ⓕ   ② ⓑ, ⓓ, ⓙ   ③ ⓒ, ⓕ, ⓖ
④ ⓒ, ⓕ, ⓘ   ⑤ ⓕ, ⓘ, ⓙ

10. 10)밑줄 친 ⓐ~ⓛ 중 어법, 혹은 문맥상 어휘의 사용이 어색한 것끼리 짝지어진 것을 고르시오. 30

While moving is difficult for everyone, it is particularly ⓐ **stressfully** for children. They ⓑ **lose** their sense of security and may feel ⓒ **disoriented** when their routine is ⓓ **disrupted** and all that is familiar is taken away. Young children, ages 3-6, are particularly ⓔ **effected** by a move. Their understanding at this stage is quite ⓕ **literal** , and it is difficult for them to imagine ⓖ **afterward** a new home and their new room. Young children may have worries such as "Will I still be me in the new place"? and "Will my toys and bed come with us"? It is important to establish a balance between ⓗ **validating** children's past experiences and focusing on helping them adjust to the new place. Children need to have opportunities to share their backgrounds in a way that ⓘ **respects** their past as an important part of who they ⓙ **are** . This ⓚ **contributes** to building a sense of community, which is essential for all children, especially those in ⓛ **transportation** .

① ⓑ, ⓒ, ⓛ   ② ⓐ, ⓑ, ⓔ, ⓚ   ③ ⓐ, ⓔ, ⓕ, ⓖ
④ ⓐ, ⓔ, ⓖ, ⓛ   ⑤ ⓔ, ⓙ, ⓚ, ⓛ

11. 11)밑줄 친 ⓐ~ⓜ 중 어법, 혹은 문맥상 어휘의 사용이 어색한 것끼리 짝지어진 것을 고르시오. 31

Many people are ⓐ **terrifying** to fly in airplanes. Often, this fear stems from a ⓑ **lack** of control. The pilot is in control, not the passengers, and this lack of control ⓒ **instills** fear. Many potential passengers are so afraid they choose to drive great distances to get to a ⓓ **destination** instead of flying. But their decision to drive is based solely on emotion, not logic. ⓔ **Logic** says that statistically, the odds of dying in a car crash ⓕ **are** around 1 in 5,000, while the odds of dying in a plane crash ⓖ **are** closer to 1 in 11 million. If you're going to take ⓗ **a risk** , especially ⓘ **one** that could possibly involve your well-being, wouldn't you want the odds ⓙ **against** your favor? However, most people choose the option that will cause them the ⓚ **least** amount of anxiety. Pay attention to the thoughts you ⓛ **have** about taking the risk and make sure you're ⓜ **based on** your decision on facts, not just feelings.

① ⓖ, ⓜ   ② ⓐ, ⓙ, ⓜ   ③ ⓕ, ⓙ, ⓚ
④ ⓖ, ⓗ, ⓘ, ⓛ   ⑤ ⓖ, ⓗ, ⓙ, ⓜ

12. 12)밑줄 친 ⓐ~ⓝ 중 어법, 혹은 문맥상 어휘의 사용이 어색한 것끼리 짝지어진 것을 고르시오. 32

The famous primatologist Frans de Waal, of Emory University, says humans ⓐ **downplay** similarities between us and other animals as a way of ⓑ **maintaining** our spot at the top of our imaginary ladder. Scientists, de Waal points out, can be some of the worst ⓒ **offenders** — employing technical language to ⓓ **distance** the other animals from us . They call "kissing" in chimps "mouth-to-mouth contact"; they call "friends" between primates "favorite ⓔ **affiliation** partners"; they interpret evidence showing that crows and chimps can make tools as being somehow ⓕ **qualitatively** different from the kind of toolmaking ⓖ **is said** to define humanity. If an animal can beat us at a cognitive task — like how ⓗ **certain** bird species can remember the precise locations of thousands of seeds — they write it off as ⓘ **instinct** , not ⓙ **instinct** . This and so many more tricks of language ⓚ **is** what de Waal has ⓛ **termed** "linguistic castration". The way we use our tongues to ⓜ **disempower** animals, the way we invent words to ⓝ **endanger** our spot at the top.

① ⓑ, ⓖ   ② ⓒ, ⓖ, ⓙ   ③ ⓓ, ⓕ, ⓘ
④ ⓔ, ⓗ, ⓙ, ⓝ   ⑤ ⓖ, ⓙ, ⓚ, ⓝ

13. 13)밑줄 친 ⓐ~ⓙ 중 어법, 혹은 문맥상 어휘의 사용이 어색한 것끼리 짝지어진 것을 고르시오. 33

A key to engagement and achievement is providing students ⓐ **with** relevant texts they will be interested in. My scholarly work and my teaching ⓑ **have been** deeply influenced by the work of Rosalie Fink. She interviewed twelve adults who were highly successful in their work, including a physicist, a biochemist, and a company CEO. All of them had dyslexia and had had significant problems with reading throughout their school years. ⓒ **While** she expected to ⓓ **find** that they had ⓔ **avoided** reading and discovered ways to bypass it or compensate with other strategies for learning, she found the opposite. "To my surprise, I found that these dyslexics were ⓕ **enthusiastic** readers...they rarely ⓖ **avoided** reading. On the contrary, they sought out books". The pattern Fink discovered was ⓗ **that** all of her subjects had been passionate in some personal interest. The areas of interest included religion, math, business, science, history, and biography. What ⓘ **is mattered** was that they read ⓙ **modestly** to find out more.

① ⓑ, ⓒ   ② ⓓ, ⓙ   ③ ⓕ, ⓘ
④ ⓖ, ⓙ   ⑤ ⓘ, ⓙ

14. 14)밑줄 친 ⓐ~ⓚ 중 어법, 혹은 문맥상 어휘의 사용이 어색한 것끼리 짝지어진 것을 고르시오. 34

For many people, ability refers to ⓐ **intellectual** competence, so they want everything they do ⓑ **to reflect** how smart they ⓒ **are** — writing a brilliant legal brief, getting the highest grade on a test, writing elegant computer code, saying something exceptionally wise or witty in a conversation. You could also ⓓ **define** ability in terms of a particular skill or talent, such as how ⓔ **well** one plays the piano, learns a language, or serves a tennis ball. Some people focus on their ability to be attractive, ⓕ **entertained** , up on the ⓖ **latest** trends, or to have the newest gadgets. ⓗ **However** ability may be ⓘ **defining** , a problem ⓙ **occurs** when it is the sole ⓚ **determinant** of one's self-worth. The performance becomes the only measure of the person; nothing else is taken into account. An outstanding performance means an outstanding person; an average performance means an average person. Period.

① ⓕ, ⓖ   ② ⓕ, ⓘ   ③ ⓖ, ⓘ
④ ⓗ, ⓘ   ⑤ ⓘ, ⓙ

15. 15)밑줄 친 ⓐ~ⓗ 중 어법, 혹은 문맥상 어휘의 사용이 어색한 것끼리 짝지어진 것을 고르시오. 35

Sensory nerves have specialized endings in the tissues that ⓐ **pick** up a particular sensation. If, for example, you step on a sharp object such as a pin, nerve endings in the skin will ⓑ **transport** the pain sensation up your leg, up and along the spinal cord to the brain. ⓒ **While** the pain itself is unpleasant, it is in fact acting as a protective mechanism for the foot. Within the brain, nerves will connect to the area ⓓ **what** controls speech, so that you ⓔ **may as well** shout 'ouch' or something rather less ⓕ **polite** . They will also connect to motor nerves that travel back down the spinal cord, and to the muscles in your leg that now ⓖ **contract** quickly to lift your foot away from the painful object. Sensory and motor nerves ⓗ **calm** almost all functions in the body — from the beating of the heart to the movement of the gut, sweating and just about everything else.

① ⓐ, ⓓ, ⓗ   ② ⓐ, ⓔ, ⓖ   ③ ⓐ, ⓑ, ⓔ, ⓕ
④ ⓑ, ⓓ, ⓔ, ⓗ   ⑤ ⓒ, ⓓ, ⓕ, ⓗ

보듬영어

16.
16)밑줄 친 ⓐ~ⓘ 중 <u>어법, 혹은 문맥상 어휘의 사용이 어색한</u> 것끼리 짝지어진 것을 고르시오. 36

Maybe you've heard this joke: " ⓐ **How** do you eat an elephant"? The answer is "one bite at a time". So, how do you "build" the Earth? That's simple, too: one atom at a time. Atoms are the basic building blocks of crystals, and since all rocks are ⓑ **made** up of crystals, the more you know about atoms, the ⓒ **well** . Crystals come in a variety of ⓓ **shape** that scientists call habits. Common crystal habits include squares, triangles, and six-sided hexagons. Usually crystals form when liquids ⓔ **cooled** , such as when you create ice cubes. Many times, crystals form in ways ⓕ **that** do not allow for perfect shapes. If conditions are too cold, too hot, or there isn't enough source material, they can form strange, twisted shapes. But when conditions are right, we see beautiful displays. Usually, this involves a slow, ⓖ **steady** environment ⓗ **where** the individual atoms have plenty of time to join and fit perfectly into what's known as the crystal lattice. This is the basic structure of atoms that ⓘ **is** seen time after time.

① ⓐ, ⓘ   ② ⓐ, ⓑ, ⓕ   ③ ⓐ, ⓓ, ⓖ
④ ⓒ, ⓓ, ⓔ   ⑤ ⓒ, ⓔ, ⓖ, ⓘ

17.
17)밑줄 친 ⓐ~ⓘ 중 <u>어법, 혹은 문맥상 어휘의 사용이 어색한</u> 것끼리 짝지어진 것을 고르시오. 37

When you pluck a guitar string it moves back and forth hundreds of times every second. Naturally, this movement is so ⓐ **fast** that you ⓑ **can** see it — you just see the blurred outline of the moving string. Strings ⓒ **vibrating** in this way on their own make ⓓ **hardly** any noise because strings are very thin and don't push much air about. But if you ⓔ **attach** a string to a big hollow box (like a guitar body), then the vibration is ⓕ **simplified** and the note is heard loud and clear. The

vibration of the string is passed on to the wooden panels of the guitar body, which ⓖ **vibrate** back and forth at the same rate as the string. The vibration of the wood creates more powerful waves in the air pressure, ⓗ **which** travel away from the guitar. When the waves ⓘ **reach** your eardrums they flex in and out the same number of ⓙ **times** a second as the original string.

① ⓐ, ⓑ   ② ⓑ, ⓕ   ③ ⓑ, ⓒ, ⓘ
④ ⓑ, ⓓ, ⓘ   ⑤ ⓒ, ⓔ, ⓖ, ⓗ

18.
18)밑줄 친 ⓐ~ⓙ 중 <u>어법, 혹은 문맥상 어휘의 사용이 어색한</u> 것끼리 짝지어진 것을 고르시오. 38

Boundaries between work and home ⓐ **are** blurring as ⓑ **portable** digital technology makes ⓒ **it** increasingly possible to work anywhere, anytime. Individuals differ in how they like to manage their time to meet work and outside responsibilities. Some people prefer to ⓓ **integrate** or segment roles so that boundary crossings are ⓔ **minimized** . For example, these people might keep separate email accounts for work and family and try to conduct work at the workplace and take care of family matters only ⓕ **during** breaks and non-work time. We've even noticed more of these " ⓖ **segmenters** " carrying two phones — one for work and one for personal use. ⓗ **Fixed** schedules work well for these individuals because they enable greater distinction between time at work and time in other roles. Other individuals prefer ⓘ **integrating** work and family roles all day long. This might ⓙ **entail** constantly trading text messages with children from the office, or monitoring emails at home and on vacation, rather than returning to work to find hundreds of messages in their inbox.

① ⓑ, ⓒ   ② ⓓ, ⓖ   ③ ⓓ, ⓗ
④ ⓗ, ⓘ   ⑤ ⓐ, ⓔ, ⓖ

19. 19)밑줄 친 ⓐ~ⓜ 중 <u>어법, 혹은 문맥상 어휘의 사용이</u> <u>어색한</u> 것끼리 짝지어진 것을 고르시오. 39

A "complementary good" is a product that is often ⓐ <u>consumed</u> alongside another ⓑ <u>products</u> . For example, popcorn is a complementary good to a movie, while a travel pillow is a complementary good for a long plane journey. When the ⓒ <u>popularity</u> of one product ⓓ <u>increases</u> , the sales of ⓔ <u>its</u> complementary good also ⓕ <u>increase</u> . By producing goods that ⓖ <u>complement</u> other products that are already (or about to be) popular, you can ⓗ <u>ensure</u> a steady stream of demand for your product. Some products enjoy perfect complementary ⓘ <u>status</u> — they have to be consumed ⓙ <u>together</u> , such as a lamp and a lightbulb. However, do not assume that a product is perfectly complementary, as customers may not be completely locked ⓚ <u>pit</u> to the product. For example, ⓛ <u>despite</u> motorists may seem required to purchase gasoline to run their cars, they can ⓜ <u>stick</u> to electric cars.

① ⓐ, ⓛ, ⓜ   ② ⓒ, ⓘ, ⓛ   ③ ⓑ, ⓓ, ⓚ, ⓜ
④ ⓑ, ⓚ, ⓛ, ⓜ   ⑤ ⓘ, ⓚ, ⓛ, ⓜ

20. 20)밑줄 친 ⓐ~ⓚ 중 <u>어법, 혹은 문맥상 어휘의 사용이</u> <u>어색한</u> 것끼리 짝지어진 것을 고르시오. 40

It's not news to anyone that we judge others based on their clothes. In general, studies that investigate these judgments find ⓐ <u>that</u> people prefer clothing ⓑ <u>that</u> matches expectations — surgeons in scrubs, little boys in blue — with one notable ⓒ <u>expectation</u> . A series of studies published in an article in June 2014 in the Journal of Consumer Research explored observers' reactions to people who broke established ⓓ <u>norms</u> only slightly. In one scenario, a man at a black-tie affair was viewed as having ⓔ <u>higher</u> status and competence when ⓕ <u>wearing</u> a red bow tie. The researchers also found that valuing ⓖ <u>uniqueness</u> increased audience members' ratings of the status and competence of a professor who wore red sneakers while giving a lecture. The results suggest that people judge these slight ⓗ <u>deviations</u> from the ⓘ <u>norm</u> as ⓙ <u>negative</u> because they suggest that the individual is powerful enough to ⓚ <u>risk</u> the social costs of such behaviors.

① ⓒ, ⓓ   ② ⓒ, ⓔ   ③ ⓒ, ⓙ
④ ⓔ, ⓙ   ⑤ ⓑ, ⓒ, ⓛ

21. ²¹⁾밑줄 친 ⓐ~ⓢ 중 어법, 혹은 문맥상 어휘의 사용이 어색한 것끼리 짝지어진 것을 고르시오. ⁴¹~⁴²

Claims that local food production ⓐ **cut** greenhouse gas emissions by reducing the burning of ⓑ **transparency** fuel ⓒ **are** usually not well founded. Transport is the source of only 11 percent of greenhouse gas emissions within the food sector, so ⓓ **reducing** the distance that food travels after it leaves the farm ⓔ **is** far ⓕ **less** important than reducing wasteful energy use on the farm. Food coming from a distance can actually be ⓖ **better** for the climate, depending on how it was grown. For example, field-grown tomatoes shipped from Mexico in the winter months will have a ⓗ **smaller** carbon footprint than local winter tomatoes ⓘ **growing** in a greenhouse. In the United Kingdom, lamb meat that travels 11,000 miles from New Zealand ⓙ **generating** only one-quarter the carbon emissions per pound compared to British lamb because farmers in the United Kingdom ⓚ **raise** their animals on feed (which must be produced using fossil fuels) rather than on clover pastureland.

When food ⓛ **does** travel, what matters most is not the distance ⓜ **traveled** but the travel mode (surface versus air), and most of all the load size. Bulk loads of food can travel halfway around the world by ocean ⓝ **fright** with a ⓞ **smaller** carbon footprint, per pound delivered, than foods ⓟ **traveling** just a ⓠ **short** distance but in ⓡ **much** smaller loads. For example, 18-wheelers carry much larger loads than pickup trucks so they can move food 100 times as far while burning only one-third as ⓢ **much** gas per pound of food delivered.

① ⓐ, ⓑ, ⓜ ② ⓑ, ⓓ, ⓙ ③ ⓓ, ⓘ, ⓡ
④ ⓑ, ⓘ, ⓙ, ⓝ ⑤ ⓕ, ⓙ, ⓝ, ⓡ

22. ²²⁾밑줄 친 ⓐ~ⓜ 중 어법, 혹은 문맥상 어휘의 사용이 어색한 것끼리 짝지어진 것을 고르시오. ⁴³~⁴⁵

Long ago, an old man built a grand temple at the center of his village. People traveled to worship at the temple. So the old man made arrangements for food and accommodation inside the temple itself. He needed someone ⓐ **who** could look after the temple, so he put up a notice: Manager needed. ⓑ **Seeing** the notice, many people went to the old man. But he ⓒ **returned** all the ⓓ **applicants** after interviews, ⓔ **telling** them, "I need a qualified person for this work". The old man would ⓕ **seat** on the roof of his house every morning, watching people go through the temple doors. One day, he saw a young man come to the temple. When that young man left the temple, the old man called him and asked, "Will you take care of this temple"? The young man was ⓖ **surprised by** the offer and replied, "I have no experience ⓗ **caring** for a temple. I'm not even educated". The old man smiled and said, "I don't want any educated man. I want a qualified person". ⓘ **Confused**, the young man asked, "But why do you consider ⓙ **me** a qualified person"? The old man replied, "I buried a brick on the path to the temple. I watched for many days as people tripped over that brick. No one thought to remove it. But you dug up that brick". The young man said, "I haven't done ⓚ **anything** great. It's the duty of every human being to think about others. I only did my duty". The old man smiled and said, "Only people who ⓛ **know** their duty and perform it ⓜ **is** qualified people".

① ⓔ, ⓙ ② ⓕ, ⓚ ③ ⓕ, ⓜ
④ ⓙ, ⓜ ⑤ ⓚ, ⓜ

(.hwp) (.pdf) ➔ www.englishmygod.com

2023 고1 9월 모의고사

❶ voca　　❷ text　　❸ [/]　　❹ ＿＿＿　　❺ quiz 1　　❻ quiz 2　　❼ quiz 3　　❽ quiz 4　　❾ quiz 5

1. 1)글의 밑줄 친 부분 중 어법, 혹은 문맥상 어휘의 쓰임이 어색한 것을 모두 고르시오. 18

Dear Professor Sanchez,

My name is Ellis Wight, and I'm the director of the Alexandria Science Museum. We are ① **holding** a Chemistry Fair for local middle school students on Saturday, October 28. The goal of the fair is to encourage them ② **being** interested in science through guided experiments. We are looking for college students who can help with the experiments ③ **while** the event. I am ④ **contacting to** you to ask you to ⑤ **recommending** some students from the chemistry department at your college who you think are qualified for this job. With their help, I'm sure the participants will have a great experience. I look forward to hearing from you soon.

Sincerely, Ellis Wight

2. 2)글의 밑줄 친 부분 중 어법, 혹은 문맥상 어휘의 쓰임이 어색한 것을 모두 고르시오. 19

Gregg and I had been rock climbing since sunrise and had had no problems. So we took a risk. "Look, the first bolt is right there. I can definitely climb out to it. Piece of cake ", I persuaded Gregg, minutes before I found ① **myself** pinned. It wasn't a piece of ② **bread**. The rock was deceptively ③ **fertile** of handholds. I clumsily moved back and forth across the cliff face and ended up with nowhere to go...but down. The bolt that would save my life, if I could get to it, was about two feet above my reach. My arms trembled from exhaustion. I looked at Gregg. My body froze with ④ **fright** from my neck down to my toes. Our rope was tied between us. If I fell, he ⑤ **would have fallen** with me.

3. 3)글의 밑줄 친 부분 중 어법, 혹은 문맥상 어휘의 쓰임이 어색한 것을 모두 고르시오. 20

We are always teaching our children something by our words and our actions. They learn from seeing. They learn from hearing and from overhearing. Children share the values of their parents about the most important things in life. Our priorities and principles and our examples of good behavior can teach our children to take the high road when other roads look ① **tempting** . Remember ② **that** children do not learn the values that make up strong character simply by being told about them. They learn by seeing the people around them ③ **action** on and ④ **uphold** those values in their daily lives. Therefore show your child good examples of life by your action . In our daily lives, we can show our children ⑤ **what** we respect others. We can show them our compassion and concern when others are suffering, and our own self-discipline , courage and honesty as we make difficult decisions.

4. 4)글의 밑줄 친 부분 중 어법, 혹은 문맥상 어휘의 쓰임 이 어색한 것을 모두 고르시오. 21

Most people have no doubt ① **heard** this question: If a tree falls in the forest and there is no one there to hear it fall, ② **is** it make a sound? The correct answer is no . Sound is more than pressure waves, and indeed there can be no sound without a hearer. And similarly, scientific communication is a ③ **one-way** process. Just as a signal of any kind is ④ **useful** unless it is perceived, a published scientific paper (signal) is useless unless it is both received and understood by its ⑤ **intended** audience. Thus we can restate the axiom of science as follows: A scientific experiment is not complete until the results have been published and understood. Publication is no more than pressure waves unless the published paper is understood. Too many scientific papers fall silently in the woods.

5. 5)글의 밑줄 친 부분 중 어법, 혹은 문맥상 어휘의 쓰임 이 어색한 것을 모두 고르시오. 22

We all negotiate every day, whether we realise it or not. Yet few people ever learn how to negotiate. Those who do usually learn the traditional, win-lose negotiating style rather than an approach that is likely to result in a win-win agreement. This old-school, ① **corresponding** approach may be useful in a one-off negotiation where you will probably not deal with that person again. However, such ② **transitions** are becoming increasingly rare , because most of us deal with the ③ **same** people repeatedly — our spouses and children, our friends and colleagues, our customers and clients. In view of this, it's essential to achieve ④ **successive** results for ourselves and maintain a ⑤ **healthy** relationship with our negotiating partners at the same time. In today's interdependent world of business partnerships and long-term relationships, a win-win outcome is fast becoming the only acceptable result.

6. 6)글의 밑줄 친 부분 중 어법, 혹은 문맥상 어휘의 쓰임 이 어색한 것을 모두 고르시오. 23

The interaction of workers from different cultural backgrounds with the host ① **popularity** might increase productivity due ② **to** positive externalities like knowledge spillovers. This is only an advantage up to a certain degree. When the variety of backgrounds is too large, fractionalization may cause excessive transaction costs for communication, which may lower productivity. ③ **Diversity** not only impacts the labour market, but may also affect the quality of life in a location. A tolerant native population may value a multicultural city or region because of an increase in the range of available goods and services. On the other hand, diversity could be perceived as an unattractive feature if natives perceive it as a ④ **preservation** of what they consider to be their national identity . They might even discriminate against other ethnic groups and they might fear that social conflicts between different foreign nationalities are ⑤ **exported** into their own neighbourhood.

7. 7)글의 밑줄 친 부분 중 어법, 혹은 문맥상 어휘의 쓰임 이 어색한 것을 모두 고르시오. 24

We think we are shaping our buildings. But really, our buildings and development are also shaping us. One of the best examples of this is the oldest-known construction: the ornately carved rings of standing stones at Göbekli Tepe in Turkey. Before these ancestors got the idea to ① **elect** standing stones some 12,000 years ago, they were hunter-gatherers. It appears that the ② **erection** of the multiple rings of megalithic stones took so long, and so many successive generations, that these innovators were forced ③ **settling** down to complete the construction works. In the process , they became the first farming society on Earth. This is an early example of a society ④ **constructing** something that ends up radically ⑤ **to remake** the society itself. Things are not so different in our own time.

(.hwp) (.pdf) ➔ www.englishmygod.com

8. 8)글의 밑줄 친 부분 중 어법, 혹은 문맥상 어휘의 쓰임이 어색한 것을 모두 고르시오. 26

American jazz pianist Bill Evans was born in New Jersey in 1929. His early training was in classical music. At the age of six, he began receiving piano lessons, later adding flute and violin. He earned bachelor's degrees in piano and music education from Southeastern Louisiana College in 1950. He went on to serve in the army from 1951 to 1954 and played flute in the Fifth Army Band. After ① **serving** in the military, he studied ② **disposition** at the Mannes School of Music in New York. Composer George Russell ③ **administered** his playing and hired Evans to record and ④ **perform** his compositions. Evans became famous for recordings made from the late-1950s through the 1960s. He won his first Grammy Award in 1964 for his album Conversations with Myself. Evans' expressive piano works and his unique harmonic approach ⑤ **inspired** a whole generation of musicians.

9. 9)글의 밑줄 친 부분 중 어법, 혹은 문맥상 어휘의 쓰임이 어색한 것을 모두 고르시오. 29

There is a reason the title "Monday Morning Quarterback" ① **exists** . Just read the comments on social media from fans discussing the weekend's games, and you quickly see how many people believe they could play, coach, and manage sport teams ② **less** successfully than those on the field. This goes for the boardroom as well. Students and professionals with years of training and specialized degrees in sport business may also find ③ **them** being given advice on how to do their jobs from friends, family, or even total strangers without any ④ **expert** . Executives in sport management have decades of knowledge and experience in their respective fields. However, many of them face criticism from fans and community members telling them how to run their business. Very ⑤ **a few** people tell their doctor how to perform surgery or their accountant how to prepare their taxes, but many people provide feedback on how sport organizations should be managed.

10. 10)글의 밑줄 친 부분 중 어법, 혹은 문맥상 어휘의 쓰임이 어색한 것을 모두 고르시오. 30

While moving is difficult for everyone, it is particularly stressful for children. They ① **gain** their sense of security and may feel disoriented when their routine is disrupted and all that is familiar is taken away. Young children, ages 3-6, are particularly affected by a move. Their understanding at this stage is quite ② **literate** , and it is difficult for them to imagine beforehand a new home and their new room. Young children may have worries such as "Will I still be me in the new place"? and "Will my toys and bed come with us"? It is important to establish a balance between validating children's past experiences and focusing on helping them adjust to the new place. Children need to have opportunities to share their backgrounds in a way that ③ **excludes** their past as an important part of who they ④ **do** . This ⑤ **contributes** to building a sense of community, which is essential for all children, especially those in transition .

11. 11)글의 밑줄 친 부분 중 어법, 혹은 문맥상 어휘의 쓰임이 어색한 것을 모두 고르시오. 31

Many people are terrified to fly in airplanes. Often, this fear stems from a lack of control. The pilot is in control, not the passengers, and this lack of control instills fear. Many potential passengers are so afraid they choose to drive great distances to get to a ① **destiny** instead of flying. But their decision to drive is based solely on emotion, not logic. ② **Logic** says that statistically, the odds of dying in a car crash ③ **is** around 1 in 5,000, while the odds of dying in a plane crash are closer to 1 in 11 million. If you're going to take a risk , especially one that could possibly involve your well-being, wouldn't you want the odds ④ **against** your favor? However, most people choose the option that will cause them the ⑤ **most** amount of anxiety. Pay attention to the thoughts you have about taking the risk and make sure you're basing your decision on facts, not just feelings.

12. 12)글의 밑줄 친 부분 중 어법, 혹은 문맥상 어휘의 쓰임이 어색한 것을 모두 고르시오. 32

The famous primatologist Frans de Waal, of Emory University, says humans ① **overestimate** similarities between us and other animals as a way of maintaining our spot at the top of our imaginary ladder. Scientists, de Waal points out, can be some of the worst offenders — employing technical language to distance the other animals from us . They call "kissing" in chimps "mouth-to-mouth contact"; they call "friends" between primates "favorite affiliation partners"; they interpret evidence showing that crows and chimps can make tools as being somehow qualitatively different from the kind of toolmaking ② **said** to define humanity. If an animal can beat us at a cognitive task — like how certain bird species can remember the precise locations of thousands of seeds — they write it off as instinct , not ③ **instinct** . This and so many more tricks of language are what de Waal has ④ **termed** "linguistic castration". The way we use our tongues to ⑤ **empower** animals, the way we invent words to maintain our spot at the top.

13. 13)글의 밑줄 친 부분 중 어법, 혹은 문맥상 어휘의 쓰임이 어색한 것을 모두 고르시오. 33

A key to engagement and achievement is providing students ① **for** relevant texts they will be interested in. My scholarly work and my teaching ② **have been** deeply influenced by the work of Rosalie Fink. She interviewed twelve adults who were highly successful in their work, including a physicist, a biochemist, and a company CEO. All of them had dyslexia and had had significant problems with reading throughout their school years. While she expected to find that they had ③ **tried** reading and discovered ways to bypass it or compensate with other strategies for learning, she found the opposite. "To my surprise, I found that these dyslexics were enthusiastic readers...they rarely ④ **enjoyed** reading. On the contrary, they sought out books". The pattern Fink discovered was that all of her subjects had been passionate in some personal interest. The areas of interest included religion, math, business, science, history, and biography. What ⑤ **mattered** was that they read voraciously to find out more.

14. 14)글의 밑줄 친 부분 중 어법, 혹은 문맥상 어휘의 쓰임이 어색한 것을 모두 고르시오. 34

For many people, ability refers to ① **instinctive** competence, so they want everything they do to reflect how smart they are — writing a brilliant legal brief, getting the highest grade on a test, writing elegant computer code, saying something exceptionally wise or witty in a conversation. You could also ② **define** ability in terms of a particular skill or talent, such as how ③ **well** one plays the piano, learns a language, or serves a tennis ball. Some people focus on their ability to be attractive, entertaining , up on the ④ **latest** trends, or to have the newest gadgets. ⑤ **However** ability may be defined , a problem occurs when it is the sole determinant of one's self-worth. The performance becomes the only measure of the person; nothing else is taken into account. An outstanding performance means an outstanding person; an average performance means an average person. Period.

15. 15)글의 밑줄 친 부분 중 어법, 혹은 문맥상 어휘의 쓰임이 어색한 것을 모두 고르시오. 35

Sensory nerves have specialized endings in the tissues that ① **pick** up a particular sensation. If, for example, you step on a sharp object such as a pin, nerve endings in the skin will transmit the pain sensation up your leg, up and along the spinal cord to the brain. While the pain itself is unpleasant, it is in fact acting as a protective mechanism for the foot. Within the brain, nerves will connect to the area ② **what** controls speech, so that you may well shout 'ouch' or something rather less ③ **polite** . They will also connect to motor nerves that travel back down the spinal cord, and to the muscles in your leg that now ④ **contract** quickly to lift your foot away from the painful object. Sensory and motor nerves ⑤ **calm** almost all functions in the body — from the beating of the heart to the movement of the gut, sweating and just about everything else.

16. 16)글의 밑줄 친 부분 중 어법, 혹은 문맥상 어휘의 쓰임이 어색한 것을 모두 고르시오. 36

Maybe you've heard this joke: " How do you eat an elephant"? The answer is "one bite at a time". So, how do you "build" the Earth? That's simple, too: one atom at a time. Atoms are the basic building blocks of crystals, and since all rocks are ① **made** up of crystals, the more you know about atoms, the ② **well** . Crystals come in a variety of ③ **shape** that scientists call habits. Common crystal habits include squares, triangles, and six-sided hexagons. Usually crystals form when liquids ④ **cooled** , such as when you create ice cubes. Many times, crystals form in ways that do not allow for perfect shapes. If conditions are too cold, too hot, or there isn't enough source material, they can form strange, twisted shapes. But when conditions are right, we see beautiful displays. Usually, this involves a slow, steady environment ⑤ **which** the individual atoms have plenty of time to join and fit perfectly into what's known as the crystal lattice. This is the basic structure of atoms that is seen time after time.

17. 17)글의 밑줄 친 부분 중 어법, 혹은 문맥상 어휘의 쓰임이 어색한 것을 모두 고르시오. 37

When you pluck a guitar string it moves back and forth hundreds of times every second. Naturally, this movement is so ① **fastly** that you ② **cannot** see it — you just see the blurred outline of the moving string. Strings ③ **vibrate** in this way on their own make hardly any noise because strings are very thin and don't push much air about. But if you attach a string to a big hollow box (like a guitar body), then the vibration is amplified and the note is heard loud and clear. The vibration of the string is passed on to the wooden panels of the guitar body, which ④ **vibrates** back and forth at the same rate as the string. The vibration of the wood creates more powerful waves in the air pressure, which travel away from the guitar. When the waves ⑤ **reach** your eardrums they flex in and out the same number of times a second as the original string.

18. 18)글의 밑줄 친 부분 중 어법, 혹은 문맥상 어휘의 쓰임이 어색한 것을 모두 고르시오. 38

Boundaries between work and home are blurring as portable digital technology makes it increasingly possible to work anywhere, anytime. Individuals differ in how they like to manage their time to meet work and outside responsibilities. Some people prefer to ① **integrate** or segment roles so that boundary crossings are minimized . For example, these people might keep separate email accounts for work and family and try to conduct work at the workplace and take care of family matters only during breaks and non-work time. We've even noticed more of these " ② **integrator** " carrying two phones — one for work and one for personal use. ③ **Flexible** schedules work well for these individuals because they enable greater distinction between time at work and time in other roles. Other individuals prefer ④ **integrating** work and family roles all day long. This might ⑤ **entail** constantly trading text messages with children from the office, or monitoring emails at home and on vacation, rather than returning to work to find hundreds of messages in their inbox.

19. ¹⁹⁾글의 밑줄 친 부분 중 <u>어법, 혹은 문맥상 어휘의 쓰임이 어색한 것을 모두 고르시오.</u> ³⁹

A "complementary good" is a product that is often ① **consuming** alongside another product . For example, popcorn is a complementary good to a movie, while a travel pillow is a complementary good for a long plane journey. When the popularity of one product increases , the sales of its complementary good also ② **increase** . By producing goods that complement other products that are already (or about to be) popular, you can ③ **ensure** a steady stream of demand for your product. Some products enjoy perfect complementary status — they have to be consumed together , such as a lamp and a lightbulb. However, do not assume that a product is perfectly complementary, as customers may not be completely locked ④ **pit** to the product. For example, ⑤ **although** motorists may seem required to purchase gasoline to run their cars, they can switch to electric cars.

20. ²⁰⁾글의 밑줄 친 부분 중 <u>어법, 혹은 문맥상 어휘의 쓰임이 어색한 것을 모두 고르시오.</u> ⁴⁰

It's not news to anyone that we judge others based on their clothes. In general, studies that investigate these judgments find that people prefer clothing that matches expectations — surgeons in scrubs, little boys in blue — with one notable ① **exception** . A series of studies published in an article in June 2014 in the Journal of Consumer Research explored observers' reactions to people who broke established norms only slightly. In one scenario, a man at a black-tie affair was viewed as having higher status and competence when ② **wore** a red bow tie. The researchers also found that valuing ③ **uniformity** increased audience members' ratings of the status and competence of a professor who wore red sneakers while giving a lecture. The results suggest that people judge these slight ④ **deviations** from the norm as positive because they suggest that the individual is powerful enough to ⑤ **risk** the social costs of such behaviors.

21. ²¹⁾글의 밑줄 친 부분 중 <u>어법, 혹은 문맥상 어휘의 쓰임이 어색한 것을 모두 고르시오.</u> ⁴¹~⁴²

Claims that local food production cut greenhouse gas emissions by reducing the burning of transportation fuel are usually not well founded. Transport is the source of only 11 percent of greenhouse gas emissions within the food sector, so reducing the distance that food travels after it leaves the farm ① **be** far ② **more** important than reducing wasteful energy use on the farm. Food coming from a distance can actually be better for the climate, depending on how it was grown. For example, field-grown tomatoes shipped from Mexico in the winter months will have a ③ **bigger** carbon footprint than local winter tomatoes grown in a greenhouse. In the United Kingdom, lamb meat that travels 11,000 miles from New Zealand generates only one-quarter the carbon emissions per pound compared to British lamb because farmers in the United Kingdom ④ **raise** their animals on feed (which must be produced using fossil fuels) rather than on clover pastureland.

When food does travel, what matters most is not the distance traveled but the travel mode (surface versus air), and most of all the load size. Bulk loads of food can travel halfway around the world by ocean ⑤ **fright** with a smaller carbon footprint, per pound delivered, than foods traveling just a short distance but in much smaller loads. For example, 18-wheelers carry much larger loads than pickup trucks so they can move food 100 times as far while burning only one-third as much gas per pound of food delivered.

22. 22)글의 밑줄 친 부분 중 어법, 혹은 문맥상 어휘의 쓰임이 어색한 것을 모두 고르시오. 43~45

Long ago, an old man built a grand temple at the center of his village. People traveled to worship at the temple. So the old man made arrangements for food and accommodation inside the temple itself. He needed someone who could look after the temple, so he put up a notice: Manager needed. ① **Seeing** the notice, many people went to the old man. But he ② **returned to** all the applicants after interviews, telling them, "I need a qualified person for this work". The old man would sit on the roof of his house every morning, watching people go through the temple doors. One day, he saw a young man come to the temple. When that young man left the temple, the old man called him and asked, "Will you take care of this temple"? The young man was surprised by the offer and replied, "I have no experience ③ **is caring** for a temple. I'm not even educated". The old man smiled and said, "I don't want any educated man. I want a qualified person". Confused , the young man asked, "But why do you consider me a qualified person"? The old man replied, "I buried a brick on the path to the temple. I watched for many days as people tripped over that brick. No one thought to remove it. But you dug up that brick". The young man said, "I haven't done anything great. It's the duty of every human being to think about others. I only did my duty". The old man smiled and said, "Only people who ④ **knows** their duty and perform it ⑤ **are** qualified people".

2023 고1 9월 모의고사

❶ voca ❷ text ❸ [/] ❹ ____ ❺ quiz 1 ❻ quiz 2 ❼ quiz 3 ❽ quiz 4 ❾ quiz 5

1. 1)밑줄 부분 중 어법, 혹은 문맥상 어휘의 쓰임이 어색한 것을 올바르게 고쳐 쓰시오. (2개) [18]

Dear Professor Sanchez,

My name is Ellis Wight, and I'm the director of the Alexandria Science Museum. We are ① **held** a Chemistry Fair for local middle school students on Saturday, October 28. The goal of the fair is to encourage them ② **to be** interested in science through guided experiments. We are looking for college students who can help with the experiments ③ **during** the event. I am ④ **contacting** you to ask you to ⑤ **recommending** some students from the chemistry department at your college who you think ⑥ **are** ⑦ **qualified** for this job. With their help, I'm sure the participants will have a great experience. I look forward to ⑧ **hearing** from you soon.

Sincerely, Ellis Wight

기호   어색한 표현   올바른 표현

(   ) _____ ⇨ _____

(   ) _____ ⇨ _____

2. 2)밑줄 부분 중 어법, 혹은 문맥상 어휘의 쓰임이 어색한 것을 올바르게 고쳐 쓰시오. (11개) [19]

Gregg and I had been rock climbing since sunrise and had had no problems. So we took a risk. "Look, the first bolt is right there. I can definitely ① **climbing** out to it. Piece of ② **bread** ", I persuaded Gregg, minutes before I found ③ **me** pinned. It wasn't a piece of ④ **bread** . The rock was ⑤ **receptively** ⑥ **fertile** of handholds. I ⑦ **skillfully** moved back and forth ⑧ **cross** the cliff face and ended up with nowhere to go...but down. The bolt that would save my life, if I could get to it, was about two feet above my reach. My arms ⑨ **were trembled** from exhaustion. I looked at Gregg. My body froze with ⑩ **fight** from my neck down to my toes. Our rope was tied between us. If I fell, he ⑪ **would have fallen** with me.

기호   어색한 표현   올바른 표현

(   ) _____ ⇨ _____

(   ) _____ ⇨ _____

(   ) _____ ⇨ _____

(   ) _____ ⇨ _____

(   ) _____ ⇨ _____

(   ) _____ ⇨ _____

(   ) _____ ⇨ _____

(   ) _____ ⇨ _____

(   ) _____ ⇨ _____

(   ) _____ ⇨ _____

(   ) _____ ⇨ _____

(.hwp) (.pdf) ➜ www.englishmygod.com

3. ³⁾밑줄 부분 중 어법, 혹은 문맥상 어휘의 쓰임이 어색한 것을 올바르게 고쳐 쓰시오. (6개) [20]

We are always teaching our children something by our words and our actions. They learn from seeing. They learn from hearing and from overhearing. Children ① **deny** the values of their parents about the most important things in life. Our priorities and principles and our examples of good behavior can teach our children ② **took** the ③ **low** road when other roads look ④ **tempting** . Remember ⑤ **that** children do not learn the values that ⑥ **makes** up strong character simply by ⑦ **being told** about them. They learn by seeing the people around them ⑧ **act** on and ⑨ **uphold** those values in their daily lives. Therefore show your child good examples of life by your ⑩ **words** . In our daily lives, we can show our children ⑪ **what** we respect others. We can show them our compassion and concern ⑫ **when** others are suffering, and our own ⑬ **self-discipline** , courage and honesty as we make difficult decisions.

기호	어색한 표현		올바른 표현
( )	_____	⇨	_____
( )	_____	⇨	_____
( )	_____	⇨	_____
( )	_____	⇨	_____
( )	_____	⇨	_____
( )	_____	⇨	_____

4. ⁴⁾밑줄 부분 중 어법, 혹은 문맥상 어휘의 쓰임이 어색한 것을 올바르게 고쳐 쓰시오. (2개) [21]

Most people have no doubt ① **heard** this question: If a tree falls in the forest and there is no one there to hear it fall, ② **is** it make a sound? The correct answer is ③ **no** . Sound is more than pressure waves, and indeed there can be no sound ④ **without** a hearer. And similarly, scientific communication is a ⑤ **two-way** process. Just as a signal of any kind is ⑥ **useless** unless it is perceived, a published scientific paper (signal) is useless ⑦ **unless** it is both received and ⑧ **understands** by its ⑨ **intended** audience. Thus we can restate the axiom of science as follows: A scientific experiment is ⑩ **not complete** until the results have ⑪ **been published** and understood. Publication is no more than pressure waves unless the published paper is understood. Too many scientific papers fall ⑫ **silently** in the woods.

기호	어색한 표현		올바른 표현
( )	_____	⇨	_____
( )	_____	⇨	_____

5. 5)밑줄 부분 중 어법, 혹은 문맥상 어휘의 쓰임이 어색한 것을 올바르게 고쳐 쓰시오. (4개) [22]

We all negotiate every day, ① **whether** we realise it or not. Yet ② **few** people ever learn how to negotiate. Those who ③ **do** usually ④ **learns** the traditional, win-lose negotiating style rather than an approach that is likely to result ⑤ **in** a win-win agreement. This old-school, ⑥ **adversarial** approach may be useful in a one-off negotiation ⑦ **where** you will probably not deal with ⑧ **that** person again. However, such ⑨ **transitions** are becoming increasingly ⑩ **rare** , because most of us deal with the ⑪ **different** people repeatedly — our spouses and children, our friends and colleagues, our customers and clients. In view of this, it's essential to achieve ⑫ **successful** results for ourselves and maintain a ⑬ **healthy** relationship with our negotiating partners at the same time. In today's ⑭ **interdependent** world of business partnerships and long-term relationships, a win-win ⑮ **income** is fast becoming the only ⑯ **acceptable** result.

기호   어색한 표현   올바른 표현

(   ) _____ ⇨ _____

(   ) _____ ⇨ _____

(   ) _____ ⇨ _____

(   ) _____ ⇨ _____

6. 6)밑줄 부분 중 어법, 혹은 문맥상 어휘의 쓰임이 어색한 것을 올바르게 고쳐 쓰시오. (1개) [23]

The ① **interaction** of workers from different cultural backgrounds with the host ② **population** might ③ **increase** productivity due ④ **to** positive ⑤ **externalities** like knowledge spillovers. This is only an advantage up to a certain degree. When the variety of backgrounds ⑥ **is** too large, ⑦ **fractionalization** may cause excessive transaction costs for communication, ⑧ **that** may ⑨ **lower** productivity. ⑩ **Diversity** not only impacts the labour market, but may also ⑪ **affect** the quality of life in a location. A ⑫ **tolerant** native population may ⑬ **value** a multicultural city or region because of an increase in the range of available goods and services. On the other hand, diversity could be ⑭ **perceived** as an unattractive feature if natives ⑮ **perceive** it as a ⑯ **distortion** of what they consider to be their national ⑰ **identity** . They might even discriminate against other ethnic groups and they might fear that social conflicts between different foreign nationalities are ⑱ **imported** into their own neighbourhood.

기호   어색한 표현   올바른 표현

(   ) _____ ⇨ _____

(.hwp) (.pdf) ➔ www.englishmygod.com

7. 7)**밑줄 부분 중 어법, 혹은 문맥상 어휘의 쓰임이 어색한 것을 올바르게 고쳐 쓰시오. (10개)** [24]

We think we are shaping our buildings. But really, our buildings and development are also shaping us. One of the best ① **example** of this is the oldest-known construction: the ornately ② **carving** rings of standing stones at Göbekli Tepe in Turkey. Before these ancestors got the idea to ③ **elect** standing stones some 12,000 years ago, they were hunter-gatherers. It appears ④ **which** the ⑤ **erection** of the multiple rings of megalithic stones took so long, and so many ⑥ **successful** generations, ⑦ **which** these innovators were forced ⑧ **settling** down to ⑨ **complete** the construction works. In the ⑩ **procession** , they became the first farming society on Earth. This is an early example of a society ⑪ **constructs** something that ends up radically ⑫ **remaking** the society itself. Things are not so ⑬ **similar** in our own time.

기호	어색한 표현		올바른 표현
( )	_____	⇨	_____
( )	_____	⇨	_____
( )	_____	⇨	_____
( )	_____	⇨	_____
( )	_____	⇨	_____
( )	_____	⇨	_____
( )	_____	⇨	_____
( )	_____	⇨	_____
( )	_____	⇨	_____
( )	_____	⇨	_____

8. 8)**밑줄 부분 중 어법, 혹은 문맥상 어휘의 쓰임이 어색한 것을 올바르게 고쳐 쓰시오. (1개)** [26]

American jazz pianist Bill Evans was born in New Jersey in 1929. His early training was in classical music. At the age of six, he began receiving piano lessons, later ① **adding** flute and violin. He earned bachelor's degrees in piano and music education from Southeastern Louisiana College in 1950. He went on to serve in the army from 1951 to 1954 and played flute in the Fifth Army Band. After ② **serving** in the military, he studied ③ **composition** at the Mannes School of Music in New York. Composer George Russell ④ **admired** his playing and hired Evans to record and ⑤ **perform** his compositions. Evans became famous for recordings ⑥ **are made** from the late-1950s through the 1960s. He won his first Grammy Award in 1964 for his album Conversations with Myself. Evans' expressive piano works and his unique harmonic approach ⑦ **inspired** a whole generation of musicians.

기호	어색한 표현		올바른 표현
( )	_____	⇨	_____

9. 9)밑줄 부분 중 어법, 혹은 문맥상 어휘의 쓰임이 어색한 것을 올바르게 고쳐 쓰시오. (7개) [29]

There is a reason the title "Monday Morning Quarterback" ① **exists** . Just read the comments on social media from fans ② **discussing about** the weekend's games, and you quickly see how many people believe they could play, coach, and manage sport teams ③ **less** successfully than those on the field. This goes for the boardroom as well. Students and professionals with years of training and specialized degrees in sport business may also find ④ **them** ⑤ **giving** ⑥ **advice** on how to do their jobs from friends, family, or even total strangers without any ⑦ **expert** . Executives in sport management have decades of knowledge and experience in their ⑧ **relative** fields. However, many of them face ⑨ **approval** from fans and community members telling them how to run their business. Very ⑩ **few** people tell their doctor how to perform surgery or their accountant how to prepare their taxes, but many people provide feedback on how sport organizations should be managed.

기호	어색한 표현		올바른 표현
(　)	＿＿＿＿＿＿	⇨	＿＿＿＿＿＿
(　)	＿＿＿＿＿＿	⇨	＿＿＿＿＿＿
(　)	＿＿＿＿＿＿	⇨	＿＿＿＿＿＿
(　)	＿＿＿＿＿＿	⇨	＿＿＿＿＿＿
(　)	＿＿＿＿＿＿	⇨	＿＿＿＿＿＿
(　)	＿＿＿＿＿＿	⇨	＿＿＿＿＿＿
(　)	＿＿＿＿＿＿	⇨	＿＿＿＿＿＿

10. 10)밑줄 부분 중 어법, 혹은 문맥상 어휘의 쓰임이 어색한 것을 올바르게 고쳐 쓰시오. (2개) [30]

While moving is difficult for everyone, it is particularly ① **stressful** for children. They ② **gain** their sense of security and may feel ③ **disoriented** when their routine is ④ **disrupted** and all that is familiar is taken away. Young children, ages 3-6, are particularly ⑤ **affected** by a move. Their understanding at this stage is quite ⑥ **literal** , and it is difficult for them to imagine ⑦ **afterward** a new home and their new room. Young children may have worries such as "Will I still be me in the new place"? and "Will my toys and bed come with us"? It is important to establish a balance between ⑧ **validating** children's past experiences and focusing on helping them adjust to the new place. Children need to have opportunities to share their backgrounds in a way that ⑨ **respects** their past as an important part of who they ⑩ **are** . This ⑪ **contributes** to building a sense of community, which is essential for all children, especially those in ⑫ **transition** .

기호	어색한 표현		올바른 표현
(　)	＿＿＿＿＿＿	⇨	＿＿＿＿＿＿
(　)	＿＿＿＿＿＿	⇨	＿＿＿＿＿＿

(.hwp) (.pdf) ➜ www.englishmygod.com

11. 11)**밑줄 부분 중 어법, 혹은 문맥상 어휘의 쓰임이 어색한 것을 올바르게 고쳐 쓰시오. (7개)** [31]

Many people are ① **terrifying** to fly in airplanes. Often, this fear stems from a ② **lack** of control. The pilot is in control, not the passengers, and this lack of control ③ **installs** fear. Many potential passengers are so afraid they choose to drive great distances to get to a ④ **destination** instead of flying. But their decision to drive is based solely on emotion, not logic. ⑤ **Emotion** says that statistically, the odds of dying in a car crash ⑥ **are** around 1 in 5,000, while the odds of dying in a plane crash ⑦ **are** closer to 1 in 11 million. If you're going to take ⑧ **a risk** , especially ⑨ **it** that could possibly involve your well-being, wouldn't you want the odds ⑩ **against** your favor? However, most people choose the option that will cause them the ⑪ **least** amount of anxiety. Pay attention to the thoughts you ⑫ **have them** about taking the risk and make sure you're ⑬ **based on** your decision on facts, not just feelings.

기호	어색한 표현		올바른 표현
( )	_____	⇨	_____
( )	_____	⇨	_____
( )	_____	⇨	_____
( )	_____	⇨	_____
( )	_____	⇨	_____
( )	_____	⇨	_____
( )	_____	⇨	_____

12. 12)**밑줄 부분 중 어법, 혹은 문맥상 어휘의 쓰임이 어색한 것을 올바르게 고쳐 쓰시오. (8개)** [32]

The famous primatologist Frans de Waal, of Emory University, says humans ① **downplay** similarities between us and other animals as a way of ② **abandoning** our spot at the top of our imaginary ladder. Scientists, de Waal points out, can be some of the worst ③ **offenders** — employing technical language to ④ **distance** the other animals from us . They call "kissing" in chimps "mouth-to-mouth contact"; they call "friends" between primates "favorite ⑤ **affliction** partners"; they interpret evidence showing that crows and chimps can make tools as being somehow ⑥ **qualitative** different from the kind of toolmaking ⑦ **is said** to define humanity. If an animal can beat us at a cognitive task — like how ⑧ **certain** bird species can remember the precise locations of thousands of seeds — they write it off as ⑨ **intelligence** , not ⑩ **instinct** . This and so many more tricks of language ⑪ **is** what de Waal has ⑫ **termed** "linguistic castration". The way we use our tongues to ⑬ **empower** animals, the way we invent words to ⑭ **maintain** our spot at the top.

기호	어색한 표현		올바른 표현
( )	_____	⇨	_____
( )	_____	⇨	_____
( )	_____	⇨	_____
( )	_____	⇨	_____
( )	_____	⇨	_____
( )	_____	⇨	_____
( )	_____	⇨	_____
( )	_____	⇨	_____

13. ¹³⁾**밑줄 부분 중 어법, 혹은 문맥상 어휘의 쓰임이 어색한 것을 올바르게 고쳐 쓰시오. (3개)** ³³

A key to engagement and achievement is providing students ① **with** relevant texts they will be interested in. My scholarly work and my teaching ② **have been** deeply influenced by the work of Rosalie Fink. She interviewed twelve adults who were highly successful in their work, including a physicist, a biochemist, and a company CEO. All of them had dyslexia and had had significant problems with reading throughout their school years. ③ **While** she expected to ④ **find** that they had ⑤ **tried** reading and discovered ways to bypass it or compensate with other strategies for learning, she found the opposite. "To my surprise, I found that these dyslexics were ⑥ **enthusiastic** readers...they rarely ⑦ **avoided** reading. On the contrary, they sought out books". The pattern Fink discovered was ⑧ **that** all of her subjects had been passionate in some personal interest. The areas of interest included religion, math, business, science, history, and biography. What ⑨ **is mattered** was that they read ⑩ **modestly** to find out more.

기호	어색한 표현		올바른 표현
( )	_____	⇨	_____
( )	_____	⇨	_____
( )	_____	⇨	_____

14. ¹⁴⁾**밑줄 부분 중 어법, 혹은 문맥상 어휘의 쓰임이 어색한 것을 올바르게 고쳐 쓰시오. (2개)** ³⁴

For many people, ability refers to ① **intellectual** competence, so they want everything they do ② **reflect** how smart they ③ **are** — writing a brilliant legal brief, getting the highest grade on a test, writing elegant computer code, saying something exceptionally wise or witty in a conversation. You could also ④ **define** ability in terms of a particular skill or talent, such as how ⑤ **well** one plays the piano, learns a language, or serves a tennis ball. Some people focus on their ability to be attractive, ⑥ **entertaining** , up on the ⑦ **last** trends, or to have the newest gadgets. ⑧ **However** ability may be ⑨ **defined** , a problem ⑩ **occurs** when it is the sole ⑪ **determinant** of one's self-worth. The performance becomes the only measure of the person; nothing else is taken into account. An outstanding performance means an outstanding person; an average performance means an average person. Period.

기호	어색한 표현		올바른 표현
( )	_____	⇨	_____
( )	_____	⇨	_____

15. 15)**밑줄 부분 중 어법, 혹은 문맥상 어휘의 쓰임이 어색한 것을 올바르게 고쳐 쓰시오. (7개)** 35

Sensory nerves have specialized endings in the tissues that ① **picks** up a particular sensation. If, for example, you step on a sharp object such as a pin, nerve endings in the skin will ② **transport** the pain sensation up your leg, up and along the spinal cord to the brain. ③ **While** the pain itself is unpleasant, it is in fact acting as a protective mechanism for the foot. Within the brain, nerves will connect to the area ④ **what** controls speech, so that you ⑤ **may as well** shout 'ouch' or something rather less ⑥ **politely** . They will also connect to motor nerves that travel back down the spinal cord, and to the muscles in your leg that now ⑦ **contact** quickly to lift your foot away from the painful object. Sensory and motor nerves ⑧ **calm** almost all functions in the body — from the beating of the heart to the movement of the gut, sweating and just about everything else.

기호   어색한 표현   올바른 표현

(   ) _____ ⇨ _____

(   ) _____ ⇨ _____

(   ) _____ ⇨ _____

(   ) _____ ⇨ _____

(   ) _____ ⇨ _____

(   ) _____ ⇨ _____

(   ) _____ ⇨ _____

16. 16)**밑줄 부분 중 어법, 혹은 문맥상 어휘의 쓰임이 어색한 것을 올바르게 고쳐 쓰시오. (9개)** 36

Maybe you've heard this joke: " ① **What** do you eat an elephant"? The answer is "one bite at a time". So, how do you "build" the Earth? That's simple, too: one atom at a time. Atoms are the basic building blocks of crystals, and since all rocks are ② **consisted** up of crystals, the more you know about atoms, the ③ **well** . Crystals come in a variety of ④ **shape** that scientists call habits. Common crystal habits include squares, triangles, and six-sided hexagons. Usually crystals form when liquids ⑤ **cooled** , such as when you create ice cubes. Many times, crystals form in ways ⑥ **how** do not allow for perfect shapes. If conditions are too cold, too hot, or there isn't enough source material, they can form strange, twisted shapes. But when conditions are right, we see beautiful displays. Usually, this involves a slow, ⑦ **drastic** environment ⑧ **which** the individual atoms have plenty of time to join and fit perfectly into what's known as the crystal lattice. This is the basic structure of atoms that ⑨ **are** seen time after time.

기호   어색한 표현   올바른 표현

(   ) _____ ⇨ _____

(   ) _____ ⇨ _____

(   ) _____ ⇨ _____

(   ) _____ ⇨ _____

(   ) _____ ⇨ _____

(   ) _____ ⇨ _____

(   ) _____ ⇨ _____

(   ) _____ ⇨ _____

(   ) _____ ⇨ _____

17. 17)**밑줄 부분 중 어법, 혹은 문맥상 어휘의 쓰임이 어색한 것을 올바르게 고쳐 쓰시오. (9개)** 37

When you pluck a guitar string it moves back and forth hundreds of times every second. Naturally, this movement is so ① **fast** that you ② **can** see it — you just see the blurred outline of the moving string. Strings ③ **vibrate** in this way on their own make ④ **hard** any noise because strings are very thin and don't push much air about. But if you ⑤ **detach** a string to a big hollow box (like a guitar body), then the vibration is ⑥ **simplified** and the note is heard loud and clear. The vibration of the string is passed on to the wooden panels of the guitar body, which ⑦ **vibrates** back and forth at the same rate as the string. The vibration of the wood creates more powerful waves in the air pressure, ⑧ **that** travel away from the guitar. When the waves ⑨ **will reach** your eardrums they flex in and out the same number of ⑩ **time** a second as the original string.

기호	어색한 표현		올바른 표현
( )	_____	⇨	_____
( )	_____	⇨	_____
( )	_____	⇨	_____
( )	_____	⇨	_____
( )	_____	⇨	_____
( )	_____	⇨	_____
( )	_____	⇨	_____
( )	_____	⇨	_____
( )	_____	⇨	_____

18. 18)**밑줄 부분 중 어법, 혹은 문맥상 어휘의 쓰임이 어색한 것을 올바르게 고쳐 쓰시오. (5개)** 38

Boundaries between work and home ① **are** blurring as ② **portable** digital technology makes ③ **it** increasingly possible to work anywhere, anytime. Individuals differ in how they like to manage their time to meet work and outside responsibilities. Some people prefer to ④ **integrate** or segment roles so that boundary crossings are ⑤ **maximized** . For example, these people might keep separate email accounts for work and family and try to conduct work at the workplace and take care of family matters only ⑥ **during** breaks and non-work time. We've even noticed more of these " ⑦ **integrator** " carrying two phones — one for work and one for personal use. ⑧ **Fixed** schedules work well for these individuals because they enable greater distinction between time at work and time in other roles. Other individuals prefer ⑨ **integrating** work and family roles all day long. This might ⑩ **refuse** constantly trading text messages with children from the office, or monitoring emails at home and on vacation, rather than returning to work to find hundreds of messages in their inbox.

기호	어색한 표현		올바른 표현
( )	_____	⇨	_____
( )	_____	⇨	_____
( )	_____	⇨	_____
( )	_____	⇨	_____
( )	_____	⇨	_____

(.hwp) (.pdf) ➔ www.englishmygod.com

19. ¹⁹⁾밑줄 부분 중 어법, 혹은 문맥상 어휘의 쓰임이 어색한 것을 올바르게 고쳐 쓰시오. (1개) ³⁹

A "complementary good" is a product that is often ① **consumed** alongside another ② **product** . For example, popcorn is a complementary good to a movie, while a travel pillow is a complementary good for a long plane journey. When the ③ **popularity** of one product ④ **increases** , the sales of ⑤ **its** complementary good also ⑥ **increase** . By producing goods that ⑦ **complement** other products that are already (or about to be) popular, you can ⑧ **disclaim** a steady stream of demand for your product. Some products enjoy perfect complementary ⑨ **status** — they have to be consumed ⑩ **together** , such as a lamp and a lightbulb. However, do not assume that a product is perfectly complementary, as customers may not be completely locked ⑪ **in** to the product. For example, ⑫ **although** motorists may seem required to purchase gasoline to run their cars, they can ⑬ **switch** to electric cars.

기호   어색한 표현   올바른 표현

( ) _____ ⇨ _____

20. ²⁰⁾밑줄 부분 중 어법, 혹은 문맥상 어휘의 쓰임이 어색한 것을 올바르게 고쳐 쓰시오. (2개) ⁴⁰

It's not news to anyone that we judge others based on their clothes. In general, studies that investigate these judgments find ① **which** people prefer clothing ② **that** matches expectations — surgeons in scrubs, little boys in blue — with one notable ③ **exception** . A series of studies published in an article in June 2014 in the Journal of Consumer Research explored observers' reactions to people who broke established ④ **norms** only slightly. In one scenario, a man at a black-tie affair was viewed as having ⑤ **higher** status and competence when ⑥ **wearing** a red bow tie. The researchers also found that valuing ⑦ **uniqueness** increased audience members' ratings of the status and competence of a professor who wore red sneakers while giving a lecture. The results suggest that people judge these slight ⑧ **unity** from the ⑨ **norm** as ⑩ **positive** because they suggest that the individual is powerful enough to ⑪ **risk** the social costs of such behaviors.

기호   어색한 표현   올바른 표현

( ) _____ ⇨ _____

( ) _____ ⇨ _____

21. 21)밑줄 부분 중 <u>어법, 혹은 문맥상 어휘</u>의 쓰임이 어색한 것을 올바르게 고쳐 쓰시오. **(14개)** 41~42

Claims that local food production ① **<u>cut</u>** greenhouse gas emissions by reducing the burning of ② **transparency** fuel ③ **<u>is</u>** usually not well founded. Transport is the source of only 11 percent of greenhouse gas emissions within the food sector, so ④ **<u>reducing</u>** the distance that food travels after it leaves the farm ⑤ **<u>be</u>** far ⑥ **<u>more</u>** important than reducing wasteful energy use on the farm. Food coming from a distance can actually be ⑦ **<u>worse</u>** for the climate, depending on how it was grown. For example, field-grown tomatoes shipped from Mexico in the winter months will have a ⑧ **<u>smaller</u>** carbon footprint than local winter tomatoes ⑨ **<u>growing</u>** in a greenhouse. In the United Kingdom, lamb meat that travels 11,000 miles from New Zealand ⑩ **<u>generating</u>** only one-quarter the carbon emissions per pound compared to British lamb because farmers in the United Kingdom ⑪ **<u>rise</u>** their animals on feed (which must be produced using fossil fuels) rather than on clover pastureland.

When food ⑫ **<u>do</u>** travel, what matters most is not the distance ⑬ **<u>traveling</u>** but the travel mode (surface versus air), and most of all the load size. Bulk loads of food can travel halfway around the world by ocean ⑭ **<u>freight</u>** with a ⑮ **<u>bigger</u>** carbon footprint, per pound delivered, than foods ⑯ **<u>travel</u>** just a ⑰ **<u>long</u>** distance but in ⑱ **<u>very</u>** smaller loads. For example, 18-wheelers carry much larger loads than pickup trucks so they can move food 100 times as far while burning only one-third as ⑲ **<u>much</u>** gas per pound of food delivered.

기호	어색한 표현	올바른 표현
(　)	_____ ⇨	_____
(　)	_____ ⇨	_____
(　)	_____ ⇨	_____
(　)	_____ ⇨	_____
(　)	_____ ⇨	_____
(　)	_____ ⇨	_____
(　)	_____ ⇨	_____
(　)	_____ ⇨	_____
(　)	_____ ⇨	_____
(　)	_____ ⇨	_____
(　)	_____ ⇨	_____
(　)	_____ ⇨	_____
(　)	_____ ⇨	_____
(　)	_____ ⇨	_____

22. 22)밑줄 부분 중 <u>어법, 혹은 문맥상 어휘의 쓰임이 어색한 것을 올바르게 고쳐 쓰시오. (4개)</u> ^{43~45}

Long ago, an old man built a grand temple at the center of his village. People traveled to worship at the temple. So the old man made arrangements for food and accommodation inside the temple itself. He needed someone ① **whom** could look after the temple, so he put up a notice: Manager needed. ② **Seen** the notice, many people went to the old man. But he ③ **returned** all the ④ **applicants** after interviews, ⑤ **telling** them, "I need a qualified person for this work". The old man would ⑥ **sit** on the roof of his house every morning, watching people go through the temple doors. One day, he saw a young man come to the temple. When that young man left the temple, the old man called him and asked, "Will you take care of this temple"? The young man was ⑦ **surprising** the offer and replied, "I have no experience ⑧ **caring** for a temple. I'm not even educated". The old man smiled and said, "I don't want any educated man. I want a qualified person". ⑨ **Confused** , the young man asked, "But why do you consider ⑩ **me** a qualified person"? The old man replied, "I buried a brick on the path to the temple. I watched for many days as people tripped over that brick. No one thought to remove it. But you dug up that brick". The young man said, "I haven't done ⑪ **anything** great. It's the duty of every human being to think about others. I only did my duty". The old man smiled and said, "Only people who ⑫ **know** their duty and perform it ⑬ **is** qualified people".

기호	어색한 표현		올바른 표현
( )	_____	⇨	_____
( )	_____	⇨	_____
( )	_____	⇨	_____
( )	_____	⇨	_____

2023 고1 9월 모의고사

❶ voca ❷ text ❸ [/] ❹ ____ ❺ quiz 1 ❻ quiz 2 ❼ quiz 3 ❽ quiz 4 ⑨ quiz 5

☑ **다음 글을 읽고 물음에 답하시오.** (2023_고1_09_18번)

Dear Professor Sanchez, My name is Ellis Wight, and I'm the ^{관장} _____ of the Alexandria Science Museum. We are ^{개최하다} _____ a Chemistry Fair for local middle school students on Saturday, October 28. The ^{목적} ____ of the fair is to ^{장려하다} _____ them to be interested in science through ^{안내적} _____ experiments. (가) <u>저희는 행사 기간 동안 실험을 도와줄 수 있는 대학생을 모집하고자 합니다.</u> I am ^{연락하다} _____ you to ask you to ^{추천하다} _____ some students from the chemistry department at your college who you think are ^{적합한} _____ for this job. With their help, I'm sure the ^{참가자들} _____ will have a great experience. I look forward to hearing from you soon. Sincerely, Ellis Wight

1. 1)힌트를 참고하여 각 <u>빈칸에 알맞은</u> 단어를 쓰시오.

2. 2)위 글에 주어진 (가)의 한글과 같은 의미를 가지도록, 각각의 주어진 단어들을 알맞게 배열하시오.

(가) the event. / with / are / college / help / experiments / We / who / can / for / students / looking / the / during

☑ **다음 글을 읽고 물음에 답하시오.** (2023_고1_09_19번)

ⓐ <u>Gregg and I had had rock climbing since sunrise and had been no problems.</u> So we took a ^{위험} ____. "Look, the first bolt is right there. I can definitely ^{올라가다} _____ to it. Piece of cake", I ^{설득하다} _____ Gregg, minutes before I found myself ^{꼼짝 못하게 되었다} _____. It wasn't a piece of cake. The rock was ^{믿을수 없게도} _____ barren of handholds. I ^{너를게} _____ moved back and forth across the cliff face and ended up with nowhere to go...but down. (가) <u>만약 내가 거기까지 갈 수 있다면, 내 목숨을 구해줄 볼트는 손이 닿을 수 있는 곳에서 약 2피트 위에 있었다.</u> My arms ^{떨렸다} _____ from ^{피로} _____. I looked at Gregg. My body froze with ^{공포} _____ from my neck down to my toes. Our rope was tied between us. If I fell, he would fall with me.

3. 3)힌트를 참고하여 각 <u>빈칸에 알맞은</u> 단어를 쓰시오.

4. 4)밑줄 친 ⓐ에서, 어법 혹은 문맥상 어색한 부분을 찾아 올바르게 고쳐 쓰시오.

   ⓐ   잘못된 표현   바른 표현

   (   ) ⇨ (   )

   (   ) ⇨ (   )

5. 5)위 글에 주어진 (가)의 한글과 같은 의미를 가지도록, 각각의 주어진 단어들을 알맞게 배열하시오.

(가) to / The +bolt / get / my / I / if / it, / about / two / feet / above / life, / reach. / could / save / would / that / was / my

(.hwp) (.pdf) ➜ www.englishmygod.com

☑ 다음 글을 읽고 물음에 답하시오. (2023_고1_09_20번)

We are always teaching our children something by our words and our actions. They learn from seeing. They learn from hearing and from ^{우연히 듣는다} _____. Children ^{공유하다} _____ the ^{가치} _____ of their parents about the most important things in life. Our ^{우선순위} _____ and ^{원칙} _____ and our examples of good behavior can teach our children to take the high road when other roads look ^{유혹적} _____. ⓐ <u>Remember that children do not learn the values what make up strong character simply by had told about them.</u> (가) <u>그들은 그들 주변 사람들이 그들의 일상생활에서 그러한 가치를 좇아 '행동'하고 '유지'하는 것을 봄으로써 배운다.</u> Therefore show your child good examples of life by your action. In our daily lives, we can show our children that we ^{존중하다} _____ others. We can show them our ^{연민} _____ and ^{걱정} _____ when others are ^{괴로움} _____, and our own ^{자제력} _____, courage and honesty as we make difficult decisions

6. 6)힌트를 참고하여 각 빈칸에 알맞은 단어를 쓰시오.

7. 7)밑줄 친 ⓐ에서, 어법 혹은 문맥상 어색한 부분을 찾아 올바르게 고쳐 쓰시오.

    ⓐ   잘못된 표현   바른 표현

    (   ) ⇨ (   )

    (   ) ⇨ (   )

8. 8)위 글에 주어진 (가)의 한글과 같은 의미를 가지도록, 각각의 주어진 단어들을 알맞게 배열하시오.

(가) act / lives. / values / those / them / daily / seeing / their / uphold / They / on / in / around / learn / and / by / the people

☑ 다음 글을 읽고 물음에 답하시오. (2023_고1_09_21번)

Most people have no ^{의심} _____ heard this question: If a tree falls in the forest and there is no one there to hear it fall, does it make a sound? The correct answer is no. Sound is more than ^{압력파} _____, and indeed there can be no sound without a ^{청취자} _____. And similarly, scientific communication is a ^{양방향} _____ ^{과정} _____. Just as a signal of any kind is useless unless it is ^{감지되다} _____, a published scientific paper (signal) is useless unless it is both received and understood by its ^{의도된 독자} _____. Thus we can ^{재진술하다} _____ the ^{이치} _____ of science as follows: (가) <u>과학 실험은 결과가 출판되고 '그리고 이해될' 때까지 완성되지 않는다.</u> Publication is no more than ^{압력파} _____ unless the published paper is understood. Too many scientific papers fall silently in the woods.

9. 9)힌트를 참고하여 각 빈칸에 알맞은 단어를 쓰시오.

10. 10)위 글에 주어진 (가)의 한글과 같은 의미를 가지도록, 각각의 주어진 단어들을 알맞게 배열하시오.

(가) and / been / is / experiment / understood. / until / A / not / published / the results / have / scientific / complete

☑ **다음 글을 읽고 물음에 답하시오.** (2023_고1_09_22번)

We all negotiate every day, whether we realise it or not. Yet few people ever learn how to ^{협상하다} _____. ⓐ <u>Those who do usually learning the traditional, win-lose negotiating style rather than an approach that is likely to resulting in a win-win agreement.</u> This old-school, ^{적대적인} _____ approach may be useful in a ^{일회성} _____ negotiation where you will probably not deal with that person again. However, such ^{거래} _____ are becoming increasingly rare, because most of us deal with the same people repeatedly — our ^{배우자} _____ and children, our friends and colleagues, our customers and clients. (가) <u>우리 자신을 위해 성공적인 결과를 얻어내는 동시에 협상 파트너들과 건전한 관계를 유지하는 것이 중요하다.</u> In today's interdependent world of business partnerships and ^{장기적} _____ relationships, a win-win ^{결과} _____ is fast becoming the only ^{받아들일 수 있는} _____ result.

11. ¹¹⁾힌트를 참고하여 각 빈칸에 알맞은 단어를 쓰시오.

12. ¹²⁾밑줄 친 ⓐ에서, 어법 혹은 문맥상 어색한 부분을 찾아 올바르게 고쳐 쓰시오.

    ⓐ 　　　잘못된 표현　　　　　　　바른 표현

    (　　　　　　　) ⇨ (　　　　　　　　)

    (　　　　　　　) ⇨ (　　　　　　　　)

13. ¹³⁾위 글에 주어진 (가)의 한글과 같은 의미를 가지도록, 각각의 주어진 단어들을 알맞게 배열하시오.

(가) this, / for / maintain / it's / successful / negotiating / with / partners / achieve / of / time. / In / at / the　　same / our / and / relationship / results / to / ourselves / a healthy / essential / view

☑ **다음 글을 읽고 물음에 답하시오.** (2023_고1_09_23번)

The interaction of workers from different ^{문화적 배경} _____ with the ^{현지 주민} _____ might increase ^{생산성} _____ due to positive ^{외부효과} _____ like knowledge ^{파급} _____. This is only an advantage up to a certain degree. When the variety of backgrounds is too large, ^{분열} _____ may cause ^{과도한} _____ ^{거래 비용} _____ for communication, which may lower productivity. (가) <u>다양성은 노동 시장에 영향을 줄 뿐만 아니라 한 지역의 삶의 질에도 영향을 미칠 수 있다.</u> A tolerant native population may value a multicultural city or region because of an increase in the ^{범위} _____ of available goods and services. ⓐ <u>On the other hand, diversity could perceive as an unattractive feature if natives have perceived it as a distortion of what they consider to be their national identity. They might even be discriminated against other ethnic groups and they might be feared that social conflicts between different foreign nationalities import into their own neighbourhood.</u>

14. ¹⁴⁾힌트를 참고하여 각 빈칸에 알맞은 단어를 쓰시오.

(.hwp) (.pdf) → www.englishmygod.com

15. 15)밑줄 친 ⓐ에서, 어법 혹은 문맥상 어색한 부분을 찾아 올바르게 고쳐 쓰시오.

ⓐ　　　잘못된 표현　　　　　바른 표현

(　　　　　　　　) ⇨ (　　　　　　　　)

(　　　　　　　　) ⇨ (　　　　　　　　)

(　　　　　　　　) ⇨ (　　　　　　　　)

(　　　　　　　　) ⇨ (　　　　　　　　)

(　　　　　　　　) ⇨ (　　　　　　　　)

16. 16)위 글에 주어진 (가)의 한글과 같은 의미를 가지도록, 각각의 주어진 단어들을 알맞게 배열하시오.

(가) life / affect / a location. / but / the labour market, / the quality / impacts / also / of / Diversity / not / may / in / only

☑ **다음 글을 읽고 물음에 답하시오.** (2023_고1_09_24번)

ⓐ We think we have been shaping our buildings. But really, our buildings and development are also have shaped us. One of the best examples of this is the oldest-known construction: the ^{화려하게} _____ carved rings of standing stones at Göbekli Tepe in Turkey. Before these ancestors got the idea to ^{세우다} _____ standing stones some 12,000 years ago, they were ^{수렵 채집인} _____. It appears that the erection of the multiple rings of ^{거석} _____ took so long, and so many ^{잇따르다} _____ generations, that these ^{혁신가} _____ were forced to ^{정착하다} _____ to complete the construction works. In the process, they became the first farming society on Earth. (가) 이것은 결국 사회 자체를 근본적으로 재구성하는 무언가를 건설하는 사회의 초기 예이다. Things are not so different in our own time.

17. 17)힌트를 참고하여 각 빈칸에 알맞은 단어를 쓰시오.

18. 18)밑줄 친 ⓐ에서, 어법 혹은 문맥상 어색한 부분을 찾아 올바르게 고쳐 쓰시오.

ⓐ　　　잘못된 표현　　　　　바른 표현

(　　　　　　　　) ⇨ (　　　　　　　　)

(　　　　　　　　) ⇨ (　　　　　　　　)

19. 19)위 글에 주어진 (가)의 한글과 같은 의미를 가지도록, 각각의 주어진 단어들을 알맞게 배열하시오.

(가) something / an / a society / constructing / radically / that / is / of / early / remaking / ends / the society / up / This / itself. / example

☑ **다음 글을 읽고 물음에 답하시오.** (2023_고1_09_26번)

ⓐ <u>American jazz pianist Bill Evans had born in New Jersey in 1929. His early training be in classical music. At the age of six, he began have received piano lessons, later adding flute and violin.</u> He earned ^{학사학위} _____ in piano and music education from Southeastern Louisiana College in 1950. He went on to serve in the ^{군대} _____ from 1951 to 1954 and played flute in the Fifth Army Band. After serving in the military, he studied ^{작곡} _____ at the Mannes School of Music in New York. Composer George Russell ^{감탄하다} _____ his playing and ^{고용하다} _____ Evans to record and perform his compositions. (가) <u>Evans는 1950년대 후반부터 1960년대 동안에 만들어진 음반으로 유명해졌다.</u> He won his first Grammy Award in 1964 for his album Conversations with Myself. Evans' ^{표현이 풍부한} _____ piano works and his unique harmonic approach ^{영감을 주다} _____ a whole ^{세대} _____ of musicians.

20. 20)힌트를 참고하여 각 빈칸에 알맞은 단어를 쓰시오.

21. 21)밑줄 친 ⓐ에서, 어법 혹은 문맥상 어색한 부분을 찾아 올바르게 고쳐 쓰시오.

ⓐ	잘못된 표현		바른 표현
(	)	⇨ (	)
(	)	⇨ (	)
(	)	⇨ (	)

22. 22)위 글에 주어진 (가)의 한글과 같은 의미를 가지도록, 각각의 주어진 단어들을 알맞게 배열하시오.

(가) recordings / the late-1950s / from / Evans / famous / through / made / for / became / 1960s. / the

☑ **다음 글을 읽고 물음에 답하시오.** (2023_고1_09_29번)

ⓐ <u>There is a reason the title "Monday Morning Quarterback" have been existing. Just read the comments on social media from fans had discussed the weekend's games, and you quickly have seen how many people believe they could play, coach, and have managed sport teams more successfully than those on the field.</u> This goes for the boardroom as well. Students and ^{전문가들} _____ with years of training and ^{전문적인 학위} _____ in sport business may also find themselves being given ^{충고,조언} _____ on how to do their jobs from friends, family, or even total strangers without any ^{전문지식} _____. ^{임원진} _____ in sport management have decades of knowledge and experience in their ^{각 분야} _____. (가) <u>하지만, 그들 중 많은 사람들이 그들에게 그들의 사업 운영 방식을 알려주는 팬들과 지역 사회 구성원들로부터의 비난에 직면한다.</u> Very few people tell their doctor how to perform surgery or their ^{회계사} _____ how to prepare their taxes, but many people provide feedback on how sport ^{조직} _____ should ^{관리되다} _____.

23. 23)힌트를 참고하여 각 빈칸에 알맞은 단어를 쓰시오.

(.hwp) (.pdf) ➔ www.englishmygod.com

24. 24)밑줄 친 ⓐ에서, 어법 혹은 문맥상 어색한 부분을 찾아 올바르게 고쳐 쓰시오.

ⓐ	잘못된 표현		바른 표현
(	)	⇨ (	)
(	)	⇨ (	)
(	)	⇨ (	)
(	)	⇨ (	)

25. 25)위 글에 주어진 (가)의 한글과 같은 의미를 가지도록, 각각의 주어진 단어들을 알맞게 배열하시오.

(가) community / fans / However, / many of / face / run / them / and / their / how to / business. / criticism / members / from / them / telling

☑ **다음 글을 읽고 물음에 답하시오.** (2023_고1_09_30번)

While ^{이사} _____ is difficult for everyone, it is particularly stressful for children. They lose their sense of ^{안심감} _____ and may feel ^{혼란스러움을 느끼다} _____ when their routine is disrupted and all that is familiar is taken away. Young children, ages 3-6, are particularly ^{영향을 받는다} _____ by a move. Their understanding at this stage is quite ^{융통성 없다} _____, and it is difficult for them to imagine ^{미리} _____ a new home and their new room. Young children may have worries such as "Will I still be me in the new place"? and "Will my toys and bed come with us"? ⓐ <u>It is important to establish a balance between have validated children's past experiences and have focused on helping them adjust to the new place.</u> (가) 아이들은 자신이 누구인지에 대한 중요한 부분으로서 자신의 과거를 존중하는 방식으로 자신의 배경을 공유할 기회를 가질 필요가 있다. This ^{기여하다} _____ building a sense of community, which is ^{필수적인, 중요한} _____ for all children, especially those in ^{변화} _____.

26. 26)힌트를 참고하여 각 빈칸에 알맞은 단어를 쓰시오.

27. 27)밑줄 친 ⓐ에서, 어법 혹은 문맥상 어색한 부분을 찾아 올바르게 고쳐 쓰시오.

ⓐ	잘못된 표현		바른 표현
(	)	⇨ (	)
(	)	⇨ (	)

28. 28)위 글에 주어진 (가)의 한글과 같은 의미를 가지도록, 각각의 주어진 단어들을 알맞게 배열하시오.

(가) backgrounds / Children / as / are. / a   way / of / to / need / past / to / who / opportunities / share / their / in / have / respects / an important / their / part / they / that

☑ **다음 글을 읽고 물음에 답하시오.** (2023_고1_09_31번)

ⓐ <u>Many people terrify to fly in airplanes. Often, this fear are stemmed from a lack of control.</u> The pilot is in control, not the passengers, and this lack of control ^{스며들다} _____ fear. Many ^{잠재적인} _____ passengers are so afraid they choose to drive great distances to get to a ^{목적지} _____ instead of flying. (가)<u>그러나 운전을 하기로 한 그들의 결정은 논리가 아닌 오직 감정에 근거한다.</u> Logic says that statistically, the ^{확률} ____ of dying in a car crash are around 1 in 5,000, while the ^{확률} ____ of dying in a plane crash are closer to 1 in 11 million. If you're going to take a risk, especially one that could possibly involve your ^{안녕} _____, wouldn't you want the odds in your ^{유리한} ____? However, most people choose the option that will cause them the least amount of ^{불안감} _____. Pay attention to the thoughts you have about taking the ^{위험} ____ and make sure you're basing your decision on facts, not just feelings.

29. ²⁹⁾힌트를 참고하여 각 <u>빈칸에 알맞은</u> 단어를 쓰시오.

30. ³⁰⁾밑줄 친 ⓐ에서, 어법 혹은 문맥상 어색한 부분을 찾아 올바르게 고쳐 쓰시오.

ⓐ	잘못된 표현	바른 표현
(	) ⇨ (	)
(	) ⇨ (	)

31. ³¹⁾위 글에 주어진 (가)의 한글과 같은 의미를 가지도록, 각각의 주어진 단어들을 알맞게 배열하시오.

(가) to / But / drive / solely / based / not / is / logic. / decision / emotion, / their / on

☑ **다음 글을 읽고 물음에 답하시오.** (2023_고1_09_32번)

The famous ^{영장류학자} _____ Frans de Waal, of Emory University, says humans ^{경시하다} _____ similarities between us and other animals as a way of ^{유지하다} _____ our spot at the top of our imaginary ^{사다리} _____. Scientists, de Waal ^{지적하다} _____, can be some of the worst offenders — ^{사용한다} _____ technical language to ^{거리를 두다} _____ the other animals from us . They call "kissing" in chimps "mouth-to-mouth contact"; they call "friends" between ^{영장류} _____ "favorite affiliation partners"; they interpret evidence showing that crows and chimps can make tools as being somehow ^{질적으로} _____ different from the kind of toolmaking said to define humanity. If an animal can beat us at a ^{인지적인} _____ task — like how certain bird species can remember the ^{정확한} _____ locations of thousands of seeds — they write it off as ^{본능} _____, not intelligence. This and so many more tricks of language are what de Waal has termed "^{언어적 거세} _____". (가)<u>우리가 동물로부터 힘을 빼앗기 위해 우리의 언어를 사용하는 방식이며, 우리가 꼭대기에서 우리의 위치를 유지하기 위해 단어들을 만드는 방식이다.</u>

32. ³²⁾힌트를 참고하여 각 <u>빈칸에 알맞은</u> 단어를 쓰시오.

33. 33)위 글에 주어진 (가)의 한글과 같은 의미를 가지도록, 각각의 주어진 단어들을 알맞게 배열하시오.

(가) tongues / use / way / the / disempower / animals, / top. / we / at / The / we / our / words / to / invent / spot / way / our / maintain / the / to

---

☑ **다음 글을 읽고 물음에 답하시오.** (2023_고1_09_33번)

A key to 참여 _____ and 성취 _____ is providing students with 적절한 _____ texts they will be interested in. ⓐ My scholarly work and my taught have been deeply influencing by the work of Rosalie Fink. She had been interviewed twelve adults who being highly successful in their work, including a physicist, a biochemist, and a company CEO. All of them had 난독증 _____ and had had 상당한 _____ problems with reading throughout their school years. While she expected to find that they had avoided reading and discovered ways to 우회하다 _____ it or compensate with other strategies for learning, she found the opposite. "To my surprise, I found that these dyslexics were enthusiastic readers...they rarely avoided reading. On the contrary, they sought out books". (가) Fink가 발견한 패턴은 그녀의 실험대상자 모두가 어떤 개인적인 관심사에 열정적이었다는 것이었다. 관심 분야는 종교, 수학, 상업, 과학, 역사 그리고 생물학을 포함했다. The areas of interest included religion, math, business, science, history, and biography. What mattered was that they read 탐욕적으로 _____ to find out more.

34. 34)힌트를 참고하여 각 빈칸에 알맞은 단어를 쓰시오.

35. 35)밑줄 친 ⓐ에서, 어법 혹은 문맥상 어색한 부분을 찾아 올바르게 고쳐 쓰시오.

ⓐ 잘못된 표현	바른 표현
(   ) ⇨ (   )
(   ) ⇨ (   )
(   ) ⇨ (   )
(   ) ⇨ (   )

36. 36)위 글에 주어진 (가)의 한글과 같은 의미를 가지도록, 각각의 주어진 단어들을 알맞게 배열하시오.

(가) in / of / all / that / pattern / some / Fink / The / was / passionate / interest. / had / been / discovered / personal / her / subjects

☑ **다음 글을 읽고 물음에 답하시오.** (2023_고1_09_34번)

For many people, ability refers to ^{지적능력}_____, so they want everything they do to ^{보여주다,반영하다} _____ how smart they are — writing a brilliant ^{법률 보고서}_____, getting the highest grade on a test, writing elegant computer code, saying something ^{비범하게}_____ wise or ^{재치있는}_____ in a conversation. You could also define ability in terms of a particular skill or talent, such as how well one plays the piano, learns a language, or serves a tennis ball. Some people focus on their ability to be attractive, entertaining, up on the latest trends, or to have the newest ^{기기}_____. (가) 능력이 어떻게 정의되든지, 그것이 자신의 가치를 결정하는 유일한 결정 요소일 때 문제가 발생한다. ⓐ The performance had become the only measure of the person; nothing else took into account. An ^{뛰어난}_____ performance means an outstanding person; an average performance means an average person. Period.

2. ³⁷⁾힌트를 참고하여 각 <u>빈칸에 알맞은</u> 단어를 쓰시오.

37. ³⁸⁾밑줄 친 ⓐ에서, 어법 혹은 문맥상 어색한 부분을 찾아 올바르게 고쳐 쓰시오.

ⓐ	잘못된 표현		바른 표현
(	) ⇨ (		)
(	) ⇨ (		)

38. ³⁹⁾위 글에 주어진 (가)의 한글과 같은 의미를 가지도록, 각각의 주어진 단어들을 알맞게 배열하시오.

(가) ability / of / occurs / when / However / be / one's / it / the sole / determinant / self-worth. / may / defined, / is / a problem

☑ **다음 글을 읽고 물음에 답하시오.** (2023_고1_09_35번)

ⓐ Sensory nerves have been specializing endings in the tissues that pick up a particular sensation. If, for example, you have stepped on a sharp object such as a pin, nerve endings in the skin will have transmitted the pain sensation up your leg, up and along the spinal cord to the brain. While the pain itself is ^{불쾌하다}_____, it is in fact acting as a protective mechanism for the foot. (가) 뇌 안에서, 신경은 언어를 통제하는 부분에 연결될 것이고, 그래서 여러분은 '아야' 또는 다소 덜 공손한 무언가를 외칠 것이다. They will also connect to ^{운동}_____ nerves that travel back down the ^{척수}_____, and to the muscles in your leg that now ^{수축하다}_____ quickly to lift your foot away from the painful object. ^{감지하는}_____ and motor nerves control almost all functions in the body — from the beating of the heart to the movement of the ^장___, sweating and just about everything else.

3. ⁴⁰⁾힌트를 참고하여 각 <u>빈칸에 알맞은</u> 단어를 쓰시오.

39. ⁴¹⁾밑줄 친 ⓐ에서, 어법 혹은 문맥상 어색한 부분을 찾아 올바르게 고쳐 쓰시오.

ⓐ	잘못된 표현		바른 표현
(	)	⇨ (	)
(	)	⇨ (	)
(	)	⇨ (	)

40. ⁴²⁾위 글에 주어진 (가)의 한글과 같은 의미를 가지도록, 각각의 주어진 단어들을 알맞게 배열하시오.

(가) the area / you / speech, / Within / shout / 'ouch' / polite. / less / that / connect / or / nerves / well / brain, / to / that / rather / will / so / controls / may / something

---

☑ **다음 글을 읽고 물음에 답하시오.** ^(2023_고1_09_36번)

Maybe you've heard this joke: "How do you eat an elephant"? The answer is "one bite at a time". So, how do you "build" the Earth? That's simple, too: one ^{원자} _____ at a time. Atoms are the basic building blocks of crystals, and since all rocks are made up of crystals, the more you know about atoms, the better. (가)<u>결정은 과학자들이 '습성'이라고 부르는 다양한 모양으로 나온다.</u> Common crystal habits include squares, triangles, and six-sided hexagons. ⓐ <u>Usually crystals are formed when liquids cool, such as when you have been created ice cubes. Many times, crystals form in ways that were not allowed for perfect shapes.</u> If conditions are too cold, too hot, or there isn't enough source material, they can ^{형성하다} _____ strange, twisted shapes. But when conditions are right, we see beautiful ^{배열} _____. Usually, this involves a slow, steady environment where the individual atoms have plenty of time to join and ^{들어맞다} _____ perfectly into what's known as the crystal ^{격자} _____. ⓑ <u>This is the basic structure of atoms that are seen time after time.</u>

41. ⁴³⁾힌트를 참고하여 각 빈칸에 알맞은 단어를 쓰시오.

42. ⁴⁴⁾밑줄 친 ⓐ~ⓑ에서, 어법 혹은 문맥상 어색한 부분을 찾아 올바르게 고쳐 쓰시오.

ⓐ	잘못된 표현		바른 표현
(	)	⇨ (	)
(	)	⇨ (	)
(	)	⇨ (	)

ⓑ	잘못된 표현		바른 표현
(	)	⇨ (	)

43. ⁴⁵⁾위 글에 주어진 (가)의 한글과 같은 의미를 가지도록, 각각의 주어진 단어들을 알맞게 배열하시오.

(가) variety / habits. / a / in / come / that / call / Crystals / of / scientists / shapes

☑ **다음 글을 읽고 물음에 답하시오.** (2023_고1_09_37번)

When you ^{뜯는다} _____ a guitar string it moves back and forth hundreds of times every second. Naturally, this movement is so fast that you cannot see it — you just see the ^{흐릿한} _____ ^{outline} ___ of the moving string. (가) <u>이렇게 스스로 진동하는 줄들은 거의 소리가 나지 않는데, 이는 줄이 매우 가늘어 많은 공기를 밀어내지 못하기 때문이다.</u> But if you attach a string to a big hollow box (like a guitar body), then the vibration is ^{증폭되다} _____ and the ^음 ____ is heard loud and clear. ⓐ <u>The vibration of the string have been passed on to the wooden panels of the guitar body, which vibrates back and forth at the same rate as the string.</u> The vibration of the wood creates more powerful waves in the air pressure, which travel away from the guitar. When the waves reach your ^{고막} _____ they ^{굽이쳐 들어오고 나가다} _____ the same number of times a second as the original string.

44. 46)힌트를 참고하여 각 <u>빈칸에 알맞은</u> 단어를 쓰시오.

45. 47)밑줄 친 ⓐ에서, 어법 혹은 문맥상 어색한 부분을 찾아 올바르게 고쳐 쓰시오.

ⓐ   잘못된 표현   바른 표현

(   ) ⇨ (   )

(   ) ⇨ (   )

46. 48)위 글에 주어진 (가)의 한글과 같은 의미를 가지도록, 각각의 주어진 단어들을 알맞게 배열하시오.

(가) this / any / way / push / and / their / much / in / don't / about. / strings / hardly / thin / on / air / noise / make / Strings / are / very / vibrating / own / because

☑ **다음 글을 읽고 물음에 답하시오.** (2023_고1_09_38번)

^{경계} _____ between work and home are ^{흐릿해지다} _____ as ^{휴대가능한} _____ digital technology makes it increasingly possible to work anywhere, anytime. (가) <u>사람들은 직장과 외부의 책임을 수행하기 위해 자신의 시간을 관리하기를 바라는 방식에 차이가 있다.</u> Some people prefer to separate or ^{분할하다} _____ roles so that ^{교차지점} _____ are minimized. For example, these people might keep separate email accounts for work and family and try to ^{수행하다} _____ work at the workplace and take care of family matters only during breaks and non-work time. We've even noticed more of these "segmenters" carrying two phones — one for work and one for personal use. ⓐ <u>Flexible schedules works well for these individuals because they have been enabled greater distinction between time at work and time in other roles.</u> Other individuals prefer to have integrated work and family roles all day long. This might ^{수반하다} _____ constantly trading text messages with children from the office, or monitoring emails at home and on vacation, rather than returning to work to find hundreds of messages in their inbox.

47. 49)힌트를 참고하여 각 빈칸에 알맞은 단어를 쓰시오.

48. ⁵⁰⁾밑줄 친 ⓐ에서, 어법 혹은 문맥상 어색한 부분을 찾아 올바르게 고쳐 쓰시오.

   ⓐ   잘못된 표현   바른 표현

   (   ) ⇨ (   )

   (   ) ⇨ (   )

   (   ) ⇨ (   )

49. ⁵¹⁾위 글에 주어진 (가)의 한글과 같은 의미를 가지도록, 각각의 주어진 단어들을 알맞게 배열하시오.

(가) manage / differ / responsibilities. / how / in / to / work / their / time / outside / like / meet / and / to / they / Individuals

---

☑ **다음 글을 읽고 물음에 답하시오.** (2023_고1_09_39번)

A "complementary good" is a product that is often consumed alongside another product. For example, popcorn is a complementary good to a movie, while a ᵛ²ᵉ ᵗⁱᵖᵉ 여행 베개 _____ is a complementary good for a long plane journey. When the ⁱⁿᵏⁱ 인기 _____ of one product increases, the ⁿᵃⁿᵐᵃᵉ 판매 _____ of its complementary good also increase. By producing goods that ᵇᵒᵂᵃⁿᵃᵈᵃ 보완하다 _____ other products that are already (or about to be) popular, you can ᵇᵒˢᵃⁿᵃᵈᵃ 보장하다 _____ a ꜰꜰꜰꜰ 꾸준한 흐름 _____ of demand for your product. ⓐ <u>Some products have enjoyed perfect complementary status — they have to be consuming together, such as a lamp and a lightbulb.</u> However, do not assume that a product is perfectly complementary, as customers may not be completely ˡᵒᶜᵏᵉᵈ locked _____ in to the product. (가) <u>예를 들어, 비록 운전자들이 자신의 차를 운전하기 위해 휘발유를 구매할 필요가 있는 것처럼 보일지라도, 그들은 전기 자동차로 바꿀 수 있다.</u>

4. ⁵²⁾힌트를 참고하여 각 <u>빈칸에 알맞은</u> 단어를 쓰시오.

50. ⁵³⁾밑줄 친 ⓐ에서, 어법 혹은 문맥상 어색한 부분을 찾아 올바르게 고쳐 쓰시오.

   ⓐ   잘못된 표현   바른 표현

   (   ) ⇨ (   )

   (   ) ⇨ (   )

51. ⁵⁴⁾위 글에 주어진 (가)의 한글과 같은 의미를 가지도록, 각각의 주어진 단어들을 알맞게 배열하시오.

(가) their / may / electric / gasoline / to / seem / they / For / motorists / example, / run / can / to / switch / cars. / although / required / cars, / purchase / to

☑ **다음 글을 읽고 물음에 답하시오.** (2023_고1_09_40번)

It's not news to anyone that we ^{판단하다} _____ others based on their clothes. In general, studies that ^{조사하다} _____ these ^{판단} _____ find that people prefer clothing that matches expectations — surgeons in scrubs, little boys in blue — with one ^{눈에 띄는} _____ exception. A series of studies published in an article in June 2014 in the Journal of Consumer Research explored observers' ^{반응} _____ to people who broke established ^{규범} _____ only slightly. ⓐ In one scenario, a man at a black-tie affair were viewed as had higher status and competence when wore a red bow tie. ⓑ The researchers also finding that valuing uniqueness have been increasing audience members' ratings of the status and competence of a professor who wore red sneakers while giving a lecture. The results suggest that people judge these slight ^{일탈들} _____ from the ^{규범} _____ as positive because they suggest that the individual is powerful enough to ^{감수하다} _____ the ^{사회적 비용} _____ of such behaviors.

5. ⁵⁵⁾힌트를 참고하여 각 빈칸에 알맞은 단어를 쓰시오.

52. ⁵⁶⁾밑줄 친 ⓐ~ⓑ에서, 어법 혹은 문맥상 어색한 부분을 찾아 올바르게 고쳐 쓰시오.

ⓐ   잘못된 표현   바른 표현
   (   ) ⇨ (   )
   (   ) ⇨ (   )
   (   ) ⇨ (   )

ⓑ   잘못된 표현   바른 표현
   (   ) ⇨ (   )
   (   ) ⇨ (   )

(.hwp) (.pdf) ➔ www.englishmygod.com

☑ **다음 글을 읽고 물음에 답하시오.** (2023_고1_09_41, 42번)

Claims that local food production cut greenhouse gas ^{배출} _____ by reducing the burning of ^{운송연료} _____ are usually not well founded. Transport is the source of only 11 percent of greenhouse gas emissions within the food sector, (가) 식품이 농장을 떠난 후 이동하는 거리를 줄이는 것은 농장에서 낭비되는 에너지 사용을 줄이는 것보다 훨씬 덜 중요하다. Food coming from a distance can actually be better for the climate, depending on how it was grown. For example, field-grown tomatoes shipped from Mexico in the winter months will have a smaller carbon ^{발자국} _____ than local winter tomatoes grown in a greenhouse. ⓐ In the United Kingdom, lamb meat that travel 11,000 miles from New Zealand generate only one-quarter the carbon emissions per pound compared to British lamb because farmers in the United Kingdom raising their animals on feed (which must produce using fossil fuels) rather than on clover pastureland. When food does travel, what matters most is not the distance traveled but the travel mode (surface versus air), and most of all the ^{적재량 규모} _____. ⓑ Bulk loads of food can travel halfway around the world by ocean freight with a smaller carbon footprint, per pound delivered, than foods have traveled just a short distance but in much smaller loads. For example, 18-wheelers have carried much larger loads than pickup trucks so they can move food 100 times as far while burnt only one-third as much gas per pound of food delivered.

53. ⁵⁷⁾힌트를 참고하여 각 빈칸에 알맞은 단어를 쓰시오.

54. ⁵⁸⁾밑줄 친 ⓐ~ⓑ에서, 어법 혹은 문맥상 어색한 부분을 찾아 올바르게 고쳐 쓰시오.

   ⓐ   잘못된 표현   바른 표현

   (   ) ⇨ (   )

   (   ) ⇨ (   )

   (   ) ⇨ (   )

   (   ) ⇨ (   )

   ⓑ   잘못된 표현   바른 표현

   (   ) ⇨ (   )

   (   ) ⇨ (   )

   (   ) ⇨ (   )

55. ⁵⁹⁾위 글에 주어진 (가)의 한글과 같은 의미를 가지도록, 각각의 주어진 단어들을 알맞게 배열하시오.

(가) is / so / the farm. / travels / food / far / less / energy / the / after / reducing / leaves / use / on / that / the distance / than / reducing / it / farm / wasteful / important

☑ **다음 글을 읽고 물음에 답하시오.** (2023_고1_09_43, 43, 45번)

Long ago, an old man built a grand temple at the center of his village. People traveled to ^{예배를 드리다} _____ at the temple. So the old man made arrangements for food and ^{숙박} _____ inside the temple itself. He needed someone who could ^{관리하다} _____ the temple, so he put up a notice: Manager needed. Seeing the notice, many people went to the old man. But he returned all the ^{지원자들} _____ after interviews, telling them, "I need a ^{자격있는} _____ person for this work". (가) <u>노인은 사람들이 사원의 문을 통과하는 것을 지켜보며 매일 아침 그의 집 지붕에 앉아 있곤 했다.</u> One day, he saw a young man come to the temple. When that young man left the temple, the old man called him and asked, "Will you take care of this temple"? The young man was surprised by the offer and replied, "I have no experience caring for a temple. I'm not even educated". The old man smiled and said, "I don't want any educated man. I want a qualified person". Confused, the young man asked, "But why do you consider me a qualified person"? The old man replied, "I buried a ^{벽돌} _____ on the path to the temple. I watched for many days as people ^{걸려 넘어지다} _____ that brick. No one thought to remove it. But you dug up that brick". The young man said, "I haven't done anything great. It's the duty of every human being to think about others. I only did my duty". The old man smiled and said, (나) <u>"자신의 의무를 알고 그 의무를 수행하는 사람만이 자격이 있는 사람이오".</u>

56. ⁶⁰⁾힌트를 참고하여 각 <u>빈칸에 알맞은</u> 단어를 쓰시오.

57. ⁶¹⁾위 글에 주어진 (가) ~ (나)의 한글과 같은 의미를 가지도록, 각각의 주어진 단어들을 알맞게 배열하시오.

(가) people / The / go / on / the / his / of / the / roof / through / doors. / house / every / watching / sit / temple / would / morning, / man / old

(나) their / people". / people / it / duty / qualified / perform / "Only / who / and / know / are

보듬영어

정답

WORK BOOK

———

2023년 고1 9월 모의고사 내신대비용 WorkBook & 변형문제

Answer Keys

Prac 1 Answers

1) holding
2) on
3) to be
4) guided
5) for
6) during
7) recommend
8) qualified
9) hearing
10) definitely
11) pinned
12) deceptively
13) was
14) at
15) was tied
16) priorities
17) principles
18) tempting
19) that
20) being *told*
21) Therefore
22) 명사절 접속사 that
23) heard
24) it
25) similarly
26) unless
27) unless
28) its
29) been published
30) whether
31) few
32) in
33) adversarial
34) 지시 형용사 that
35) transactions
36) successful
37) interdependent
38) productivity
39) to
40) advantage
41) is
42) excessive
43) which
44) lower
45) affect
46) unattractive
47) diversity
48) what
49) imported
50) erect
51) they
52) appears
53) erection
54) successive
55) that
56) were forced
57) remaking
58) receiving
59) adding
60) played
61) composition
62) **George Russell**
63) late
64) exists
65) discussing
66) successfully
67) those
68) specialized
69) themselves
70) being given
71) respective
72) telling
73) Executives in sport management
74) run
75) disoriented
76) away
77) literal
78) it
79) for
80) validating
81) focusing
82) adjust
83) building
84) which
85) terrified
86) instills
87) destination
88) are
89) are
90) involve
91) Pay
92) basing
93) says
94) similarities
95) imaginary
96) employing
97) affiliation
98) that
99) it
100) termed
101) with
102) 목적격 관계대명사 that / which
103) highly
104) reading
105) reading
106) that
107) voraciously
108) competence
109) smart they are
110) exceptionally
111) terms
112) learns
113) However
114) defined
115) determinant
116) nothing
117) specialized
118) transmit
119) itself
120) well
121) less
122) contract
123) are made
124) more
125) variety
126) 목적격 관계대명사 that
127) include
128) for
129) twisted
130) as
131) is
132) that
133) vibrating
134) make
135) hardly
136) much
137) attach
138) is passed
139) which
140) creates
141) which
142) reach
143) are
144) makes
145) 가목적어 it
146) how
147) minimized
148) during
149) carrying
150) entail

(.hwp) (.pdf) ➔ www.englishmygod.com

151) monitoring
152) consumed
153) increases
154) its
155) increase
156) ensure
157) be consumed
158) However
159) required
160) their
161) to
162) exception
163) published
164) explored
165) having
166) competence
167) wearing
168) increased
169) while
170) deviations
171) powerful enough
172) production
173) emissions
174) transportation
175) are
176) founded
177) Transport
178) leaves
179) reducing
180) how
181) grown
182) emissions
183) compared
184) freight
185) delivered
186) while
187) accommodation
188) after
189) Seeing
190) applicants
191) qualified
192) go
193) come
194) that
195) caring
196) Confused
197) to remove
198) anything
199) being
200) are

Answers

1) holding
2) on
3) to be
4) guided
5) for
6) during
7) recommend
8) qualified
9) hearing
10) definitely
11) pinned
12) deceptively
13) was
14) at
15) was tied
16) priorities
17) principles
18) tempting
19) that
20) being *told*
21) Therefore
22) 명사절 접속사 that
23) heard
24) it
25) similarly
26) unless
27) unless
28) its
29) been published
30) whether
31) few
32) in
33) adversarial
34) 지시 형용사 that
35) transactions
36) successful
37) interdependent
38) productivity
39) to
40) advantage
41) is
42) excessive
43) which
44) lower
45) affect
46) unattractive
47) diversity
48) what
49) imported
50) erect
51) they
52) appears
53) erection
54) successive
55) that
56) were forced
57) remaking
58) receiving
59) adding
60) played
61) composition
62) **George Russell**
63) late
64) exists
65) discussing
66) successfully
67) those
68) specialized
69) themselves
70) being given
71) respective
72) telling
73) Executives in sport management

74) run
75) disoriented
76) away
77) literal
78) it
79) for
80) validating
81) focusing
82) adjust
83) building
84) which
85) terrified
86) instills
87) destination
88) are
89) are
90) involve
91) Pay
92) basing
93) says
94) similarities
95) imaginary
96) employing
97) affiliation
98) that
99) it
100) termed
101) with
102) 목적격 관계대명사 that / which
103) highly
104) reading
105) reading
106) that
107) voraciously
108) competence
109) smart they are
110) exceptionally
111) terms
112) learns
113) However
114) defined
115) determinant
116) nothing
117) specialized
118) transmit
119) itself
120) well
121) less
122) contract
123) are made
124) more
125) variety
126) 목적격 관계대명사 that
127) include
128) for
129) twisted
130) as
131) is
132) that
133) vibrating
134) make
135) hardly
136) much
137) attach
138) is passed
139) which
140) creates
141) which
142) reach
143) are
144) makes
145) 가목적어 it
146) how
147) minimized
148) during
149) carrying
150) entail

151) monitoring
152) consumed
153) increases
154) its
155) increase
156) ensure
157) be consumed
158) However
159) required
160) their
161) to
162) exception
163) published
164) explored
165) having
166) competence
167) wearing
168) increased
169) while
170) deviations
171) powerful enough
172) production
173) emissions
174) transportation
175) are
176) founded
177) Transport
178) leaves
179) reducing
180) how
181) grown
182) emissions
183) compared
184) freight
185) delivered
186) while
187) accommodation
188) after
189) Seeing
190) applicants
191) qualified
192) go
193) come
194) that
195) caring
196) Confused
197) to remove
198) anything
199) being
200) are

Prac 2 Answers

1) director
2) holding
3) local
4) goal
5) encourage
6) contacting
7) recommend
8) department
9) qualified
10) participants
11) since
12) risk.
13) definitely
14) persuaded
15) pinned.
16) deceptively
17) clumsily
18) cliff
19) reach
20) trembled
21) exhaustion.
22) tied
23) *overhearing*
24) priorities
25) principles
26) tempting.
27) character
28) *told*
29) *act*
30) *uphold*
31) daily
32) respect
33) compassion
34) concern
35) suffering,
36) honesty
37) doubt
38) pressure
39) scientific
40) signal
41) perceived,
42) paper
43) intended
44) restate
45) axiom
46) complete
47) Publication
48) silently
49) negotiate
50) *how*
51) learn
52) traditional,
53) adversarial
54) one-off
55) transactions
56) increasingly
57) colleagues,
58) clients.
59) essential
60) maintain
61) interdependent
62) long-term
63) outcome
64) interaction
65) productivity
66) externalities
67) spillovers
68) fractionalization
69) excessive
70) lower
71) Diversity
72) labour
73) tolerant

74) multicultural
75) increase
76) diversity
77) unattractive
78) feature
79) distortion
80) national
81) discriminate
82) conflicts
83) nationalities
84) imported
85) shaping
86) construction:
87) ornately
88) ancestors
89) erect.
90) erection
91) multiple
92) successive
93) that
94) innovators
95) settle
96) farming
97) constructing
98) radically
99) remaking
100) receiving
101) degrees
102) serving
103) military,
104) composition
105) admired
106) perform
107) for
108) made
109) expressive
110) harmonic
111) inspired
112) generation
113) comments
114) discussing
115) manage
116) successfully
117) boardroom
118) specialized
119) being
120) expertise
121) Executives
122) decades
123) respective
124) face
125) criticism
126) few
127) accountant
128) but
129) organizations
130) managed
131) particularly
132) disoriented
133) disrupted
134) literal,
135) beforehand
136) establish
137) validating
138) backgrounds
139) contributes
140) essential
141) stems
142) passengers,
143) instills
144) potential
145) destination
146) logic.
147) odds
148) involve
149) anxiety.
150) basing

151) downplay
152) maintaining
153) imaginary
154) offenders
155) primates
156) interpret
157) crows
158) cognitive
159) precise
160) disempower
161) engagement
162) achievement
163) relevant
164) scholarly
165) influenced
166) dyslexia
167) significant
168) bypass
169) compensate
170) enthusiastic
171) sought
172) passionate
173) voraciously
174) refers
175) competence,
176) reflect
177) brief
178) elegant
179) exceptionally
180) witty
181) define
182) attractive,
183) entertaining
184) latest
185) gadgets.
186) defined,
187) determinant
188) measure
189) account
190) outstanding
191) Period.
192) Sensory
193) nerves
194) specialized
195) tissues
196) sensation.
197) transmit
198) sensation
199) spinal
200) unpleasant,
201) mechanism
202) polite.
203) motor
204) spinal
205) contract
206) control
207) functions
208) gut,
209) atom
210) crystals,
211) made
212) *habits*
213) include
214) hexagons.
215) liquids
216) conditions
217) source
218) twisted
219) displays.
220) steady
221) individual
222) fit
223) structure
224) pluck
225) second
226) that
227) blurred

228) vibrating
229) hardly
230) much
231) attach
232) hollow
233) vibration
234) amplified
235) vibration
236) passed
237) which
238) vibration
239) waves
240) which
241) reach
242) eardrums
243) flex
244) times
245) original
246) Boundaries
247) blurring
248) portable
249) increasingly
250) differ
251) meet
252) prefer
253) separate
254) segment
255) crossings
256) minimized.
257) separate
258) conduct
259) noticed
260) segmenters
261) Flexible
262) greater
263) distinction
264) integrating
265) entail
266) trading
267) monitoring
268) returning
269) complementary
270) consumed
271) alongside
272) complementary
273) pillow
274) complementary
275) journey.
276) popularity
277) sales
278) ensure
279) steady
280) status
281) lightbulb.
282) assume
283) complementary
284) locked
285) motorists
286) purchase
287) electric
288) judge
289) investigate
290) judgments
291) prefer
292) expectations
293) scrubs,
294) notable
295) exception
296) broke
297) norms
298) affair
299) status
300) competence
301) valuing
302) uniqueness
303) competence
304) lecture.

305) judge
306) deviations
307) norm
308) positive
309) risk
310) costs
311) greenhouse
312) emissions
313) reducing
314) transportation
315) sector,
316) distance
317) wasteful
318) climate,
319) shipped
320) carbon
321) footprint
322) lamb
323) generates
324) compared
325) raise
326) pastureland.
327) matters
328) distance
329) surface
330) air),
331) load
332) Bulk
333) halfway
334) freight
335) loads
336) carry
337) burning
338) temple
339) worship
340) arrangements
341) accommodation
342) applicants
343) qualified
344) offer
345) replied,
346) Confused
347) consider
348) tripped
349) remove
350) duty

1) director
2) holding
3) local
4) goal
5) encourage
6) contacting
7) recommend
8) department
9) qualified
10) participants
11) since
12) risk.
13) definitely
14) persuaded
15) pinned.
16) deceptively
17) clumsily
18) cliff
19) reach
20) trembled
21) exhaustion.
22) tied
23) *overhearing*
24) priorities
25) principles
26) tempting.
27) character
28) *told*
29) *act*
30) *uphold*
31) daily
32) respect
33) compassion
34) concern
35) suffering,
36) honesty
37) doubt
38) pressure
39) scientific
40) signal
41) perceived,
42) paper
43) intended
44) restate
45) axiom
46) complete
47) Publication
48) silently
49) negotiate
50) *how*
51) learn
52) traditional,
53) adversarial
54) one-off
55) transactions
56) increasingly
57) colleagues,
58) clients.
59) essential
60) maintain
61) interdependent
62) long-term
63) outcome
64) interaction
65) productivity
66) externalities
67) spillovers
68) fractionalization
69) excessive
70) lower
71) Diversity
72) labour

73) tolerant
74) multicultural
75) increase
76) diversity
77) unattractive
78) feature
79) distortion
80) national
81) discriminate
82) conflicts
83) nationalities
84) imported
85) shaping
86) construction:
87) ornately
88) ancestors
89) erect
90) erection
91) multiple
92) successive
93) that
94) innovators
95) settle
96) farming
97) constructing
98) radically
99) remaking
100) receiving
101) degrees
102) serving
103) military,
104) composition
105) admired
106) perform
107) for
108) made
109) expressive
110) harmonic
111) inspired
112) generation
113) comments
114) discussing
115) manage
116) successfully
117) boardroom
118) specialized
119) being
120) expertise
121) Executives
122) decades
123) respective
124) face
125) criticism
126) few
127) accountant
128) but
129) organizations
130) managed
131) particularly
132) disoriented
133) disrupted
134) literal,
135) beforehand
136) establish
137) validating
138) backgrounds
139) contributes
140) essential
141) stems
142) passengers,
143) instills
144) potential
145) destination
146) logic.
147) odds
148) involve
149) anxiety.

150) basing
151) downplay
152) maintaining
153) imaginary
154) offenders
155) primates
156) interpret
157) crows
158) cognitive
159) precise
160) disempower
161) engagement
162) achievement
163) relevant
164) scholarly
165) influenced
166) dyslexia
167) significant
168) bypass
169) compensate
170) enthusiastic
171) sought
172) passionate
173) voraciously
174) refers
175) competence,
176) reflect
177) brief
178) elegant
179) exceptionally
180) witty
181) define
182) attractive,
183) entertaining
184) latest
185) gadgets.
186) defined,
187) determinant
188) measure
189) account
190) outstanding
191) Period.
192) Sensory
193) nerves
194) specialized
195) tissues
196) sensation.
197) transmit
198) sensation
199) spinal
200) unpleasant,
201) mechanism
202) polite.
203) motor
204) spinal
205) contract
206) control
207) functions
208) gut,
209) atom
210) crystals,
211) made
212) *habits*
213) include
214) hexagons.
215) liquids
216) conditions
217) source
218) twisted
219) displays.
220) steady
221) individual
222) fit
223) structure
224) pluck
225) second
226) that

(.hwp) (.pdf) → www.englishmygod.com

227) blurred
228) vibrating
229) hardly
230) much
231) attach
232) hollow
233) vibration
234) amplified
235) vibration
236) passed
237) which
238) vibration
239) waves
240) which
241) reach
242) eardrums
243) flex
244) times
245) original
246) Boundaries
247) blurring
248) portable
249) increasingly
250) differ
251) meet
252) prefer
253) separate
254) segment
255) crossings
256) minimized.
257) separate
258) conduct
259) noticed
260) segmenters
261) Flexible
262) greater
263) distinction
264) integrating
265) entail
266) trading
267) monitoring
268) returning
269) complementary
270) consumed
271) alongside
272) complementary
273) pillow
274) complementary
275) journey.
276) popularity
277) sales
278) ensure
279) steady
280) status
281) lightbulb.
282) assume
283) complementary
284) locked
285) motorists
286) purchase
287) electric
288) judge
289) investigate
290) judgments
291) prefer
292) expectations
293) scrubs,
294) notable
295) exception
296) broke
297) norms
298) affair
299) status
300) competence
301) valuing
302) uniqueness
303) competence

304) lecture.
305) judge
306) deviations
307) norm
308) positive
309) risk
310) costs
311) greenhouse
312) emissions
313) reducing
314) transportation
315) sector,
316) distance
317) wasteful
318) climate,
319) shipped
320) carbon
321) footprint
322) lamb
323) generates
324) compared
325) raise
326) pastureland.
327) matters
328) distance
329) surface
330) air),
331) load
332) Bulk
333) halfway
334) freight
335) loads
336) carry
337) burning
338) temple
339) worship
340) arrangements
341) accommodation
342) applicants
343) qualified
344) offer
345) replied,
346) Confused
347) consider
348) tripped
349) remove
350) duty

Answer Keys

quiz 1 Answers

1) ③
2) ③
3) ④
4) ③
5) ③
6) ③
7) ③
8) ④
9) ⑤
10) ②
11) ③
12) ⑤
13) ③
14) ③
15) ④
16) ②
17) ③
18) ④
19) ②
20) ④
21) ③
22) ③
23) ②
24) ③
25) (D)-(E)-(B)-(C)-(A)
26) (D)-(A)-(E)-(B)-(C)
27) (D)-(C)-(A)-(B)
28) (A)-(C)-(D)-(B)-(E)
29) (B)-(A)-(C)
30) (C)-(A)-(D)-(B)-(E)
31) (B)-(A)-(C)-(D)-(E)
32) (C)-(A)-(B)-(D)
33) (C)-(A)-(B)
34) (A)-(B)-(C)
35) (A)-(D)-(C)-(E)-(B)
36) (A)-(D)-(C)-(B)
37) (D)-(C)-(A)-(B)
38) (D)-(C)-(A)-(B)
39) (B)-(D)-(C)-(A)
40) (B)-(A)-(C)
41) (E)-(D)-(B)-(A)-(C)
42) (C)-(A)-(B)
43) (A)-(D)-(C)-(B)
44) (A)-(B)-(C)
45) (A)-(D)-(B)-(C)
46) (D)-(A)-(C)-(B)

quiz 2 Answers

1)
[정답] ② ⓑ, ⑨
[해설]
ⓑ being ⇨ to be
⑨ quantified ⇨ qualified

2)
[정답] ④ ⓑ, ⓓ, ⓕ, ⓗ
[해설]
ⓑ bread ⇨ cake
ⓓ bread ⇨ cake
ⓕ fertile ⇨ barren
ⓗ cross ⇨ across

3)
[정답] ② ⓐ, ⓑ, ⓓ, ①
[해설]
ⓐ deny ⇨ share
ⓑ took ⇨ to take
ⓓ temptation ⇨ tempting
① that ⇨ when

4)
[정답] ⑤ ⓓ, ⓕ, ⓗ, ⓙ
[해설]
ⓓ with ⇨ without
ⓕ useful ⇨ useless
ⓗ understands ⇨ understood
ⓙ complete ⇨ not complete

5)
[정답] ⑤ ⓑ, ⓔ, ⑨, ⓞ
[해설]
ⓑ little ⇨ few
ⓔ from ⇨ in
⑨ which ⇨ where
ⓞ income ⇨ outcome

6)
[정답] ⑤ ⓕ, ⓜ, ⓞ, ⓡ
[해설]
ⓕ are ⇨ is
ⓜ desert ⇨ value
ⓞ receive ⇨ perceive
ⓡ exported ⇨ imported

7)
[정답] ① ⓓ, ⓜ
[해설]
ⓓ which ⇨ that
ⓜ similar ⇨ different

8)

(.hwp) (.pdf) ➔ www.englishmygod.com

[정답] ④ ⓒ, ⓓ, ⓕ
[해설]
ⓒ disposition ⇨ composition
ⓓ administered ⇨ admired
ⓕ are made ⇨ made

9)
[정답] ⑤ ⓕ, ⓘ, ⓙ
[해설]
ⓕ advise ⇨ advice
ⓘ approval ⇨ criticism
ⓙ a few ⇨ few

10)
[정답] ④ ⓐ, ⓔ, ⓖ, ⓘ
[해설]
ⓐ stressfully ⇨ stressful
ⓔ effected ⇨ affected
ⓖ afterward ⇨ beforehand
ⓘ transportation ⇨ transition

11)
[정답] ② ⓐ, ⓙ, ⓜ
[해설]
ⓐ terrifying ⇨ terrified
ⓙ against ⇨ in
ⓜ based on ⇨ basing

12)
[정답] ⑤ ⓖ, ⓙ, ⓚ, ⓝ
[해설]
ⓖ is said ⇨ said
ⓙ instinct ⇨ intelligence
ⓚ is ⇨ are
ⓝ endanger ⇨ maintain

13)
[정답] ⑤ ⓘ, ⓙ
[해설]
ⓘ is mattered ⇨ mattered
ⓙ modestly ⇨ voraciously

14)
[정답] ② ⓕ, ⓘ
[해설]
ⓕ entertained ⇨ entertaining
ⓘ defining ⇨ defined

15)
[정답] ④ ⓑ, ⓓ, ⓔ, ⓗ

[해설]
ⓑ transport ⇨ transmit
ⓓ what ⇨ that
ⓔ may as well ⇨ may well
ⓗ calm ⇨ control

16)
[정답] ④ ⓒ, ⓓ, ⓔ
[해설]
ⓒ well ⇨ better
ⓓ shape ⇨ shapes
ⓔ cooled ⇨ cool

17)
[정답] ② ⓑ, ⓕ
[해설]
ⓑ can ⇨ cannot
ⓕ simplified ⇨ amplified

18)
[정답] ③ ⓓ, ⓗ
[해설]
ⓓ integrate ⇨ separate
ⓗ Fixed ⇨ Flexible

19)
[정답] ④ ⓑ, ⓚ, ⓛ, ⓜ
[해설]
ⓑ products ⇨ product
ⓚ pit ⇨ in
ⓛ despite ⇨ although
ⓜ stick ⇨ switch

20)
[정답] ③ ⓒ, ⓙ
[해설]
ⓒ expectation ⇨ exception
ⓙ negative ⇨ positive

21)
[정답] ④ ⓑ, ⓘ, ⓙ, ⓝ
[해설]
ⓑ transparency ⇨ transportation
ⓘ growing ⇨ grown
ⓙ generating ⇨ generates
ⓝ fright ⇨ freight

22)
[정답] ③ ⓕ, ⓜ
[해설]
ⓕ seat ⇨ sit
ⓜ is ⇨ are

Answer Keys

quiz 3 Answers

1)
[정답] ②③④⑤
[해설]
② being ⇨ to be
③ while ⇨ during
④ contacting to ⇨ contacting
⑤ recommending ⇨ recommend

2)
[정답] ②③⑤
[해설]
② bread ⇨ cake
③ fertile ⇨ barren
⑤ would have fallen ⇨ would fall

3)
[정답] ③⑤
[해설]
③ action ⇨ act
⑤ what ⇨ that

4)
[정답] ②③④
[해설]
② is ⇨ does
③ one-way ⇨ two-way
④ useful ⇨ useless

5)
[정답] ①②④
[해설]
① corresponding ⇨ adversarial
② transitions ⇨ transactions
④ successive ⇨ successful

6)
[정답] ①④⑤
[해설]
① popularity ⇨ population
④ preservation ⇨ distortion
⑤ exported ⇨ imported

7)
[정답] ①③⑤
[해설]
① elect ⇨ erect
③ settling ⇨ to settle
⑤ to remake ⇨ remaking

8)
[정답] ②③
[해설]
② disposition ⇨ composition
③ administered ⇨ admired

9)
[정답] ②③④⑤
[해설]
② less ⇨ more
③ them ⇨ themselves
④ expert ⇨ expertise
⑤ a few ⇨ few

10)
[정답] ①②③④
[해설]
① gain ⇨ lose
② literate ⇨ literal
③ excludes ⇨ respects
④ do ⇨ are

11)
[정답] ①③④⑤
[해설]
① destiny ⇨ destination
③ is ⇨ are
④ against ⇨ in
⑤ most ⇨ least

12)
[정답] ①③⑤
[해설]
① overestimate ⇨ downplay
③ instinct ⇨ intelligence
⑤ empower ⇨ disempower

13)
[정답] ①②①
[해설]
① for ⇨ with
③ tried ⇨ avoided
④ enjoyed ⇨ avoided

14)
[정답] ①
[해설]
① instinctive ⇨ intellectual

15)
[정답] ②⑤
[해설]
② what ⇨ that
⑤ calm ⇨ control

16)
[정답] ②③④⑤
[해설]
② well ⇨ better
③ shape ⇨ shapes

보듬영어

④ cooled ⇨ cool
⑤ which ⇨ where

17)
[정답] ①③④
[해설]
① fastly ⇨ fast
③ vibrate ⇨ vibrating
④ vibrates ⇨ vibrate

18)
[정답] ①②
[해설]
① integrate ⇨ separate
② integrator ⇨ segmenters

19)
[정답] ①④
[해설]
① consuming ⇨ consumed
④ pit ⇨ in

20)
[정답] ②③
[해설]
② wore ⇨ wearing
③ uniformity ⇨ uniqueness

21)
[정답] ①②③⑤
[해설]
① be ⇨ is
② more ⇨ less
③ bigger ⇨ smaller
⑤ fright ⇨ freight

22)
[정답] ②③④
[해설]
② returned to ⇨ returned
③ is caring ⇨ caring
④ knows ⇨ know

quiz 4 Answers

1)
[정답]
① held ⇨ holding
⑤ recommending ⇨ recommend

2)
[정답]
① climbing ⇨ climb
② bread ⇨ cake
③ me ⇨ myself
④ bread ⇨ cake
⑤ receptively ⇨ deceptively
⑥ fertile ⇨ barren
⑦ skillfully ⇨ clumsily
⑧ cross ⇨ across
⑨ were trembled ⇨ trembled
⑩ fight ⇨ fright
⑪ would have fallen ⇨ would fall

3)
[정답]
① deny ⇨ share
② took ⇨ to take
③ low ⇨ high
⑥ makes ⇨ make
⑩ words ⇨ action
⑪ what ⇨ that

4)
[정답]
② is ⇨ does
⑧ understands ⇨ understood

5)
[정답]
④ learns ⇨ learn
⑨ transitions ⇨ transactions
⑪ different ⇨ same
⑮ income ⇨ outcome

6)
[정답]
⑧ that ⇨ which

7)
[정답]
① example ⇨ examples
② carving ⇨ carved
③ elect ⇨ erect
④ which ⇨ that
⑥ successful ⇨ successive
⑦ which ⇨ that
⑧ settling ⇨ to settle

Answer Keys

⑩ procession ⇨ process
⑪ constructs ⇨ constructing
⑬ similar ⇨ different

8)
[정답]
⑥ are made ⇨ made

9)
[정답]
② discussing about ⇨ discussing
③ less ⇨ more
④ them ⇨ themselves
⑤ giving ⇨ being given
⑦ expert ⇨ expertise
⑧ relative ⇨ respective
⑨ approval ⇨ criticism

10)
[정답]
② gain ⇨ lose
⑦ afterward ⇨ beforehand

11)
[정답]
① terrifying ⇨ terrified
③ installs ⇨ instills
⑤ Emotion ⇨ Logic
⑨ it ⇨ one
⑩ against ⇨ in
⑫ have them ⇨ have
⑬ based on ⇨ basing

12)
[정답]
② abandoning ⇨ maintaining
⑤ affliction ⇨ affiliation
⑥ qualitative ⇨ qualitatively
⑦ is said ⇨ said
⑨ intelligence ⇨ instinct
⑩ instinct ⇨ intelligence
⑪ is ⇨ are
⑬ empower ⇨ disempower

13)
[정답]
⑤ tried ⇨ avoided
⑨ is mattered ⇨ mattered
⑩ modestly ⇨ voraciously

14)
[정답]
② reflect ⇨ to reflect
⑦ last ⇨ latest

15)

[정답]
① picks ⇨ pick
② transport ⇨ transmit
④ what ⇨ that
⑤ may as well ⇨ may well
⑥ politely ⇨ polite
⑦ contact ⇨ contract
⑧ calm ⇨ control

16)
[정답]
① What ⇨ How
② consisted ⇨ made
③ well ⇨ better
④ shape ⇨ shapes
⑤ cooled ⇨ cool
⑥ how ⇨ that
⑦ drastic ⇨ steady
⑧ which ⇨ where
⑨ are ⇨ is

17)
[정답]
② can ⇨ cannot
③ vibrate ⇨ vibrating
④ hard ⇨ hardly
⑤ detach ⇨ attach
⑥ simplified ⇨ amplified
⑦ vibrates ⇨ vibrate
⑧ that ⇨ which
⑨ will reach ⇨ reach
⑩ time ⇨ times

18)
[정답]
④ integrate ⇨ separate
⑤ maximized ⇨ minimized
⑦ integrator ⇨ segmenters
⑧ Fixed ⇨ Flexible
⑩ refuse ⇨ entail

19)
[정답]
⑧ disclaim ⇨ ensure

20)
[정답]
① which ⇨ that
⑧ unity ⇨ deviations

21)
[정답]
② transparency ⇨ transportation
③ is ⇨ are
⑤ be ⇨ is
⑥ more ⇨ less

⑦ worse ⇨ better
⑨ growing ⇨ grown
⑩ generating ⇨ generates
⑪ rise ⇨ raise
⑫ do ⇨ does
⑬ traveling ⇨ traveled
⑮ bigger ⇨ smaller
⑯ travel ⇨ traveling
⑰ long ⇨ short
⑱ very ⇨ much

22)
[정답]
① whom ⇨ who
② Seen ⇨ Seeing
⑦ surprising ⇨ surprised by
⑬ is ⇨ are

---

quiz 5 **Answers**

1) 관장 - director // 개최하다 - holding // 목적 - goal // 장려하다 - encourage // 안내적 - guided // 연락하다 - contacting // 추천하다 - recommend // 적합한 - qualified // 참가자들 - participants

2)
(가) We are looking for college students who can help with the experiments during the event.

3) 위험 - risk // 올라가다 - climb out // 설득하다 - persuaded // 꼼짝 못하게 되었다 - pinned // 믿을수 없게도 - deceptively // 서툴게 - clumsily // 떨렸다 - trembled // 피로 - exhaustion // 공포 - fright

4)
ⓐ
had had ⇨ had been
had been ⇨ had had

5)
(가) The bolt that would save my life, if I could get to it, was about two feet above my reach.

6) 우연히 듣는다 - overhearing // 공유하다 - share // 가치 - values // 우선순위 - priorities // 원칙 - principles // 유혹적 - tempting // 존중하다 - respect // 연민 - compassion // 걱정 - concern // 괴로움 - suffering // 자제력 - self-discipline

7)
ⓐ
what ⇨ that
had told ⇨ being told

8)
(가) They learn by seeing the people around them act on and uphold those values in their daily lives.

9) 의심 - doubt // 압력파 - pressure waves // 청취자 - hearer // 양방향 - two-way // 과정 - process // 감지되다 - perceived // 의도된 독자 - intended audience // 재진술하다 - restate // 이치 - axiom // 압력파 - pressure waves

10)
(가) A scientific experiment is not complete until the results have been published and understood.

11) 협상하다 - negotiate // 적대적인 - adversarial // 일회성 - one-off // 거래 - transactions // 배우자 - spouses // 장기적 - long-term // 결과 - outcome // 받아들일 수 있는 - acceptable

12)
ⓐ
learning ⇨ learn
resulting in ⇨ result in

13)
(가) In view of this, it's essential to achieve successful results for ourselves and maintain a healthy relationship with our negotiating partners at the same time.

14) 문화적 배경 - cultural backgrounds // 현지 주민 - host population // 생산성 - productivity // 외부효과 - externalities // 파급 - spillovers // 분열 -

fractionalization // 과도한 - excessive // 거래비용 - transaction costs // 범위 - range

15)

ⓐ

perceive ⇨ be perceived

have perceived ⇨ perceive

be discriminated ⇨ discriminate

be feared ⇨ fear

import ⇨ are imported

16)

(가) Diversity not only impacts the labour market, but may also affect the quality of life in a location.

17) 화려하게 - ornately // 세우다 - erect // 수렵 채집인 - hunter-gatherers // 거석 - megalithic stones // 잇따르다 - successive // 혁신가 - innovators // 정착하다 - settle down

18)

ⓐ

have been shaping ⇨ are shaping

have shaped ⇨ shaping

19)

(가) This is an early example of a society constructing something that ends up radically remaking the society itself.

20) 학사학위 - bachelor's degrees // 군대 - army // 작곡 - composition // 감탄하다 - admired // 고용하다 - hired // 표현이 풍부한 - expressive // 영감을 주다 - inspired // 세대 - generation

21)

ⓐ

had born ⇨ was born

be ⇨ was

have received ⇨ receiving

22)

(가) Evans became famous for recordings made from the late 1950s through the 1960s.

23) 전문가들 - professionals // 전문적인 학위 - specialized degrees // 충고,조언 - advice // 전문지식 - expertise // 임원진 - executives // 각 분야 - respective fields // 회계사 - accountant // 조직 - organizations // 관리되다 - be managed

24)

ⓐ

have been existing ⇨ exists

had discussed ⇨ discussing

have seen ⇨ see

have managed ⇨ manage

25)

(가) However, many of them face criticism from fans and community members telling them how to run their business.

26) 이사 - moving // 안심감 - security // 혼란스러움을 느끼다 - disoriented // 영향을 받는다 - affected // 융통성 없다 - literal // 미리 - beforehand // 기여하다 - contributes to // 필수적인, 중요한 - essential // 변화 - transition

27)

ⓐ

have validated ⇨ validating

have focused ⇨ focusing

28)

(가) Children need to have opportunities to share their backgrounds in a way that respects their past as an important part of who they are.

29) 스며들다 - instills // 잠재적인 - potential // 목적지 - destination // 확률 - odds // 확률 - odds // 안녕 - well-being // 유리한 - favor // 불안감 - anxiety // 위험 - risk

30)

ⓐ

terrify ⇨ are terrified

are stemmed ⇨ stems

31)

(가) But their decision to drive is based solely on emotion, not logic.

32) 영장류학자 - primatologist // 경시하다 - downplay // 유지하다 - maintaining // 사다리 - ladder // 지적하다 - points out // 사용한다 - employing // 거리를 두다 - distance // 영장류 - primates // 질적으로 - qualitatively // 인지적인 - cognitive // 정확한 - precise // 본능 - instinct // 언어적 거세 - linguistic castration

33)

(가) The way we use our tongues to disempower animals, the way we invent words to maintain our spot at the top.

34) 참여 - engagement // 성취 - achievement // 적절한 - relevant // 난독증 - dyslexia // 상당한 - significant // 우회하다 - bypass // 탐욕적으로 - voraciously

35)

ⓐ

taught ⇨ teaching

influencing ⇨ influenced

had been interviewed ⇨ interviewed

being ➡ were

36)

(가) The pattern Fink discovered was that all of her subjects had been passionate in some personal interest.

37) 지적능력 - intellectual competence // 보여주다,반영하다 - reflect // 법률 보고서 - legal brief // 비범하게 - exceptionally // 재치있는 - witty // 기기 - gadgets // 뛰어난 - outstanding

38)

ⓐ

had become ⇨ becomes

took ⇨ is taken

39)

(가) However ability may be defined, a problem occurs when it is the sole determinant of one's self-worth.

40) 불쾌하다 - unpleasant // 운동 - motor // 척수 - spinal cord // 수축하다 - contract // 감지하는 - Sensory // 장 - gut

41)

ⓐ

have been specializing ⇨ have specialized

(.hwp) (.pdf) → www.englishmygod.com

have stepped ⇨ step
have transmitted ⇨ transmit

42)

(가) Within the brain, nerves will connect to the area that controls speech, so that you may well shout 'ouch' or something rather less polite.

43) 원자 - atom // 형성하다 - form // 배열 - displays // 들어맞다 - fit // 격자 - lattice

44)

ⓐ
are formed ⇨ form
have been created ⇨ create
were not allowed ⇨ do not allow
ⓑ
are ⇨ is

45)

(가) Crystals come in a variety of shapes that scientists call habits.

46) 뜯는다 - pluck // 흐릿한 - blurred // outline - 윤곽 // 증폭되다 - amplified // 음 - note // 고막 - eardrums // 굽이쳐 들어오고 나가다 - flex in and out

47)

ⓐ
have been passed ⇨ is passed
vibrates ⇨ vibrate

48)

(가) Strings vibrating in this way on their own make hardly any noise because strings are very thin and don't push much air about.

49) 경계 - Boundaries // 흐릿해지다 - blurring // 휴대가능한 - portable // 분할하다 - segment // 교차지점 - boundary crossings // 수행하다 - conduct // 수반하다 - entail

50)

ⓐ
works ⇨ work
have been enabled ⇨ enable
to have integrated ⇨ integrating

51)

(가) Individuals differ in how they like to manage their time to meet work and outside responsibilities.

52) 여행 베개 - travel pillow // 인기 - popularity // 판매 - sales // 보완하다 - complement // 보장하다 - ensure // 꾸준한 흐름 - steady stream // locked - locking

53)

ⓐ
have enjoyed ⇨ enjoy
consuming ⇨ consumed

54)

(가) For example, although motorists may seem required to purchase gasoline to run their cars, they can switch to electric cars.

55) 판단하다 - judge // 조사하다 - investigate // 판단 - judgments // 눈에 띄는 - notable // 반응 - reactions // 규범 - norms // 일탈들 - deviations // 규범 - norm // 감수하다 - risk // 사회적 비용 - social costs

56)

ⓐ

were viewed ⇨ was viewed
had ⇨ having
wore ⇨ wearing
ⓑ
finding ⇨ found
have been increasing ⇨ increased

57) 배출 - emissions // 운송연료 - transportation fuel // 발자국 - footprint // 적재량 규모 - load size

58)

ⓐ
travel ⇨ travels
generate ⇨ generates
raising ⇨ raise
produce ⇨ be produced
ⓑ
have traveled ⇨ traveling
have carried ⇨ carry
burnt ⇨ burning

59)

(가) so reducing the distance that food travels after it leaves the farm is far less important than reducing wasteful energy use on the farm.

60) 예배를 드리다 - worship // 숙박 - accommodation // 관리하다 - look after // 지원자들 - applicants // 자격있는 - qualified // 벽돌 - brick // 걸려 넘어지다 - tripped over

61)

(가) The old man would sit on the roof of his house every morning, watching people go through the temple doors.

(나) "Only people who know their duty and perform it are qualified people".